c

D1560117

Prudentius' *Psychomachia*

Prudentius' *Psychomachia,*
A REEXAMINATION

MACKLIN SMITH

PRINCETON UNIVERSITY PRESS
PRINCETON, NEW JERSEY

Copyright © 1976 by Princeton University Press
Published by Princeton University Press, Princeton, New Jersey
In the United Kingdom: Princeton University Press, Guildford, Surrey
All Rights Reserved

Library of Congress Cataloging in Publication Data will
be found on the last printed page of this book

Publication of this book has been aided by a grant from
the Andrew W. Mellon Foundation

This book has been composed in Linotype Janson

Printed in the United States of America
by Princeton University Press, Princeton, New Jersey

To My Mother and Father

Et quis est usque adeo sapiens ut contra libidines
nullum habeat omnino conflictum?

St. Augustine, *De Civitate Dei* XIX. 4.

CONTENTS

THIS critical study of the *Psychomachia*, the first published
in English, joins a handful of articles and monographs whose
appearance during the past decade witnesses a steady but
slight interest in Prudentius. I hope that my book will help
increase Prudentius' readership, for he deserves to be read.
He is the best Latin poet between the Augustan Age and
the twelfth century. His corpus can be anatomized profit-
ably by historians intent on knowing why Rome fell and
how orthodox Christianity rose. Classicists know him as the
only poet of Late Antiquity (perhaps rivaled by Claudian)
who could successfully imitate Vergil and Horace; medievalists know him as the creator of personification allegory,
the first theological poet, one of the first hymnists, the
source of a rich iconography of the virtues and vices. My
intent is to persuade both classicists and medievalists that
the *Psychomachia* is a fine poem for reasons that may surprise them: its skillful imitation of Vergil is anti-Vergilian;
its allegory cannot be understood in medieval terms, but
needs to be referred to a special historical context, that is,
the Church's struggle against pagan institutions and ideals
at the close of the fourth century.

Because many people actually or potentially interested in
Prudentius are not classicists or medievalists, I have provided translations of Latin texts wherever needed. I am especially grateful to Harvard University Press for permission
to use the Loeb Classical Library *Prudentius*, with its
English translations by H. J. Thomson, and for permission
to use other Loeb translations that I have indicated in notes.
Catholic University of America Press has kindly let me use
translations from its Fathers of the Church series. My friend
Robert G. Moran has my thanks for his help on the translations from St. Ambrose's *De Abraham*.

My interest in the *Psychomachia* I owe to Robert Hollander, Department of Comparative Literature, Princeton University. In his graduate seminar on allegory, he encouraged my comparison of the biblical typology and the Vergilian allusions in the *Psychomachia*; since then, he has commented astutely on no less than four of my written attempts to interpret the relationship, as Prudentius structured it, between Scripture and the *Aeneid*. This book would not have been written without Professor Hollander's help, and many of its virtues, but not its vices, are his.

I am also grateful to John V. Fleming, J. Arthur Hanson, and Janet Martin for reading part or all of the manuscript and offering encouragement and criticism. The most helpful reader next to Robert Hollander—and the best listener by far—has been my wife Sallie, without whose loving patience I could not have written this book. My fundamental and greatest debt I am happy to acknowledge in the dedication.

MACKLIN SMITH

Prudentius' *Psychomachia*

CRITICAL INTRODUCTION

LITERARY historians know Prudentius' *Psychomachia*[1] (c. 405) as the first sustained personification allegory, one notable for its powerful influence upon medieval and Renaissance culture; they have viewed it as a poetic representation of animated virtues and vices who fight for dominion over the mind of a Christian everyman.[2] The action of the allegory is

[1] Text used is *Prudentius* (Loeb Classical Library), ed. and trans. H. J. Thomson, 2 vols. (London, 1961). Citations will be by title and line numbers in parentheses. The Loeb edition has been chosen as the most accessible and as the most convenient for readers with inadequate Latin. Thomson's translation is probably the best in any modern language: it captures the literal meaning of the original without claiming for itself high literary value, and it is especially good in its sensitivity to Prudentius' figural use of Scripture and exegetical vocabulary. No important scholarly obstacles prevent our using the Loeb edition. The textual tradition of Prudentius is sound in comparison with that of most classical authors; interpolations are not a problem; variant readings are for the most part inconsequential for our interpretation. But readers may wish to consult the authoritative Latin edition of Ioannes Bergman, *Aurelii Prudentii Clementis Carmina*, CSEL, Vol. 61 (Vienna, 1926). The edition of Arevalo (1788) reprinted in *Patrolgia Latina*, ed. Migne, Vols. 59, 60 (Paris, 1847), has been superseded yet retains a certain usefulness because of its apparatus of early Latin and German glosses. That of Maurice P. Cunningham, *Corpus Christianorum*, Series Latina, 126 (Turhout, 1966), is in my view the best, but it remains controversial—see, e.g., Christian Gnilka, review of R. Herzog, *Die allegorische Dichtkunst bei Prudentius*, in *Gnomon*, 40 (1968), n. 2; and see Cunningham's defense and corrigenda of his edition in "The Problem of Interpolation in the Textual Tradition of Prudentius," *Transactions and Proceedings of the American Philological Association*, 99 (1968), 119-141. A modern language edition comparable to Thomson's is that of Maurice Lavarenne, *Prudence*, 4 vols. (Paris: Budé, 1943-1951). The *Psychomachia* has been edited separately by Lavarenne (Paris, 1933). Other editions exist. Bibliographical notes follow, but readers should consult the full bibliography in Cunningham's edition.

[2] For the idea of animated personifications, I am indebted to Mor-

3

simple: despite near reversals, the Christian virtues led by Faith win a series of epic combats over the vices, after which the victorious army constructs a holy city (in the mind) on whose citadel stands a glorious temple dedicated to Wisdom.

The meaning of this psychic narrative is more complex than it initially seems, however, because the poet relates his personification allegory to scriptural and ecclesiastical history. His prefatory narration of the career of Abraham, interspersed with scriptural emblems and contemporary allusions, indicates that the allegory participates in universal salvation-history. And inspired as it is—or so the poet claims—by Christ, this allegory is meant to aid in the salvation of its Christian audience. Thus the poem, its scriptural and liturgical context, and its effect on others' souls all exist in one continuum of spiritual reality. Scanning its entire range of spirituality, we observe that the *Psychomachia* is no simple narrative, but a sophisticated version of Christian history operative in several moral senses.

In order to do full justice to the complexity of the *Psychomachia*, another large context must be considered in addition to Christian history—the entire Roman literary tradition, that is, the epic tradition, and particularly its paragon Vergil. Prudentius has obviously absorbed, imitated, and—not to exaggerate—mastered this tradition. He follows Roman, not scriptural, models when he employs dactylic hexameter as the vehicle for a narrative of arms and civilization-building. He imitates certain features of Vergilian prosody to achieve epic effects. And he borrows half-lines and phrases from the *Aeneid*, weaving them into his own narrative. Such practices have been explained as stemming from a profound Christian humanism, from the desire to incorporate the cultural excellences of pagan Rome into the new Christian civilization. This thesis I find unsound. It is quite probable that Prudentius' audience was aristo-

---

ton W. Bloomfield, "A Grammatical Approach to Personification Allegory," *Modern Philology*, 60 (1962-1963), 161-171.

cratic and senatorial, therefore imbued with the Roman tradition and expectant of its imitation. But to posit this sociology for the work is not to restrict questions of literary criticism, and we must therefore ask how the poet responds to the expectations of his audience. Is the quotation of Vergil in the *Psychomachia* merely a pleasant embellishment upon the Christian allegory? Is the *imitatio* straightforward? I hope to demonstrate convincingly that such is not the case, that Prudentius' stance towards his Roman literary tradition is fundamentally ironic.

If my reading of the *Psychomachia* is correct, there exists a range of correspondence—from typological to parodic, from sacramental to ironic—between the personification allegory and the rival testaments of sacred and profane culture. Charles Witke, commenting on the literature that Prudentius brought to bear on his poetic production, offers this formulation: "His own private synthesis is between the Bible and Vergil, between his God and his culture."[3] My agreement with the basic elements here identified does not extend to the analysis of the compound. It seems to me that no "synthesis" occurs precisely because the poet cannot conceive his culture apart from his God, that his cultural orientation is exclusively Christian. For clarification's sake I anticipate my findings: By simultaneous use of different linguistic modes, Prudentius relates his allegory of soul-struggle to divinely revealed salvation-history and to the pagan distortion of history as embodied in Vergil's *Aeneid*. This concomitant struggle of historical analogies is not statically expressed; rather, evolving interpretations of sacred and profane literature accompany the progress of the personification allegory, and these interpretations are completed when the allegorical struggle is resolved in holy peace. As the scriptural illumination of the allegory brightens, Vergil's old heroic monument to Augustan Rome is

[3] Charles Witke, *Numen Litterarum: The Old and the New in Latin Poetry from Constantine to Gregory the Great* (Leiden, 1971), p. 105.

cast in ever darkening moral shadow. Thus, out of this one Christian Latin text emerges a contrast of opposing visions, and this contrast places the microcosmic personification allegory in the perspective of macrocosmic struggle. The warfare in everyman's soul implies the war of the Church against the forces of Satan, a war indeed being fought in literary circles c. 405. The allegorical process, ending in a return to the arena of the putative reader's mind, is intended to have a moral effect on his sense of duty to embrace the Word of God and to reject the false pleasures and teachings discovered from the masterwork of Roman literature.

The complexity of Prudentian allegory has gone unnoticed for want of determined analysis, the reason probably being that few literary historians specialize in late antiquity, and thus classicists, medievalists, and general readers tend to neglect this period. Considered merely as personification allegory, the *Psychomachia* is manifestly original; and, it is revolutionary in its impact, being the major source of a rich allegorical tradition extending through the Middle Ages and into the eighteenth century. Therefore, many modern scholars have been able to remark on its importance in literary history and in the history of art; but few have investigated its poetic workings, and fewer still have appreciated its intrinsic worth. There are three problems with the pigeonhole "medieval personification allegory": it hides the document, discouraging analysis; it misclassifies historically; and it oversimplifies generic classification. Perhaps our uncertainties about the Early Christian Period or about "the nature of allegory" have more strongly impelled us to pigeonhole the *Psychomachia*. Clearly the very feature—allegory—that has guaranteed it a place in literary history has retarded literary criticism and, in turn, appreciative reading. The allegorical mode, unpopular for two centuries, still confounds our critical senses—and our historical senses as well. In truth, Prudentius' place in literary history has been poorly defined. To categorize the

Psychomachia as the first personification allegory is not to explain the conditions that gave rise to it. What poetic mentality could conceive the *Psychomachia*? What historical conditions at the beginning of the fifth century prepared an audience to receive it?

Such areas of inquiry, largely unexplored, have determined in part the organizational logic of my study. Chapter divisions follow the assumption that an appreciation of the personification allegory itself and of its special complexities requires prior knowledge of motivating historical forces. The poet's will is one such force, and the social conditions affecting him another. So Chapter I treats the poet in his times, analyzing Prudentius' sense of poetic purpose from the evidence of his *opera*, and describing in some detail two major threats, heresy and paganism, which were subjectively recognized by the poet and objectively faced by the Church at the close of the fourth century. Chapter II, a general consideration of the allegory, treats the nature of the personifications and the Christian metaphors by which these personifications are animated to perform their moral roles in the basic plot of spiritual conversion. Discussions of scriptural and Vergilian elements fill the concluding chapters, III and IV, respectively. These discussions are complementary excursions from Chapter II, but insofar as the anti-Vergilian irony is significant mainly as an adjunct to the scriptural imagery and structure, Chapter IV may truly be said to follow and depend on Chapter III. It will be evident that my treatment is not exhaustive in terms of either historical or literary analysis: The complete story of Prudentius' times cannot be told adequately by treating the Church's struggle against paganism and heresy; many interesting elements in the *Psychomachia*, such as metrics, vocabulary, and non-Vergilian allusions, are not dealt with here, and while these particular topics have received some critical attention, others, such as the relation of sound to meaning, have not. I do believe, however, that the topics I discuss are of sufficient weight to yield a satisfying reading of the *Psychomachia*, and at the same time suggest further lines of inquiry.

Before taking up these topics, I should like to comment on two vexed issues: Prudentius' historical period and the nature of his allegory.

Aurelius Prudentius Clemens (348-c. 410) wrote in troubled times. In all probability he died in the very year that Alaric's Visigothic army sacked Rome, till then the *urbs aeterna*, afterwards of problematic destiny. All of Prudentius' verse is the product of these late and last years (c. 392 and after), a period of political and economic uncertainty in his native Spain as well as in the Roman metropolis so important (biographically and symbolically) to his poetic culture. Under the weak and divided rule of Honorius and Arcadius, the Western and Eastern empires were politically unstable and subjected to a series of intriguing regents, generals, and ministers. War against the Visigoths and Huns was an almost yearly occurrence. The hazards of travel, the stagnation of commerce, the deterioration of city life, the flight into the countryside to avoid taxation—these are the well-known features of late Roman life.[4]

Within this unstable environment, Prudentius composed for a cultivated audience whose social class at least approached his own—that is, for the aristocracy and for the

[4] For a survey of these times, see, e.g., A.H.M. Jones, *The Later Roman Empire, 284-602* (Oxford, 1964), and Henry Chadwick, *The Early Church*, Pelican History of the Church, Vol. 1 (London, 1967); also the highly detailed study of Alan Cameron, *Claudian: Poetry and Propaganda at the Court of Honorius* (Oxford, 1970), with bibliography; the fuller bibliography in François Paschoud, *Roma Aeterna: Études sur le patriotisme romain dans l'occident latin à l'époque des grandes invasions*, Bibliotheca Helvetica Romana, Vol. 7 (1967); Lynn White, ed., *The Transformation of the Roman World: Gibbon's Problem After Two Centuries* (Los Angeles, 1966); and A. Momigliano, ed., *The Conflict between Paganism and Christianity in the Fourth Century* (Oxford, 1963).

high administrators of Empire and Church.[5] This class had
no solid ideological unity. It was torn by the Christian-
pagan struggle, to some extent by heresy within the Christian group, and it was troubled by uncertainty of its social
destiny. Indeed, its very existence as a class was being under-
mined by changes, including barbarian invasions, which
were to cause the collapse of the Roman order. That our
lay poet and many of his contemporaries in the Church
hierarchy could share firm hope in the legacy of the powerful Emperor Theodosius—one universal Christian Empire—
confirms the transitoriness of this class's subjective outlook.
Documentation of the subjective change can be found in
St. Augustine's *City of God*. Although *Romanitas* persisted through later centuries, no longer (at least till the
time of Charlemagne) was this ideal reflective of political
institutions.[6]

It may seem paradoxical that in this brief period of flux
would flourish the most traditionally Latin poet—formally
speaking—of the entire three centuries' span conventionally
known as the Early Christian Period. Prudentius did not
write (as St. Ambrose wrote his hymns) as a representative
of a Church office, but surely his work was in some way
guided or overseen by the Church. Unfortunately, Prudentius' status as layman has encouraged the attribution of special qualities in his works to individual genius per se, and
this has of course been accompanied by a minimizing of

[5] With Sidonius' testimony (below, nn. 8, 9) may be placed the
hard evidence of the Rustic Capital script—that script usually reserved for Vergil—in the earliest Prudentius manuscript.

[6] The Roman senatorial aristocracy, however, persisted intact into
the sixth century; see P.R.L. Brown, "Aspects of the Christianization
of the Roman Aristocracy," *Journal of Roman Studies*, 51 (1961), 1-
11, and Paschoud, cited above n. 4. My general point is that despite
the continuity of the "Romans of Rome," urban life changed dras-
tically throughout the Empire in the fifth century. For internal transformation of the Roman aristocracy, see especially Herbert Bloch,
"The Pagan Revival in the West at the End of the Fourth Century,"
in Momigliano (cited n. 4), pp. 193-218.

historical considerations. Granted that Prudentius' formal classicism is atypical, a transitory phenomenon in the tradition of Early Christian poetry, it can be explained as resulting not only from a personal engagement with literary ancestors, but from a timely responsiveness to his audience's desperate need for stability.

In any case, the uniqueness of Prudentius underscores the real brevity of his proper period. Time soon passed him by: not that his reputation was anything but strong and enduring, but his full achievement could not be understood. In response to the drastic fifth-century shift in the politico-economic order,[7] there occurred a comparable shift in Christian spirituality. The socially organized asceticism of the monastic movement soon could satisfy men's psychological (and material) needs better than an illusory hope for a Church triumphant in this world. Therefore much of the topicality—ecclesiastical as well as political—of Prudentius' works became obscure. Another change affected understanding of his use of classical models and allusions. With the dissolution of the Roman bureaucracy, the homogeneous Roman educational system and the class of *rhetores* ceased to exist. Education became Church-sponsored (except in senatorial families), and in monastic and ecclesiastical centers the favorite subjects of the antique schools of rhetoric received considerably less attention than before. A few decades after the composition of the *Psychomachia*, the intensive literary knowledge required for its full appreciation (especially vis-à-vis the use of Vergil) had become practically unattainable.[8] Interpretation of the allegory was

---

[7] The intolerability of fifth-century life is well pictured in the *De Gubernatione Dei* by Salvian the Presbyter.

[8] Boethius is the exception to the decline of learning, because the senatorial aristocracy to which he belonged was the social exception. The erudition of Sidonius should be noted as well, but his frozen panegyrics signal a dying culture rather than a vital literary tradition. Alan Cameron, *Claudian* (cited n. 4), p. 318, calls Sidonius' verse "precious and monotonous in the extreme."

then limited to exposition of ascetic psychology, and this narrow appreciation of the *Psychomachia* persisted, in the main, throughout the medieval period.

Two early notices of Prudentius show that by the second half of the fifth century his works were being appreciated according to divergent standards, neither of which adequately captured the range of meaning intended by the poet. The first notice is that of Sidonius Apollinaris. In one of his elegant epistles, Sidonius describes a delightful sojourn [*tempus voluptuosissimum*] on the estates of sympathetic hosts. Here to be enjoyed, along with the pleasures of gaming and country dining, is a library worthy of comparison to the Athenaeum. "The arrangement was such that the manuscripts near the ladies' seats were of a devotional type, while those among the gentlemen's benches were works distinguished by the grandeur of Latin eloquence; the latter, however, included certain writings of particular authors which preserve a similarity of style though their doctrines are different [*in causis disparibus dicendi parilitatem*]; for it was a frequent practice to read writers whose artistry was of a similar kind—here Augustine, there Varro, here Horace, there Prudentius."[9]

By writing of authors *in causis disparibus dicendi parilitatem*, Sidonius anticipated the modern commonplace of Prudentius scholarship: Christian content in classical form. There can be no denying that Prudentius uses classical forms and presents a Christian message, yet the observation of these elements does not explain *how* or *why* Prudentius chose to emulate the eloquence of traditional Latin poetry. Sidonius is not interested in such considerations, and perhaps he has no way of knowing that only some decades before him the juxtaposition of classical form and Christian content could signify something in addition to, or other than, iden-

[9] Letter II, 9. Trans. from *Sidonius: Poems and Letters* (Loeb Classical Library), ed. W. B. Anderson, 2 vols. (London, 1936-1965), Vol. 1, pp. 453-455.

tification with the Roman literary tradition. It should be
noted that his library classification system is based primarily
on levels of style. The *stilus religiosus* is for women; while
the women are denied all the pagan authors, only certain
Christian works of quality (and hence of generic distinction) are deemed fit for the men. Whatever the sociological
basis of this reading arrangement, Sidonius' aesthetic assumptions are clear enough. With a certain wit, the bishop asserts
the effeminacy of "merely Christian" writings while recognizing the vigor of certain exceptionally eloquent Christian
writings—this from the standpoint of proper literary taste
based on a typically Roman sense of literary history. His
standards of judgment for Christian literature are thus literary rather than religious.

Our other fifth-century notice of Prudentius hints at a
different critical standpoint. Avitus of Vienne also observes
in Prudentius the coexistence of great artistry and Christian
doctrine, but his priorities of importance reverse those of
Sidonius. Here the context is monastic. Prudentius in this
case is recommended for a female reader's moral instruction
(which involves no relegation of the poet to a lower order).
The following lines occur in Avitus' verse epistle *De Vir-
ginitate*, addressed to one sister Fuscina, and are in praise
of the *Psychomachia*:

> Hae virtutis opes, haec sunt solatia belli,
> Quis dubium adversus mentis cum corpore bellum
> Ipsa suos armat clamantis buccina Pauli,
> Quae prudenti olim cecinit Prudentius ore.

> [These are the strengths of virtue, these the reliefs of war,
> by means of which the very trumpet of Paul crying forth
> arms its own forces for the uncertain war of mind against
> body—these Prudentius with prudent lips once sang.][10]

[10] Text from Arevalo's *Prolegomena in Editionem Prudentii, Patrologia Latina*, Vol. 59, col. 752; trans. mine. In *Oeuvres complètes de
Saint Avit*, ed. Ulysse Chevalier (Lyon, 1890), line 3 of our passage
is excised as an interpolation.

A composer of a biblical epic himself, Avitus could not fail to recognize that the *Psychomachia* is imitative of the *Aeneid* and that it is scattered through with Vergilian quotations and themes. But he chooses not to make the comparison. Given his totally different treatment of epic mode in the *De Mosaicae Historiae Gestis*, Avitus may not have fully understood Prudentius' use of Vergil. Certainly he would have been better attuned to Prudentius' use of scriptural allegory. With the reference to the Apostle Paul, he links Prudentius to the biblical rather than the classical tradition. Avitus' concern is less with the style—the rhetorical nicety of the pun on the poet's name notwithstanding—than with the moral reality (*solatia belli*) of the *Psychomachia* in terms of religious experience. Rather than a discrete fictional or rhetorical construct, he finds the *Psychomachia* a version of Christian truth.

Both fifth-century ecclesiastics have judged Prudentius from a standpoint external to the age of Prudentius: Sidonius from that of the Roman literary tradition emanating from the Augustan Age, Avitus from that of a monastic Christian morality detached from immediate temporal and literary issues. Both have contributed correct observations, but these observations cannot constitute a total interpretation because they ignore the poet's historical situation, especially his role in the Church's task c. 400 of defining the position of pagan literature versus Scripture. Not that Sidonius and Avitus should be faulted for failing to be historical critics; the necessary historical relativism was outside the ken of fifth-century Christendom and would remain so until modern times.[11]

Nor should modern commentators be blamed for having acquired standpoints external to Prudentius' times. Scholarship has suffered from a factor largely beyond the control of literary scholars: Prudentius straddles the boundary be-

[11] A convenient introduction to this method of literary analysis is D. W. Robertson, Jr., "Historical Criticism," *English Institute Essays: 1950*, ed. Alan S. Downer (New York, 1951), pp. 3-31.

13

tween two historical periods of which he was entirely ignorant, the ancient and medieval periods. No matter how useful this periodization is generally, it has proved a culprit or
at least a nuisance in our particular area of study.

Ever since the great Bentley (following Sidonius?) called
Prudentius "the Horace and Vergil of the Christians,"[12]
classicists have tended to investigate the *Psychomachia* in
terms of its Roman ancestry. Their contributions have been
extremely useful in the matter of specific data. Having
known that Prudentius was totally familiar with Augustan
literature, classicists have identified Horatian and Vergilian
elements—vocabulary, meter, *topoi*, allusions, quotations—
in his works.[13] But interpretation of these elements has
floundered. Is Prudentius Horatian because he uses the
meters and language of Horace, or is he Vergilian because
he quotes Vergil and employs an epic mode in the *Psychomachia*? Such reductive conclusions have continually been
drawn.[14] Even Charles Witke, who has written with fine
sensitivity on Prudentius' lyrics and who is deeply informed
about the history of Christian hexameters, vastly misjudges
Prudentius' classicism: thus Prudentius "is a Christian poet
because of his ability to write within a culture which was

[12] *Christianorum Maro et Flaccus*—Richard Bentley, *Horatius Flaccus* (Cambridge, 1711), on *Carm.* II. 2. 15.

[13] For Horace in Prudentius, see Herrmann Breidt, *De Aurelio
Prudentio Clemente Horatii Imitatione* (Diss., Heidelberg, 1887); L.
Strezelecki, *De Horatio Rei Metricae Prudentianae Auctore* (Krakow,
1935). For Vergil in Prudentius, see Christian Schwen, *Vergil bei
Prudentius* (Diss., Leipzig, 1937); Albertus Mahoney, *Virgil in the
Works of Prudentius* [Diss.], The Catholic University of America
Patristic Studies, Vol. 39 (Washington, D.C., 1934). Similarly, Marie
L. Ewald, *Ovid in the Contra Orationem Symmachi of Prudentius*
[Diss.], The Catholic University of America Patristic Studies, Vol. 66
(Washington, D.C., 1942); Stella Marie [Hanley], "Prudentius and
Juvenal," *Phoenix*, 16 (1962), 41-52. The editions of Bergman, Lava-
renne, and Cunningham all contain useful *indices auctorum*.

[14] But for a denial of the Horatian character of Prudentius, see
Ilona Opelt, "Prudentius und Horaz," *Forschungen zur römischen
Literatur: Festschrift Karl Büchner* (Wiesbaden, 1970), pp. 206-213.

for him Christian. His relationship with God is his outlook. He does not teach or justify. He writes, and writes conventionally, out of the possibilities set up by this outlook. The conventions adhere in the Latin language's resources, in the world of poems written before Prudentius, and in Prudentius' own practice. He is a Christian poet because he is not trying to be anything except a Latin poet. . . ."[15] And again: "Prudentius is no foe of poetry in the Latin tradition. His use of classical lines for important sacred events shows as much, as does his careful use of meter and sense of symmetry in strophic composition. Almost every aspect of his poetry is classical in basis."[16] Such an interpretation precludes the possibility of mere formal appropriation, of a cynical Christian use of classical elements. The classical bias is present also in an otherwise admirable monograph, Klaus Thraede's *Studien zu Sprache und Stil des Prudentius*. For example, Thraede devotes great attention to the classical *topos* of false modesty which he discerns in the *Epilogus*, but meanwhile he passes over the New Testament concept of humility.[17] Thraede also treats Prudentius' conception of poetry as an offering to God, so he is not unaware of its essentially religious nature; yet he misjudges the spirituality

[15] Charles Witke, "Prudentius and the Tradition of Latin Poetry," *Transactions and Proceedings of the American Philological Association*, 99 (1968), 513-514.

[16] Witke, "Prudentius and the Tradition of Latin Poetry," 524. This language, and that of the preceding quotation, is repeated almost verbatim in *Numen Litterarum* (cited n. 3), pp. 110, 143-144. Other moderns have shown a "humanist" appreciation of Prudentius. See Gaston Boissier, *La fin de paganisme*, 2 vols. (Paris, 1891), Vol. 2, p. 175; and H. J. Thomson's *Prudentius* (Loeb Classical Library), pp. xiii-ix: "He regards the pagan literature and art not as things to be rejected but as part of the inheritance into which Christian Rome enters. . . . It is as a poet in whom is embodied a reconciliation between the new faith and the old culture, and in whom Christian thought claims rank in the world of letters, that Prudentius is historically important."

[17] Klaus Thraede, *Studien zu Sprache und Stil des Prudentius*, Hypomnemata, 13 (Göttingen, 1965), pp. 48-72 *passim*.

of the modesty *topos*. With Witke, Thraede tends to over-stress the positive meaningfulness of the classical form at the expense of the Christian content.[18]

Oriented in the other direction, medievalists have tended to study the *Psychomachia* in terms of its iconographic or generic offspring. Their orientation also is not without basis in literary history. Just as classical scholars point to Pruden-tius' proficiency in traditional Latin forms of poetry, so medievalists point to his inventiveness and originality. So Prudentius justly joins Ambrose and Hilary as an inventor of the Christian hymn. His *Peristephanon Liber* is the first collection (discounting Pope Damasus' inscriptions) of poetic celebrations of the Christian martyrs. And the doc-trinal anti-pagan and anti-heretical hexameter compositions are original in several respects. But for the medievalists, of course, the *Psychomachia* is Prudentius' major achievement because of its influence. Raby's *Christian Latin Poetry* (1927) summarizes a strain of scholarly opinion on the *Psychomachia*: "[It] has been described . . . as aesthetically the weakest, but the most important from the literary and historical standpoint. For it presents the first poetical Chris-tian allegory, an original creation, which caught the fancy of the Middle Ages and inspired many imitations."[19] Even today, the majority of readers approach the *Psychomachia* because of an interest in medieval allegory and theory of allegory: What did this distant ancestor of the *Roman de la Rose* look like?[20] Given this and other oblique paths toward

[18] Witke and Thraede are members of a new movement apprecia-tive of Prudentius. The earlier French scholars have valued the poet mainly as an interesting example of decadence. So Aimé Puech, *Prudence: Étude sur la poésie latine chrétienne au IVe siècle* (Paris, 1888); P. de Labriolle, *Histoire de la littérature latine chrétienne*, 3rd ed. (Paris, 1947); and, in large measure, the editor Lavarenne.

[19] F.J.E. Raby, *Christian Latin Poetry* (Oxford, 1927), p. 61.

[20] The most comprehensive treatment of the influence of the *Psychomachia* up to the fourteenth century is the unpublished dis-sertation of Eugene B. Vest, "Prudentius in the Middle Ages" (Har-vard University, 1932).

the *Psychomachia*, it is surprising that some of the best criticism of the poem is embedded in treatments of much later literature.[21]

But the dangers in this outside orientation should be recognized. Experience with later Christian literature does not necessarily guarantee an understanding of early Christian literature. The social basis of poetry in the High Middle Ages, the period of Dante, Jean de Meun, Chaucer, is different enough even from that of the early medieval period of monastic poetry; and Prudentius almost antedates, and in temperament is totally removed from, the age of monasticism. He has not witnessed the fall of Rome, and he believes deeply, despite his orientation toward the afterlife, in his citizenship in a Roman Christian Empire, which after centuries of misbelief now follows Christ. Clearly an interpretation of Prudentius according to monastic or later medieval conventions must be shunned. If classicists have much to learn from medievalists in the area of early patristic materials, medievalists have much to learn from classicists specializing in late antiquity in the matter of Prudentius' historical context.

What then is Prudentius' period? The units of periodization smaller than "classical" and "medieval" have their drawbacks: "late classical" (*spätantike*) invariably evokes the idea of decadence; "early Christian" evokes ideas of naiveté, immaturity, undevelopment. Although such sub-periods bring us closer to the object of study, still the question

---

[21] Thus Hans Robert Jauss, "Form und Auffassung der Allegorie in der Tradition der *Psychomachia*," *Medium Aevum Vivum: Festschrift für Walther Bulst*, ed. Jauss and Schaller (Heidelberg, 1960), pp. 179-206; Jauss, "La transformation de la forme allégorique entre 1180 et 1240: d'Alain de Lille à Guillaume de Lorris," *L'humanisme médiéval dans les littératures romanes du XIIe au XIVe siècle*, Actes et Colloques du Centre de Philologie et de Littératures romanes de l'Université de Strasbourg, Fasc. 3 (Paris, 1964), pp. 107-146; Marc-René Jung, *Études sur le poème allégorique en France au moyen âge*, Romanica Helvetica, series linguistica, Vol. 82 (Berne, 1971), pp. 25-34.

remains: if within the sub-period there exist heterogeneous religious and cultural forces, what does the sub-periodization contribute to our understanding of their relationship? Prudentius and Claudian both called themselves Christians and both were first-rate poets. Whence their differences? Even more striking are the differences between Prudentius and the Christian hexameter poets from Juvencus to Arator. A symptom of the problem of periodizing early Christian poetry is seen in Charles Witke's great contribution to the literary history of these times, *Numen Litterarum*, where Prudentius is discussed in one chapter and the history of Christian hexameter poets from Juvencus onward in another. There is of course a generic distinction at work between scriptural paraphrase and original composition based on classical models. But if Prudentius cannot be treated in critical terms applicable to his fellow poets and fellow Christians, of what use is the sub-period that unites them? Perhaps none.

The excursus on "Early Christian Poetry" in Ernst Robert Curtius' *European Literature and the Latin Middle Ages* further illustrates these difficulties. Curtius discerns "two directions" possible in that poetry between Constantine's reign and A.D. 600 which was not cult poetry but was "conceived as literature." "On the one hand, the Christian poet could treat the matter of Christian piety (sanctification of daily work, cult of martyrs) and of Christian dogma and ethics (doctrine of the Trinity, the origin of sin, apologetics, battle of the vices and virtues). It was Prudentius' great accomplishment that he followed this path. With full command of classical literary style he opened up great new realms to poetry. High gifts and intense experience were the springs of his creation. The rich flood of his poetry is independent of the system of the antique genres and hence is not forced to come to terms with antique literary theory. He is the most important and most original of the early Christian poets. But he is also a solitary phenomenon. The majority of the early Christian poets followed another path:

18

that of keeping to the antique genres and filling them with Christian matter."[22] Of the two paths said to be open during this 300-year period, the one was chosen just once, by Prudentius, the other by all the other poets. We must ask: since Prudentius was unique in having chosen the path of "independence from antique genres"[23] (a path described tautologically in terms of his *opera*), in what sense can this path have existed for the other poets? If Prudentius was indeed a solitary phenomenon, it seems rather more likely that the path in question was open for only a short period during the 300-year span. If so, then perhaps the other Christian poets did not have a choice and, conversely, perhaps when Prudentius lived the path of biblical epic, which Curtius proceeds to describe, was closed. It is hard to avoid suspecting that even the sub-period of Early Christian Poetry is too broad a category to apply to Prudentius. This suggests that the works of Prudentius should be examined in relation to contemporary texts and events, to a really quite brief period of time.

The value of a restricted historical scope is further confirmed by Curtius' discussion of biblical epic before and after Prudentius. The major figures, Juvencus and Sedulius, are contrasted without mention of the fact that no writers of biblical epic flourish alongside of Prudentius, a fact that suggests that this tradition is discontinuous. (Only scattered hexameters on biblical themes survive from the end of the fourth century; these are all brief, with little narrative movement.) Curtius describes Juvencus' admiration for antique poetry and his desire to create its Christian counterpart, to build up "literature of Christian content in antique form." He next contrasts Sedulius "to Juvencus' smooth, clear poetic language, elevated by Virgilian echoes, to Pruden-

[22] Ernst Robert Curtius, *European Literature and the Latin Middle Ages*, trans. Willard R. Trask, Bollingen Series 36 (New York, 1953), pp. 458-459.
[23] But Charles Witke, *Numen Litterarum*, p. 144, claims: "Prudentius invents no new genres." I discuss Prudentius' genres in Chapter I.

19

tius' ringing Christian Classicism. . . ." Sedulius does not mention the names of Vergil and Homer, as Juvencus does, but instead proclaims that he will sing in the manner of David. "These statements," Curtius concludes, "are significant. They contain the germ of a Christian theory of literature (sacred subjects should be treated after the model of the Biblical bard). But they also announce a rigoristic rejection of antique poetry and the antique pantheon. This is the sign of a new period."[24] Thus the Early Christian Period of 300 years is split in half, Prudentius with his "ringing Christian Classicism" joining Juvencus, Sedulius launching a sub-sub-period. Yet the very signs of this new period are evident in Prudentius: rejection of the antique pantheon, emulation of the biblical bard, conspicuous refraining from mention of Vergil. This does not mean that Prudentius launches a new period himself, but that his works display radical differences from those of poets on either side of him.

My working hypothesis is that two significant shifts in poetic outlook bracket the career of Prudentius, giving late fourth-century Christian literature certain characteristics of its own. The first shift, separating Prudentius from Juvencus, is marked by a sharp ideological break with Roman liberalism by the Church and by Theodosius and his successors. This break with Roman liberalism included an attack not only against the pagan ritual long sheltered by it, but against its characteristic philosophical eclecticism and secular historical outlook. The polemical nature of much of Prudentius' verse should be seen in this anti-liberal context. His anti-Vergilianism responds to a quiet but firm aristocratic movement gathering all the grand old—and by now outlawed—pagan traditions under the cultural aegis of Vergil. To a degree, the Church-State coalition under Theodosius and his heirs anticipated Alaric's sacking of the pagan tem-

---

[24] *European Literature and the Latin Middle Ages*, pp. 459-462. Boethius' *De Consolatione Philosophiae* is the last major work of late antiquity produced outside the Church's secular and regular organizations.

ples in Rome. Not all the outlawed pagan idols were placed in art museums as the Theodosian edicts had instructed: the cultural program of the Church opposed not only the religious observances of paganism but, in part, the art and literature associated with them.[25] Prudentius, I shall attempt to show, was a willing participant in the activity against pagan culture—not perhaps as a hammer-wielding iconoclast, but as a cultivated, sophisticated man of letters.

The second shift in poetic outlook takes place after Prudentius' death, and is signaled by rejection of Theodosian political piety in favor of other-worldly Christian asceticism.[26] This second shift will not concern us much, for it falls beyond the object of our inquiry; but certain features of Prudentius' poetry may be partly explicable— for example, his interest in the immediate worldly relevance

[25] Only in part. Examples of the tolerance of pagan culture are given in Chadwick (cited n. 4), pp. 171-173; see also Brown (cited n. 6) for pagan culture in the fifth century and generally for the Church's liberalism (e.g., towards mixed marriages) as a means of gradually converting the Roman aristocracy. If the late dating of Macrobius' *Saturnalia* is correct, we have a certainly pagan work produced by a certainly pagan high official c. 430; and the sixth-century historian Zosimus is a pagan who attempts to demonstrate that the fall of Rome resulted from abandonment of the old religion. At the end of the fourth century, the aged Ausonius and the young Claudian were, whatever their professed belief, not more than lukewarm Christians, at least in their verse. But if the break with liberalism may be said to have hardly affected a poet like Claudian, perhaps his special role as Stilicho's propagandist (involving a narrowness of poetic task, of audience) disqualifies him from being considered representative of his period; on this matter, and on the more basic question of whether Christian-pagan cultural relations are to be characterized by struggle or peaceful coexistence, I disagree with Alan Cameron (cited n. 4). Further discussion in notes below.

[26] Christian asceticism was still considered a rather exotic, Egyptian phenomenon in late fourth-century Rome. It had Roman adherents, as witnesses the correspondence of Jerome; and see D. Gordini, "Origine e sviluppo del monachesimo a Roma," *Gregorianum*, 37 (1956), 220-260. Augustine himself records the conversion of two centurions upon reading the *Life of St. Anthony*—see *Confessions* VIII; but the ascetic movement was new, radical, atypical.

21

of scriptural typology—by the fact that the broad social impact of monastic values had not yet been felt.

Prudentius' own concept of periodization is that he lives in the era of the New Law, of fulfilled prophecy, of the Church founded by Christ for the salvation of souls. He sees his own existence within the Church, which moves on the advancing stream of time between the Incarnation and the Last Judgment. He understands the moral significance of his life (including the writing of poems) in relation to the contemporary Church and, beyond this, in relation to these supreme events—the cardinal and the last—of sacred history. The poet's response to literature and language is therefore first and foremost a response to Scripture, where the New Law is supremely revealed. The present study will show that the major themes of the *Psychomachia* are scriptural; it will consider how the manifold presence of scriptural allusions and language operates upon these themes. The writings of the Church Fathers are ancillary in defining the meaning of the *Psychomachia*; if (as the *Psychomachia*'s poet also claims) inspired by God's grace, these writings are nevertheless inferior to the unique Word of God.[27] In relation to both Scripture and patristic writings, however, literature produced by pagans is outside the fold of truth. Insofar as Prudentius conceives the *Psychomachia* as an expression of orthodox Christian faith, his allusions to pagan literature must be qualitatively different from allusions to scriptural or patristic writings. The Latin literary heritages available to the poet are thus not only varied but conflicting. When joined together they are able to create strong crosscurrents, literary turbulence. Why this turbulence was created at the close of the fourth century will be a topic of historical investigation in the first chapter; after-

[27] The excellent recent article of P. F. Beatrice, "L'allegoria nella *Psychomachia* di Prudenzio," *Studia Patavina*, 18 (1971), 25-73, is unfortunately marred by its overemphasis on the influence of patristic writers—in this case, problematically, of Origen—on Prudentius; yet many of the key scriptural references are provided in footnotes.

wards the actual presence of scriptural, patristic, and pagan literary elements in the text of the *Psychomachia* will be treated.

If the *Psychomachia* is such a battle between literatures, between the Word of God and the words of Satan's followers, then the definition of its literary genre vis-à-vis the scriptural and classical traditions becomes crucially important. Take the genre classification often used: "allegorical epic." In what sense "allegorical" and in what sense an "epic"? Do these terms refer to the Roman literary tradition, in which case the *Psychomachia* is at least recognizable by its classical form? Or is the *Psychomachia* instead a poem of a new type, allegorical and epic in ways beyond and outside of the classical tradition, in imitation of Scripture? Or—and this is my understanding—does the *Psychomachia* refer to both profane and sacred traditions in radically different ways?

C. S. Lewis, in his influential *The Allegory of Love*, has termed the *Psychomachia* "the fully-fledged allegorical poem."[28] He refers to the significant presence of abstract personifications who move within a consistent world defined by their existence, a fictional space-time continuum. The origin of allegory he explains this way: ". . . you can start with an immaterial fact, such as the passions which you actually experience, and can then invent *visibilia* to express them. If you are hesitating between an angry retort and a soft answer, you can express your state of mind by inventing a person called *Ira* with a torch and letting her contend with another invented person called *Patientia*. This is allegory. . . ."[29] Elsewhere Lewis remarks that allegory is "simile seen from the other end,"[30] a representation rather than a mode of expression. According to this viewpoint, allegory achieves the embodiment of immaterial experience only at the cost of abstracting, of distancing, of making less

[28] C. S. Lewis, *The Allegory of Love* (Oxford, 1936), p. 66. Likewise Raby, see n. 19.

[29] Lewis, pp. 44-45.　　　　　[30] Lewis, p. 125.

real the psychological reality of the mind. Given this basis, allegory will be either good or bad depending upon the extent to which it captures the fundamental equivalence between experience and the abstraction of experience.[31]

Lewis's characterization of the *Psychomachia*'s personification allegory encapsulates nineteenth-century charges of artificiality—and lends them theoretical sophistication. Over the past decade and a half, however, Lewis's views have been challenged theoretically by the view that ancient and medieval allegory, far from being an abstracting representation, is a mode of expression equally or perhaps more "real" (to its audience) than quotidian experience. And Lewis's views have been challenged practically by investigation in the *Psychomachia* of another sort of "allegory" besides personification allegory, that is, scriptural allegory. St. Paul allegorized events and persons of the Old Testament in terms of their fulfillment in the events and persons—especially Christ—of the Gospels. This figural relationship St. Paul in turn applied to contemporary moral problems. An intelligible pattern of scriptural history was thus capable of fulfillment in the life of the individual Christian. It goes without saying that this sort of "allegory" is unlike that described by C. S. Lewis, for it in no way permits a lessening of the reality of events in the moral scheme of things. We shall deal with the scriptural allegory of the *Psychomachia* in later pages; here it will suffice to indicate recent advances

[31] Lewis's conviction that the *Psychomachia* does not capture this fundamental equivalence is evident from his commentary on pp. 68-69. Lewis's deprecation of Prudentian allegory and, by extension, much medieval allegory, has been unfortunately influential. It ends with this treatment of a "mechanical defect in the pitched battle": "that fighting is an activity that is not proper to most of the virtues. Courage can fight, and perhaps we can make a shift with Faith. But how is Patience to rage in battle? How is Mercy to strike down her foes, or Humility to triumph over them when fallen? Prudentius is almost everywhere embarrassed by this difficulty, and his attempts to solve it are failures because they betray his deficiency in humour."

in understanding the figural relationship of the *Psychomachia* to Scripture.

Scholars have for some time noticed and commented briefly on the existence of biblical characters and symbols in the poem, but these elements have been considered merely "allusions," rhetorical flourishes meant to decorate the personification allegory.[32] Little effort was made to understand the relation between scriptural allegory and personification allegory until Henri de Lubac, in his monumental *Exégèse médiévale: les quatre sens de l'Écriture*, pointed to the Old Testament characters Judith, Job, David, and Samuel "solemnly drawn" beneath the figures of Pudicitia, Patientia, Sobrietas: this was biblical typology grafted onto Vergilian language.[33] Laura Cotogni had suggested some twenty years prior to Lubac that the *Psychomachia* was "a poetic elaboration of allegorical exegesis" and had pointed to its typological "Praefatio" by way of evidence—but Cotogni's suggestion was not followed by others until recently.[34] Contemporaneously with Lubac, Hans Robert Jauss echoed

[32] Such is the attitude of Lavarenne. Even Auerbach, amazingly, errs: "Prudentius [in the *Psychomachia*] does not seem to recognize figural interpretation."—"Figura," trans. Ralph Manheim, in *Scenes from the Drama of European Literature* (New York, 1959), n. 36. In the same footnote the *Dittochaeon* of Prudentius is mentioned as an exception. Auerbach finds only personification allegory in the *Psychomachia*. He attaches the footnote to general remarks: "Most of the allegories we find in literature or art represent a virtue (e.g. wisdom), or a passion (jealousy), an institution (justice), or at most a very general synthesis of historical phenomena (peace, the fatherland)—almost never a definite event in its full historicity. Such are the allegories of late antiquity and the Middle Ages, extending roughly from the *Psychomachia* of Prudentius to Alain de Lille and the *Roman de la Rose*" ("Figura," p. 54).

[33] Henri de Lubac, *Exégèse médiévale: les quatre sens de l'Écriture*, 2 Parts [2 vols. in each] (Paris, 1959-1964), Part 2, Vol. 2, p. 214.

[34] Laura Cotogni, "Sovrapposizione di visioni e di allegorie nella *Psychomachia* de Prudenzio," *Rendiconti della R. Accademia Nazionale dei Lincei, classe di scienze morali, storiche e filologiche*, Serie 6, Vol. 12 (1936), 441.

Cotogni: the poet's intention was to expound typological exegesis of Scripture in the epic mode.[35] Since Lubac and Jauss, it has become a critical commonplace to speak of the typology or scriptural allegory or exegetical structure of the *Psychomachia*. This positive development has changed our conception of the allegory and our appreciation of its sophisticated structure. Yet scriptural allegory in Prudentius requires much more attention. Even the recent treatments of this matter have been hasty and superficial, the monograph of Gnilka being the only exception.[36] Too often the presence of typology in the *Psychomachia* has been treated as structural framework, as mere form, rather than as an impulse behind the moral content of the poem. And the influence of the Epistles upon the allegory has not been appreciated. Specifically, the Old Testament themes of warfare and temple-building, interpreted by Pauline exegesis, should be seen as the major Christian metaphors animating the *Psychomachia*; of equal impact is Paul's interpretation of Abraham, the father of Israel, the spiritual type of all Christian faithful. The mere presence of the Old Testament characters mentioned by Lubac is secondary in relation to this dynamic Christian typology. Finally, the anagogic pull of the Apocalypse of John is strong indeed; while a number of scholars have pointed to allusions to this book of future history, they have not explored the relation of such to scriptural allegory. Chapters II and III of this study treat such matters in order to gain a general understanding of how Prudentius employs Scripture in the *Psychomachia*.

After discussion of personification allegory and scriptural allegory, there remains the problem of the poem's epic form and mode. Given the vital scriptural presence in the *Psychomachia*, to what degree is depiction of heroic conventions

[35] Jauss, "Form und Auffassung der Allegorie in der Tradition der *Psychomachia*" (cited n. 21), p. 188.
[36] Christian Gnilka, *Studien zur Psychomachie des Prudentius*, Klassisch-Philologische Studien, 27 (Wiesbaden, 1963).

contingent upon scriptural themes? Does Prudentius intend to ennoble his scriptural allegory by means of the epic mode as he borrows it from the Roman literary tradition? Or rather, does he intend the scriptural allegory to generate a revised conception of the heroic in the minds of his readers? Such questions have never been seriously addressed, possibly on account of an entrenched belief that Prudentius is the preeminent poet of Christian humanism, the poet who could join the best features of Roman civilization and Christian spirituality. E. K. Rand writes: "I look with sympathy on the attempt of the Church to guard its peculiar treasure with zeal, but to treasure no less devoutly its heritage in the culture of the past."[37] By culture is meant, of course, Roman culture, but did Prudentius, a poet of the Church, treasure this culture? History suggests, and Prudentius' text proves, that he did not. My concluding topic is the status of Vergil at the close of the fourth century and of Vergil in the works of Prudentius. Although several detailed studies have been published on Prudentius' use of Vergil, these have not evidenced a critical understanding of the poet's reaction against the late fourth-century cult of Vergil.[38] Prudentius' use of Vergil has been treated either as a purely rhetorical device, or as thematically important only very locally in the context of this or that passage. My intention is to uncover the deeper anti-Vergilian ironies contained in the epic mode generally and in the Vergilian quotations specifically.

To reveal the scriptural and Vergilian presences in the *Psychomachia* as essentially antagonistic is to challenge the view of Prudentius as humanist. The poet is in fact fervently anti-pagan because he connects the salvation of his own soul with the preservation of his embattled Church. He writes on behalf of both. Possessing great poetic gifts and a com-

[37] E. K. Rand, "Prudentius and Christian Humanism," *Transactions and Proceedings of the American Philological Association*, 51 (1920), 72.
[38] For bibliographical discussion of Vergil in the works of Prudentius, see Chapter IV.

27

plete grasp of the literary tradition in which he has been trained, Prudentius is most willing to use these gifts and this literary tradition against the culture in which he was raised and on behalf of that culture which, for him, is alone worthy: the culture of souls in the Church.

The Christian Poet in His Times

JUDGING from the kinds of poems he produced and from his attitudes and statements about poetry, Prudentius' self-consciousness as a poet is fundamentally Christian. By this I mean that he is not simply a poet professing and occasionally expressing a religious point of view (as Claudian does), but one who in writing is primarily motivated by religious concerns. The purpose of this chapter is to define these religious concerns, especially in respect to their individual and social dimensions. Such definition is important background to an interpretation of the *Psychomachia* that links psychology directly to ecclesiastical history. In order to claim that in following the soul's progress Prudentius is also tracing the current history of the Church after the conversion of Rome—a Church invaded by the vices of success, indulgence, greed, and hypocrisy; fighting to return to a life of devotion but falling into the discords of heresy; and finally overcoming heresy and accomplishing the conversion of the temple of paganism—in order to claim such a connection, it will be necessary first to establish Prudentius' norms of individual and social spirituality. These norms are implicit in the range of genre in his works, explicit in the many references to his personal status in Roman Christian society.

The content and arrangement of Prudentius' *opera* conform with the range of Christian living as set forth in the Gospel. To love God and neighbor is, in terms of poetry, to set one's words moving in two directions, heavenward and through the world. Thus the lyrics are generally conceived as directed toward God: the hymns of the *Liber Cathemerinon* sounding the *canticum novum*, the liturgical

29

music of the Church in tune with God; in the *Peristephanon Liber*, celebrations of the Christian martyrs whose names are heard in heaven. The hexameter compositions are generally conceived as directed to men in the here and now: the *Apotheosis* and *Hamartigenia*, polemics against heresy and theological expositions of Nicene orthodoxy; the two books *Contra Orationem Symmachi*, polemics against the pagan revival of the nineties, advocating non-compromise on the restoration of pagan rights and propagating a vision of a unified, glorious Christian Empire. But this generic distinction, according to heavenly or worldly end, is neither clear-cut nor entirely consistent, and is perhaps paradoxical: for the hymns are also to be sung, and the martyrs to be emulated in this world; the polemics are designed to save souls for the world to come. So it is with the audience use of the finished poems: the hexameter pieces, with their orator's voice of public engagement, were most likely read in small groups, if not privately,[1] while the hymns, often expressive of individual devotion, were chanted en masse during church worship.[2] This crossover and simultaneity of public and private voices are typically Prudentian.

Prudentius wishes[3] to define his role as a poet in relation to both his language and its uses. He does not detach himself from his creation, and he does place his persona in a number of passages perhaps best characterized as sincere

[1] This is not to rule out the possibility of an initial public reading by the poet—as Claudian orated his occasional pieces—at some date before they were published as collected works (c. 405). Poetry in late antiquity was only rarely read in private.

[2] *Cath.* V, VI, VII, IX, and X are included in the Mozarabic Rite. See Bernard Peebles, *The Poet Prudentius* (New York, 1951), p. 142, for a discursive note on this subject. Peebles's study contains excellent and full notes on the sociology of the works, on biography, and on the vexed matter of Prudentian dating and chronology; it summarizes the range of modern speculation. A more recent study of the Church's use of Prudentius' lyrics is Maurice P. Cunningham, "The Nature and Purpose of the *Peristephanon* of Prudentius," *Sacris Erudiri*, 14 (1963), 40-45.

[3] I do not subscribe to Wimsatt's theory of "intentional fallacy."

statements of aim. These passages reveal a poet (or at least a poet's self-portrait) of intense individualism and of intense concern with public service, a poet who mingles the two aims not out of subjectivism or philosophical confusion, but out of Christian morality. For surely the poet's faith is the main cause of his poetry. Prudentius accepts the doctrine of the Trinity, and he loves and wishes to glorify Christ: note for example, the *Apotheosis*, a complete Christology prefaced by the exquisite "Hymnus de Trinitate." But this faith is not solely a private matter. Prudentius believes the Church to be the mystical Bride of Christ, continuing the redemptive work of the Incarnation in human history; and he conceives himself as a member of this mystical body, dependent upon it for his own salvation. As a poet in, of, and for the Church, he understands that his works should further the works of the Church, the saving of souls now and in the future. The very social-historical context of the Church suggests that immersion in carnal particulars is essential to its culture. So Prudentius composes polemics against whatever forces threaten the Church; he expounds the theological issues of the moment. His panegyrics in praise of martyrs proclaim new heroes for a changing society. When he gives notice of his collected works in the *Praefatio*, he shows more than a general awareness of ecclesiastical politics. He alludes to a paganism flourishing in Rome and to heresy—these are the timely enemies against whom he will hurl his darts of language. In sum, his poetry will serve God and the Church not only in universal and sacred language (liturgical, scriptural) befitting the eternal Creator, but in the particular language needed by the embattled Church. Both modes are necessary in Christian poetry, and the poet believes that his own salvation is involved in both.

Praefatio

Prudentius introduces the public to his collected works with an autobiographical lyric. Here, the end of Christian

31

poetry is characterized as daily and unceasing praise of God, and the various genres (a catalogue of the works to follow) are presented as manifestations of this basic spiritual end. That this summary of poetic theory and practice is grafted to the poet's life history and is offered to his audience as the fruition of that life is significant. I assume that Prudentius considers that the display of his past career and present intent will function as an example or lesson, one that will put his audience in the right frame of mind to understand and enjoy his poems. Simple pride of authorship can hardly have been Prudentius' motivation, since that motivation conflicts with the self-image he draws for our scrutiny: a sober, humble Prudentius, who confesses doubt about the worth of his past life, who acknowledges present sinfulness, who hopes that his poetic career may answer and atone for his career in the Roman administration, and who prays that the following poems will be judged worthy by God. Granting the didactic purpose of all this, I sense that the religious sentiment is sincere and the autobiography probably accurate. The subject of this reflective lyric is, it seems to me, the birth of poetry in Christian conversion, a subject wholly relevant to the Prudentian corpus.[4]

Autobiography of course has a traditional and dignified place in classical Roman lyric. Several modern commentators on the *Praefatio* have pointed to its Horatian imagery and form, and Charles Witke's full and astute analysis includes discussion of specific Horatian reminiscences.[5] As Witke has demonstrated, there is nothing gratuitous about

[4] My understanding of the spirituality of the *Praefatio* is generally indebted to Isidoro Rodriguez-Herrera, *Poeta Christianus: Prudentius' Auffassung vom Wesen und von der Aufgabe des christlichen Dichters* [Diss.] (Munich, 1936). For an opposing view, that Prudentius does not depict his spiritual conversion, see Emanuelo Rapisarda, "La *Praefatio* de Prudenzio," *Nuovo Didaskaleion*, 2 (1948), 51-61. Neither of these scholars sees the *Praefatio* as a statement in contradiction to the classical tradition.

[5] See Critical Introd., n. 13; and *Numen Litterarum* (cited Critical Introd., n. 3), pp. 107-113.

such reminiscences: an Horatian situation is called forth typically in order to be revised, transformed, and converted by the poet's Christian outlook. I would submit that much else is happening in the course of the *Praefatio*. The conspicuousness of the classical conventions within which Prudentius' language strains should not obscure the source of that language's energy. Commenting on lines 22-27, Witke calls the movement "unusual in that it brings forward a personal insight stated in lyrical terms into an official context of career-summary."[6] And on the succeeding strophe: "This passage from life to death is explicit, classical in its preparation and execution and language. . . . But the sentiment, as the succeeding strophe shows, is Christian."[7] This "personal insight" and "sentiment" are translatable, I should think, into Christian individualism. Prudentius portrays himself in the *Praefatio* as fearing God, considering the limitations of the world, pondering the fate of his soul after death. Such sentiment is indeed non-classical, and it is embodied in a separate literary tradition; the Psalms and prophetic books of the Old Testament and the Pauline Epistles are its major components.[8] This is not to claim that the *Praefatio* is generically a psalm, penitential or otherwise; but it does dramatize the soul's conversion toward God, its becoming an instrument of song. Its essential plot is one of movement away from Roman political life and, as a poet of the Church, toward communion with God. The Horatian retreat to a country villa is avoided, as are several other Horatian conceits. Accompanying the change in orientation is a change in literary expression: the conventional imagery and restrained tone associated with Prudentius' Roman career yield to personal and fervent devotion. This turn happens midpoint in the *Praefatio*, which gives the conversion a symmetrical structure and antistrophic movement.

The first seven of fifteen stanzas contain the poet's announcement of his old age, his typically Roman question

---

[6] *Numen Litterarum*, p. 108.   [7] *Numen Litterarum*, p. 109.
[8] And the *Confessions* of St. Augustine, discussed p. 245.

about his life's meaning (*quid nos utile tanti spatio temporis egimus?*), and his summarized public career (early education, training in rhetoric, the classic sins of manhood—*lasciva protervitas / et luxus petulans*, success as a lawyer, governorship over two cities, and finally his "greater elevation" by the Emperor).[9] Charles Witke has correctly observed: "These strophes are not unlike a Roman funeral-inscription, particularly in the self-characterization in line 18 [*ius civile bonis reddidimus, terruimus reos*]. Prudentius is objectively setting forth his life's work in answer to one set of possible responses to the question *quid utile?* So far his measured response has been no more unclassical than any careerist's; even the modest disassociation from and gentle castigation of youth's excesses, the *concessa Venus* of Horace ('heu pudet ac piget') is not far from Pliny himself commenting on his *nugae*, a standard pose."[10] But Witke, recognizing the subsequent shift to the personal and lyrical, seems not always to appreciate the fragility of this "standard pose"—and its capacity for irony—in the context of the poet's contrition. Prudentius' sentiments toward his prior cupidity are restrained and dignified, yet they are enough to make plausible the powerful drama of the conversion. And as Witke himself has commented, even before the shift in tone, each strophe dealing with Prudentius' advance in the Roman administration "ends with words which signify the drawbacks or bad features now seen in the perspective of the poet's present view."[11] Now with the stylistic about-face, Prudentius forces a negation of the conventional, classical, Roman associations of the first half of the *Praefatio*.

Summarizing this secular career just prior to his direct

[9] "It is probable, on chronological grounds, that the emperor who elevated him [to an honorable post of unknown nature] was Theodosius."—Peebles, *The Poet Prudentius*, pp. 17-18.

[10] "Prudentius and the Tradition of Latin Poetry" (cited Critical Introd., n. 15), pp. 511-512; similarly, *Numen Litterarum*, p. 108.

[11] "Prudentius and the Tradition of Latin Poetry," p. 511; *Numen Litterarum*, p. 107.

consideration of poetry, the poet presents himself as con-
trite in the remembrance of sin and death:

> numquid talia proderunt
>> carnis post obitum vel bona vel mala
>> cum iam, quidquid id est quod fueram, mors aboleverit?
> dicendum mihi: quisquis es,
>> mundum, quem coluit, mens tua perdidit.
>> non sunt illa Dei, quae studuit, cuius habeberis. (28-33)

[Will such things, good or bad, be of any profit after my
flesh is dead, when death shall have wiped out all that I
was? It must be said to me: "Whomsoever thou art, thy
soul hath lost the world it cherished; not to God, who will
claim thee as His, belong the things for which it was
zealous."]

The morality is straightforward: a person is not justified
before God by having possibly done some good—*vel bona
vel mala*—in the world, but by the goodness of what he
cherishes. This is the concept of *caritas*. The poet explicitly
admits to an improper love of the world and, so doing, displays the endangered state of his soul; secondarily, he casts
doubt on the effects of his political career—they are good
or bad. His attitude, from which arises the will to sing, is
penitential. In the tradition of David, Prudentius offers his
voice to God as surrogate good works, and from this new
voice of charity come all the genres of Christian poetry.

> atqui fine sub ultimo
>> peccatrix anima stultitiam exuat:
>> saltem voce Deum concelebret, si meritis nequit.
> hymnis continuet dies,
>> nec nox ulla vacet quin Dominum canat;
>> pugnet contra hereses, catholicam discutiat fidem,
> conculcet sacra gentium,
>> labem, Roma, tuis inferat idolis,
>> carmen martyribus devoveat, laudet apostolos.

35

haec dum scribo vel eloquor,
  vinclis o utinam corporis emicem
  liber, quo tulerit lingua sono mobilis ultimo! (34-45)

[Yet as my last end draws near let my sinning soul put
off her folly. With voice at least let her honour God, if
with good deeds she cannot. With hymns let her link
the days together, and no night pass without singing of
her Lord. Let her fight against heresies, expound the
Catholic faith, trample on the rites of the heathen, strike
down thy idols, O Rome, devote song to the martyrs,
and praise the apostles. And while I write or speak of
these themes, O may I fly forth in freedom from the
bonds of the body, to the place whither my busy tongue's
last word shall tend.]

"The last strophe," comments Charles Witke, "stands in the
place of the conventional apotheosis of the poet, as Horace
Carmina 3.30, 2.20, 11.35ff., where elevation implies approaching the divine. In contrast, Prudentius does not point
to his poems to justify or anticipate his flight to heaven. . . .
His art is the scene of his flight to heaven just like poets of
the Latin tradition. But by poising the act of moving *quo
tulerit lingua sono mobilis ultimo* in the context of continuous service to the divine in poetry, Prudentius puts the
creative act into a personal light: it is no longer the effect,
a publicly accessible monument, the text, that liberates
from this world's limits, but rather liberation may come
(and is implored to come) in the midst of poetic endeavor
privately and individually going forward in the praise of
God. Prudentius integrates art into a total seamless continuum of life, and literature thus reasserted as the significance of Prudentius' existence, comes to characterize it
exclusively."[12] If I may Christianize these perceptive observations somewhat, Prudentius' radical alteration of the
Horatian (and pagan) apotheosis of the poet signals his

[12] *Numen Litterarum*, pp. 112-113.

THE CHRISTIAN POET IN HIS TIMES

identification of poetry with *caritas*, which has the inevitable effect of negating the value of the conventions and formalism of the past worldly career.[13] Poetry, says Prudentius, is not at all what it used to be: no longer of the world, its origin is in the charitable soul, its end is in God, and its reward is, with God's grace, salvation.

This anagogic conclusion confirms the negating rather than synthesizing effect of the *Praefatio*'s antistrophe. The counterposed political and poetic careers involve alternate attitudes toward the world. Thus each part opens with a statement of the poet's advancing age, first through cold, rarified planetary imagery, second through the natural imagery of frost, roses, snow—

> sub quo prima dies mihi
>   quam multas hiemes volverit, et rosas
>   pratis post glaciem reddiderit, nix capitis probat.

$$(25\text{-}27)$$

[Under him (Salia) my time began, and how many winters it has seen roll on, how often seen the roses given back to the meadows after the frost, the snow on my head proves.][14]

Next the question, *quid utile?*, is posed in two contrary ways: first, with a restrained conventionality suggesting no more than concern for the dignity of appearance, then with fear against the soul's condition after death. Most important, of Prudentius' careers, the one has ended already in the past, the other is only about to begin and is set in the subjunctive mood. This shift in verb tense sets Prudentius between two states, and thus conveys not only the psychological decisiveness of his conversion but the problematic hope against eter-

---

[13] The title, *Apotheosis*, represents a similarly bold alteration of the traditional Latin meaning to a theological one. See p. 114, n. 5.

[14] Charles Witke has commented on the "deliberately evoked warm feeling" of this stanza. *Numen Litterarum*, p. 109.

nity. Although Prudentius' first career might have seemed the great Roman success story of late antiquity, its inadequacy becomes increasingly clear as the poetic career, motivated by love of God and hope of salvation, answers and atones for it. Having once learned to utter sinful falsehoods in the *rhetores'* school—*mox docuit toga / infectum vitiis falsa loqui, non sine crimine*—he would use his voice to praise God and defend the Church *contra hereses*. Having served *Romanitas*, he would cast down Rome's idols. Having governed two cities in Spain, possibly even with high standards of equity, he would celebrate martyrs who themselves had once been oppressed by the municipal principalities. Finally, having once been elevated by the Emperor to the nearest rank (*ordine proximo*), he rejects all such worldly profit and prays for his soul's elevation to its desired proximity to the King of Heaven.

Is it farfetched to suppose that Prudentius' writing of deeply felt Christian poems late in life grew out of intense spiritual crisis and conversion? Not that he was ever a pagan, but for most of his lifetime he may have been a nominal Christian, unbothered by the spiritual implications of Christianity and comfortably at home with traditional pagan culture. There were many such. And not that it was impossible to maintain a strong Christian faith while serving as a high Roman official, for the Empire was, of course, officially Christian; but Prudentius does not testify that he was then a fervent Christian, and seems to suggest the opposite. Perhaps the intensifying struggle between the Church and pagan organizations at the close of the fourth century brought to a head a religious struggle within the poet's own mind. We cannot know the genesis of Prudentius' spiritual conversion, only its probable effects upon his poetry.

THE INDIVIDUAL POET IN SOCIETY

One such effect on his poetry would be the strong Christian individualism obvious in the *Praefatio*, in the lyric hymns, and even in hexameter compositions such as the *Contra Orationem Symmachi*. Prudentius' willingness to display inner religious fears and hopes, to trace the motions of his soul, is of course not simply a matter of private revelation or confession. It is the creation of a typical Christian psyche for didactic purposes. Because Prudentius views his own soul as one of a community of Christian souls, he is able as an individual both to feel ultimate moral responsibility for his soul and to conceive of it as typically created in God's image, typically fallen into the state of sin, and typically redeemed by Christ. These perceptions of self and of general humanity are simultaneous. The *Psychomachia* is accordingly Prudentius' most complete treatment of the typical psychology, yet here as elsewhere the representation of the soul is not distanced from actuality: the poet includes his own soul with that represented by the allegory, and he expects his readers to do likewise.

It is important not to lose sight of the genuineness of the poet's personal sentiments even when these sentiments are seen to serve as general moral instruction. Being mature in years as he writes, and believing that his poetry has marked a new phase in his life, his individualistic expression of salvational desires is wholly natural and meaningful to his own situation. Frequent references to the Last Judgment at the conclusions of his poems should not be imputed solely to a Christian poet's duty to warn his audience; in fact, most apocalyptic scenes occasion—and perhaps are occasioned by—Prudentius' prayers for his own salvation. These lines, for example, end his hymn in honor of three martyrs of Tarraco:

> olim tempus erit ruente mundo,
> cum te, Tarraco, Fructuosus acri
> solvet supplicio tegens ab igni.
> fors dignabitur et meis medellam
> tormentis dare prosperante Christo,
> dulces hendecasyllabos revolvens. (*Per.* VI, 157-162)

39

[One day will come a time when in the dissolution of the world Fructuosus will free thee, Tarraco, from sore distresses, covering thee from fire; and perchance under Christ's favour he will deign to give relief to my torments too, as he recalls my sweet hendecasyllables.]

Prudentius has just imagined the population of Tarraco hymning in unison their martyr-heroes. The gilded roofs of the church reecho, and the joyous seas contribute their song. Here Prudentius relates his moral situation to that of the Christian community, praying that the martyr will intercede on the Day of Doom on behalf of the city collectively and himself individually. He expresses humility by suggesting that his own fate is more problematic (*fors*) than that of Tarraco. There is no cause to doubt the sincerity of such statement. Prudentius believes with his contemporaries in the martyr's power of intercession: the martyrs of Tarraco can and will intercede for Christians who address them by name, but especially for Christians at, or identified with, the locality of their martyrdom. By having composed the hymn of praise by which the citizens will address their martyr, Prudentius can hopefully partake of their spiritual benefits; and by also addressing the martyr in his own person he further increases the possibilities of his salvation.

Personal religious emotion is likewise evident in the unique passage where Prudentius names himself. At the end of *Peristephanon* II, the citizens of Rome are pictured celebrating the passion of St. Lawrence when the poet, now including himself among them (*hos inter*, 573), addresses the martyr directly. He skillfully contrasts the martyr's proximity to Christ with his own distance by means of the apostrophe, "thou glory of Christ" (*o Christi decus*, 573), followed by self-characterization as a *poetam rusticam*—the topos is now moralized—who acknowledges a sinful heart and unworthy deeds (*cordis fatentem crimina / et facta prodentem sua*). The final strophe contains the self-naming.

audi benignus supplicem
Christi reum Prudentium,
et servientem corpori
absolve vinclis saeculi. (*Per.* II, 581-584)

[Be thou gracious and hear the prayer of Prudentius who stands arraigned by Christ, and set him free from the fetters of the world where he is in bondage to the body.]

A shared feature of these examples of Christian individualism is their avoidance of the isolationism characteristic of modern (or Romantic) individualism. Crowds of the faithful are ubiquitous in Prudentius' poems. The *fideles*, for example, provide the opening setting of his celebration of Peter and Paul: *Romam per omnem cursitant ovantque* (*Per.* XII, 2). Prudentius typically places himself *inter hos*. Logically so, since he, with them, composes the Church, and since the unified Church on earth prefigures the unified society of the saved in heaven. This close corollation between individual and social welfare is a factor of Prudentius' self-consciousness as a Christian poet, and it governs his poetic logic. Our own appreciation of this poetic logic is hindered by our habit of thinking of the individual and society as dialectical opposites. Not only does Prudentius sense no "tension" between the two, but he can understand the one as necessarily involved in and implying the other.

The *Contra Orationem Symmachi* illustrates this association of self with the social order. Each book of this hexameter polemic handles the matter under debate—that is, whether the Christian Roman emperor should legally suppress the old state religion—differently. My interest is in the suitability of different roles the poet takes in each book. Book I presents the historical background of Book II. This background is the struggle over senatorial restoration of the Altar of Victory, a struggle temporarily and (we discover in Book II) tenuously resolved in the defeat of Symmachus (394) by the Emperor Theodosius. The greater portion of

41

this first book is historical or mythic narration of the kind employed by Ovid in the *Metamorphoses*. Successive tales about the Roman divinities are told in the typically ridiculing manner of Christian apologetic. These narrations prepare for the main action of the book by discrediting the grotesque morality of the Olympian gods. Enter Theodosius, whose speech summarizes the meaning of pagan religious history. The emperor resolves to rid Rome of the throngs of monsters and devils who, by offending Christ, have been preventing the flowering of civil peace. Events now unfold swiftly as a spiritual consequence of Theodosius' speech. The noble senatorial class, with the lone and ludicrous exception of Symmachus, has joined the plebs in whole-hearted allegiance to Christ. Through all this, the poet has narrated the background and the more recent action in his own voice; there is nothing remarkable about his role, which is simply that of the conventional narrator. But the happy conclusion of Book I is of course idealized. Its reversal in Book II will carry the action forward to present actuality, and this will necessitate a new role for the Christian poet.

Conventional Christian apologetic now yields to debate over the specific points advocated by the pagan Symmachus, and this debate refers to certain issues (such as the banning of gladiatorial contests) current at the time of writing (c. 403).[15] As Prudentius focuses on contemporary problems, he alters his narrative technique and his mode of self-

[15] For the dating of Prudentius' works, see Rodriguez-Herrera, *Poeta Christianus*, pp. 15-18; the edition of Bergman (cited Critical Introd., n. 1), p. xiii; and Peebles, *The Poet Prudentius*, pp. 115-121. The place of pagan cults in the gladiatorial games and the importance of these games in the interpretation of the *Contra Orationem Symmachi* are treated by Friedrich Solmsen, "The Powers of Darkness in Prudentius' *Contra Symmachum*," *Vigiliae Christianae*, 19 (1965), 237-257. Solmsen's n. 7 gives bibliography useful for dating the disappearance of the games. Emperor Honorius is traditionally credited with ending the contests in 404, but recent historians have disputed this, arguing for a natural death after 410.

presentation. He becomes more visible and more important. For a short while the earlier straight narration persists as the poet, speaking in his own voice, presents discourse by the brother emperors, Honorius and Arcadius. But their speech contrasts markedly in effect with that of Theodosius. Far from accomplishing the total conversion of Rome, Honorius and Arcadius are ineffective even in silencing Symmachus. Ultimately, then, the unlimited secular power of Roman emperors cannot cope even with the social manifestations of this essentially spiritual crisis. The edicts of Theodosius are discovered not to have prevented the recrudescence of paganism; what is worse, the brother leaders are themselves seduced by Symmachus' arguments. At this dangerous impasse the social role of the Christian poet emerges in all its importance.

The solution of the social conflict comes about through the poet's inner conflict, which he dramatizes in response to Symmachus' speech. Prudentius suspends objective narration and speaks not in one voice, but in several. This shift he introduces as follows:

his tam magnificis tantaque fluentibus arte
respondit vel sola Fides doctissima primum
pandere vestibulum verae ad penetralia sectae.

(C. Symm. II, 91-93)

[To these fine words flowing with such art Faith has given the answer, for she before all has skill to open the first approach to the heart of the true belief.]

Prudentius presents arguments in the person of Fides, thereby distancing himself from human error. The voice of the poet inspired by Fides is authoritative, and offers a convincing Christian rebuttal to Symmachus. But the matter does not end here, for it is not so simple as this. If the poet can possess Faith, he cannot be identified with her—not, at least, without abandoning his claim to truthfulness. And there is a counter force within the poet, the uninspired voice of sin, the voice not inspired by Faith. After the authoritative speech is concluded, the poet argues in the person of his bestial nature which, having discovered that it is mortal, gleefully anticipates wicked acts it can perform in the absence of an afterlife: "I shall go with burning passion from one unclean indulgence to another. . . ." (*ibo per inpuros fervente libidine luxus* [II, 172]). In the course of its hypothetical meditation, the bestial nature argues increasingly against the Christian responsibility to a higher moral law and a higher Judge. As if caught in a network of suggestions of judgment and Hell, a network of words like *lex, crimen, poena . . . iudex* (179-181), this sinful meditation ceases. Suddenly the voice of the poet becomes penitential, and this change sets the psychological stage for the action of Christian conversion, possible by divine agency. Into the mind of the poet comes the inspiration of the Trinity. This extraordinary speech of God comes not as if it were an imagining but a real religious event in the mind of the imperfect, sinful poet.[16]

> sed quid ego haec meditor? revocat Deus ecce severa
> maiestate minax, negat interitura meorum
> per mortem monumenta operum. non occidet,
>   inquit,
> interior qui spirat homo; luet ille perenne
> supplicium quod subiectos male rexerit artus.
>   (*C. Symm.* II, 182-186)

[But why do I meditate such acts? There is God calling me back with the menace of his stern majesty; He tells me that the record of my works will not be done away by my death. "The man who breathes within," He says, "will not die; he will pay an everlasting penalty for misguiding the body placed under his control."]

[16] Prudentius' relation to God is typologically anticipated by St. Peter's. See discussion of the "Praefatio" of *C. Symm.* II below.

God presents himself as the Lord of Creation with absolute power over the fate of men's souls. He defines his nature and persons, and He explains the mission of Christ. His moral command to the poet concerns the ordering of the interior temple of the soul.

> quare age, mortalis, soli mihi construe templum,
> meque unum venerare Deum. caementa remitto,
> et quae saxa Paros secat et quae Punica rupis,
> quae viridis Lacedaemon habet maculosaque Synna;
> nativum nemo scopuli mihi dedicet ostrum.
> templum mentis amo, non marmoris: aurea in illo
> fundamenta manent fidei; structura nivali
> consurgit pietate nitens, tegit ardua culmen
> iustitia, interius spargit sola picta rubenti
> flore pudicitiae pudor almus et atria servat.
> haec domus apta mihi est, haec me pulcherrima sedes
> accipit, aeterno caelestique hospite digna.
> nec novus hic locus est; fluxit mea gloria in artus
> et lux vera Dei.   (*C. Symm.* II, 244-257)

[Come then, O mortal, build a temple to me alone and worship me as the one God. I seek no quarried stones, neither the rock that Paros or the Punic cliff cuts, nor that which green Lacedaemon or stained Synna possesses; let no man consecrate natural red stone to me. I love a temple of the heart, not one of marble. In it stand firm the golden foundations of faith, the lofty building shines with holiness snow-white, righteousness covers its roof high up, and within it life-giving purity colours the floor with blushing flowers of modesty scattered over it, and keeps the courts. This is the house that befits me, the beauteous abode which I enter, worthy of its everlasting heavenly guest. Nor is it a new seat. My glory and the true light of God flowed into the flesh.]

These are the metaphorical foundations upon which the *Psychomachia* also is built. As in the *Psychomachia*, the

45

entry of Faith is not unchallenged by the forces of sin; yet the resolution of worshipful peace has made the struggle itself worth waging.

Amazing is that this whole dramatization of individual conversion, inspiration, and moral introspection occurs at the crisis of a public debate over urgent matters of Roman religious policy. Having already answered the arguments of Symmachus through the personified figure of Fides (whose arguments correspond with those of Bishop Ambrose),[17] the poet suddenly turns inward. God enters his mind. God's moral solution for the poet is non-public, like the poet's introspection and the penitence that occasioned it. God mentions neither Rome, nor the pagan gods, nor the Church; instead, he stresses the primacy of inner spirituality, the metaphorical *templum* of the soul.

Yet the social action of the poem continues and under the direction of a new sort of poet. The message of God's speech is not that Church affairs are irrelevant but that they must proceed from the affairs of the individual soul. Having impersonated inner forces, Prudentius now can impersonate the characters of ideas larger than himself. Thus this dramatic presentation:

si vocem simulare licet, nempe aptior ista
vox Romae est, quam nunc eius sub nomine promam.
(*C. Symm*. II, 649-650)

[If one may assume a voice, surely more befitting Rome is the voice which I shall now put forth in her name.]

The poet is able to take on the public *vox Romae* because he has been inspired inwardly by the *vox Domini*. The relation of the two voices is one of cause and effect: moral

17 "Both verbal parallels and the method and content of his arguments put it beyond doubt that Prudentius had open in front of him as he wrote a copy of both Symmachus' *Relatio* and Ambrose's refutation of it."—Alan Cameron, *Claudian* (cited Critical Introd., n. 4), p. 240.

conversion precedes divine inspiration, which confers on the poet the power of prophesy and teaching. However, the relation is also one of mystical correspondence, of typology, between psychological and social conversion. Accordingly, Prudentius' "simulation" of the speech of Roma is structurally parallel to his previous speech of moral introspection. The poet has acknowledged his tendency to sin; as Roma he acknowledges the evil of Roman history:

> crimen enim, piget heu, crimen persuaserat atrox
> Iuppiter, ut sacro iustorum sanguine tincta
> adsuetum bellis scelerarem funere ferrum.
>
> (*C. Symm.* II, 666-668)

[For it was to sin (alas, to my sorrow now!), it was to sin that savage Jupiter led me on, to stain my hands with the holy blood of the righteous and defile with the guilt of their death the sword that had its proper use in war.]

Just as the poet has allied himself with Fides and then experienced Christian conversion with the grace of God, so Roma experiences a mass conversion to the faith. Just as the poet has rejoiced in the newly inspired power of his polemic, Roma rejoices in greater success in just warfare under Stilicho and the Christian emperors. Finally, the temple imagery recurs: negatively, in respect to the destruction of pagan temples; and positively, in respect to the Christian worship of the Empire. Roma and her emperor are joined in worship (*devotos*) to God—

>   cui sordida templa
> clausimus et madidas sanie deiecimus aras.
> unus nostra regat servetque palatia Christus;
> ne quis Romuleas daemon iam noverit arces,
> sed soli pacis Domino mea serviat aula.
>
> (*C. Symm.* II, 764-768)

[in whose honour we have closed the foul temples and cast down the blood-soaked altars. Let Christ alone rule

and keep our palaces, let no evil spirit any longer know
the strongholds of Romulus, but my court serve the Lord
of peace alone.]

At the conclusion of this speech, the conversion of Roma
has been achieved and Symmachus defeated. Now speaking
in his own voice once again, the poet urges the emperor to
wipe out such pagan vestiges as the Vestal Virgins and the
gladiatorial contests. Needless to say, such urging requires
great authority. Prudentius himself expresses no doubt that
the emperor, having sincerely accepted Roma's ideal of
Christian rule, will hear and respond to the *vox Domini* as
it has been voiced through the poet.[18]

With clear relevance to the *Psychomachia*, Prudentius in
Praefatio and in *Contra Orationem Symmachi* has insisted
on the priority of internal moral states. Good works, poetic
or otherwise, proceed from inner conversion—the poet's,
the emperor's—rather than vice versa. Beyond cause and
effect, however, psychological and social manifestations of
sin and Christian charity are figurally proximate. The same
metaphors refer to both realms of moral action, so that
psychological and social conversion form essentially the
same *historia*.

The two are interexpressive. Metaphorical interrelation
reflects the poet's conviction that there exists a real moral-
spiritual continuum, and this conviction is supported by the
authority of metaphorical transfigurations in Scripture.
When the poet chooses the word *templum* as a metaphor
for the soul in a state of charity, he inevitably borrows

---

[18] So *Per.* X, 21-25, about which Charles Witke comments in *Numen
Litterarum*, p. 129: "The poet will become the *lingua* while Christ
will be the *rhetor*." Witke goes on to write of the "inspiration of
the poet-prophet of the Judaic tradition," but unfortunately he fails
to give sufficient weight to the comparison. That Christ speaks
through Prudentius is "purely a conventional claim." Yet: "Nevertheless, the implication is clear: Prudentius was not disturbed at the
thought of Christ expressing himself through polymetric strophic
poems."

associations from scriptural history. The building of the temple by Solomon, its reestablishment by Christ, its future and eternal existence in the heavenly Jerusalem at the Last Judgment—all of these are figurations of the temple in the soul. And Prudentius is not simply borrowing these associations, he is imitating St. Paul by applying them to moral states. Exciting things happen when the Christian poet brings this web of significations into an oration on the destruction of pagan temples. Roman history is made to conform with salvation history. The pagan temples partake of the typology of the *templum*—but antitypically. Jupiter is Satan, the Roman temples have been prefigured by the temples of Baal, the spilling of martyrs' blood is perpetuated by the black sacrament of the *taurobolium*.

Such networks of meaning give narrative the tendency to circulate back upon itself or to move forward in a number of spiritual senses at once. To a reader unappreciative of the metaphorical complexity of Prudentius' work, the narrative may seem to become choked on its own language. Of course the *Contra Orationem Symmachi* explicitly segregates psychological from social conversion by means of structural parallelism; but in other poems there may exist ambiguity of locus.

By way of example, in *Peristephanon* XII the architectural details of the churches of Saint Peter and Saint Paul—the golden ornaments, white pillars, mosaic patternings—may describe actual (as well as symbolic) features of the buildings, or moral features in the souls of Christians entering the buildings, or both. In the *Psychomachia*, where there apparently exists one consistently mental locus of action, a series of analogies from ecclesiastical history refers this mental locus to the Church in society; yet it is sometimes uncertain when or in what detail the psychological reality is meant to further signify the historical.

Prudentius' insistence upon the continuity of inner and outer events is hardly idiosyncratic; it is shared by Christian writers from St. Paul to St. Augustine (and by the much later William Langland). The outlook is at bottom that of Christianity, not simply that of the poetic personality, because what makes it poetically true is the faith that one God has intervened and will intervene anywhere and everywhere: on Mount Sinai, in Bethlehem, on the road to Damascus, at the Milvian Bridge, in the soul of every Christian, on the Day of Doom. Especially between A.D. 313 and A.D. 410, when the empire is energetically and aggressively Christian, and the ascetic movement not yet dominant, the most intense inner spirituality is readily translatable to the precincts of public, urban Christendom. Prudentius' greater contemporary, St. Augustine, however moved he may have been by Athanasius' *Life of Saint Anthony*, was in the end converted in Milan, and converted by St. Ambrose, whose moral exegesis of Scripture as psychological *historia* was composed amidst the most energetic activity in Church-State politics.

The range of Prudentius' activity, generically speaking, is extraordinary in comparison with other Christian poets; yet it is what we might expect from a "total poet" c. 400, a poet who envisions his various works as answerable to the various needs of the Church. Later in this chapter I will argue that the *Hamartigenia* and *Apotheosis* respond to an actual threat of heresy, the *Contra Orationem Symmachi* to an actual threat of paganism. But it is perhaps methodologically inaccurate to consider the objective situation when dealing with a poet committed to the idea that subjective and objective reality is continuous. Therefore two points of caution. First, actuality is a larger category for Prudentius (or Theodosius, or Augustine) than for us. We would agree with Prudentius that Symmachus (or the memory of Symmachus, or his ideas) is part of the objective context of the pagan revival of the nineties, and hence of the *Contra Orationem Symmachi*. But the "Praefatio" of the *Hamartigenia* contains earnest polemic against Marcion, a second-century heretic long since discredited by the Church. In this case the objective context is fourth-century heresy, which would seem to exclude Marcion from any claim to relevance. Yet Prudentius and others earnestly believe that Marcion's gnostic teachings have a vigorous afterlife, that the arch-heretic (like the Fiend who inspired him) is spiritually embodied or fulfilled in contemporary Manichean teachers. We moderns who disbelieve in the power and persistence of Satan will dispute Prudentius' objectivity in our capacity as historians, but as literary critics we should grant the poet his own vision of spiritual truth.

THE ESSENCE AND FORMS OF POETRY

The second point of caution in treating the historicity of Prudentius' *opera* is that he views his particular poems less as responses to particular occasions than as particular manifestations of one basic activity, poetry. As the *Praefatio* characterizes it, this activity begins inwardly. Prudentius summons his own soul (*anima*) to use her voice to honor God. But *anima*'s "voice" is purely spiritual in that it precedes or generates the symbols for vocalization, that is, the actual voicing by the poet's lips or the setting down by the poet's hand. The process of translating *anima*'s music into written words for the Church's use is not described, but it is clear that poetry is in some sense already in existence in the soul and continues to exist when verbalized. This range of reality is perhaps Platonic; yet the actualization of poetry is analogous to Judeo-Christian ideas of Creation and Incarnation, to wit, that a spiritual substance enters and affects men's lives morally. The *Praefatio* suggests that the substance of poetry is independent of its assumed forms, the written genres of Christian poetry. Insofar as *anima*'s music imitates or emulates heavenly music, poetry can be said to exist prior to the poet's soul being inspired (by God's grace) with it—and there are many passages indicative of such a theory. Taking the soul as poetry's place of origin, the world outside the poet is where poetry is manifested. This is so as a matter of common sense, for poetry once inscribed

51

or vocalized is brought outside the mind and into the perceivable world; but Prudentius also seems intent on emphasizing this. The hymn is the first genre named. It is the most individualistic genre, for it involves direct lyric expression toward the divine. The genres that follow are unimaginable in purely individualistic terms. To expound the Catholic faith, to fight against heresies, to cast down Rome's idols—such are the songs of the Church militant, time-bound poetry of political necessity. In the *Praefatio*'s outline, the naming of the hymn has been transitional between the soul's inner music and the polemic of the Christian orator. The range of poetry, then, moves from within the poet (or above him) outward; and from purely spiritual substance to material actualization. This range of locus and ontology does little to encourage an interpretation of Prudentius as primarily responsive to external or worldly particulars, despite the fact that he is far more responsive to such than other poets of his age; this range suggests, instead, that he is primarily responsive to God.

It will be noticed that, although his poetic practice reveals him to be highly sensitive to generic expectations inherent in the different classical forms, Prudentius' conception of genre is not based on form. It is based on prospective audience or end, on whether it is to be received by God or by men. And secondarily, within the human sphere, it is based on topic: the origin of sin, the divinity of Christ, the nature of the soul. As I pointed out at the beginning of this chapter, these distinctions of audience and subject are not hard and fast because of ideas basic to Christianity, for example, the continguousness of God and man (implying that the audience or end of a poem may be twofold), and the subordination of moral laws and ideas to a universal truth (implying that a discrete topic may be infinitely expanded). However provisional or pragmatic these Prudentian genres be, they arise from his sense of duty as a Christan poet to speak charitably to God and neighbor and to serve the Church. As Prudentius defines these genres, they will not conform to formal classical standards. Charles Witke is both right and wrong in claiming that the poet invents no new genres;[19] for he invariably uses meters from the past. Or, if classical genre be given a broader meaning, he uses the conventions of epic in the *Psychomachia*, of Horatian lyric in the *Liber Cathemerinon*, of Lucretian hexameter for the theological exposition of the *Apotheosis*, of Juvenalian satire for its mode of dominant anti-heretical polemic. Prudentius' works are unthinkable without such formal and conventional components, and without the poetic diction of Latin. So what did he invent? Accepting the poet's own generic definitions, every work is new. Prudentius composed the first collection or cycle of hymns, containing the first structurally ode-like hymns; the first literary panegyrics of the martyrs; the first long anti-pagan polemic; the first theological expositions in hexameter; and the first long poem about the soul (in a genre new by any standard: the first personification allegory). The appreciation of his full originality clearly depends upon an evaluation of him not simply as a Latin poet, but as a Christian poet, and upon an understanding that this distinction is one of substance.

Prudentius, I am convinced, was deeply aware of this substantive distinction. The proof lies in his troubled attitude toward classical form. Willingness to serve the public needs of the Church of course demands the use of conventional language; the soul's inner music must somehow be voiced to be received by the community. If poetry as a spiritual substance is formless, as it were, and capable of being voiced according to the conventions of either prose or poetry, then it is a matter of interest when Prudentius chooses to express himself within poetic conventions. Here the positive impact of classical forms is felt, for language to be sung must be metrical, public polemic (as opposed to private controversy) must be hexametric, and so on. Prudentius' modes and subjects require meter. By why does Prudentius so far

[19] See Critical Introd., n. 23; similarly, Curtius' assertion that Prudentius "was independent of the system of antique genres."

overstep the generic norms already appropriated by Christian poets? Why in the *Liber Cathemerinon* does he go beyond Ambrosian meter, which had only recently served the needs of the Church so well, to imitate the complex meters of Horace? Why are his hexameters so resonant, as those of his predecessors are not, with Vergilian tone and rhythm? I submit that these elements are functions of the poet's acquired skill (rather than conviction) and of his audience's expectation. If an aristocratic audience is posited, one including nominal Christians and even pagans, then his mastery of classical meters makes sense in terms of the Church's social mission, and need not be interpreted as a product of artistic conviction. If my reading is correct, Prudentius views the difference between classical and scriptural form as that between surface attraction, which is to be used, and substantial beauty, which is to be loved.

Miracles aside, it is inconceivable that Prudentius in his late fifties began composing verse without having already achieved considerable competence. I imagine him an amateur of poetry, both as an avid reader and imitator, from his early days in the school of rhetoric. (If he published poems prior to his career as a serious Christian poet, these have been lost.) Assuming such past exposure to the Latin tradition, it is curious that Prudentius never names a classical author. Yet he often names such scriptural authors as Moses and the bard David, thereby perpetuating their just fame. We have already seen that his attitude toward his past life is anything but nostalgic, and there is no warmth of affection (such as Augustine admits) toward the Roman school days that imbued his senses with Vergil and Horace. Prudentius' attitude toward the literary tradition is that of the possessor of a certain skill which happens to be useful but not in itself worthy. Augustine's remarks on the subject of eloquence in *On Christian Doctrine* are apt: ". . . for it is a mark of good and distinguished minds to love the truth within words and not the words. Of what use is a gold key if it will not open what we wish? Or what objection is there

to a wooden one which will, when we seek nothing except
to open what is closed? But since there is some comparison
between eating and learning, it may be noted that on account of the fastidiousness of many even that food without
which life is impossible must be seasoned."[20] Although Prudentius' scattered references to his poetic craft lack Augustine's explicitness, they convey his basic idea. The fastidiousness of Prudentius' audience, roughly the same as Claudian's,
is hardly open to dispute, and we have seen that Prudentius
is desirous of the "food without which life is impossible"
and of sharing it with others. What does he reveal about his
skills in "seasonings"?

In a passage quoted above, he imagines the martyr Fructuosus recalling the "sweet hendecasyllables" composed in
his honor and therefore granting relief from torments. Since
the poetry is (it is hoped) to be instrumental in the salvation or damnation of the poet, it would be most inappropriate to interpret the phrase as putting primary stress on the
meter. No one was ever graced by God for having composed hendecasyllables of high quality; even the scattered
medieval attempts to make a Christian poet out of Vergil
were based not on poetic craft but on meaning, *sententia*.
No orthodox Christian of Prudentius' intelligence would
claim spiritual worth for a form of poetry per se. The essential fact about the hendecasyllables is that they are sweet,
and the nature of their sweetness is—again judging from the
context—a function of having borne praise of the martyrs
and of Christ.

Other references to poetic form are located just where
the religious aim of a poem is revealed. Thus in the *Liber
Cathemerinon* Prudentius draws attention to his meter just
before evoking the essential nature of hymnody. This juxtaposition signals no happy reconcilation of Christian and
classical values, rather, the conversion of the meter to an
unprecedented religious use. Only the use makes the meter

[20] *De Doctrina Christiana* IV, 11 (27); trans. D. W. Robertson, Jr.,
Saint Augustine: On Christian Doctrine (New York, 1958), p. 136.

55

worthy. "Mystic" poetry—the term comes from scriptural
exegesis, where it denotes the hidden Christological or sacramental sense—emerges only after the ivy-leaves of Roman
tradition are spurned:

> sperne, Camena, leves hederas,
> cingere tempora quis solita es,
> sertaque mystica dactylico
> texere docta liga strophio,
> laude Dei redimita comas.
>
> quod generosa potest anima,
> lucis et aetheris indigena,
> solvere dignius obsequium,
> quam data munera si recinat
> artificem modulata suum? (*Cath.* III, 26-35)

[Put away, my Muse, the paltry ivy-leaves wherewith
thou hast been wont to encircle thy brows; learn to weave
mystic garlands and tie them with a band of dactyls, and
wear thy hair wreathed with the praise of God. What
worthier service can the highborn soul, native of light
and heaven, pay, than to chant the gifts she has received,
singing of her Creator?]

By advertising his meter even as he rejects the old pagan
poetic, Prudentius points to the alien nature of what Augustine calls "Egyptian gold," refusing to let its recasting into
religious vessels pass unnoticed.[21] A similar passage characterizes the garlands of dactyls offered to Eulalia as joyous
on account of their spiritual fervor but intrinsically poor
and unbeautiful.

> ast ego serta choro in medio
> texta feram pede dactylico,
> vilia, marcida, festa tamen. (*Per.* III, 208-210)

[21] For Augustine's allegorization of the Egyptian gold in Exodus,
see *De Doctrina Christiana*, II, 40 (60).

[But I in the midst of your company will bring garlands
wreathed of dactylic measures, of little worth and faded,
but still joyous.]

Far from "Christian Classicism," we perceive Christianity
despite classicism, new wine marketed in old bottles.

There is an incongruity in the product, an awkwardness
apparent in its making. Charles Witke has observed that the
classical convention of alluding to names that cannot scan
is followed by Prudentius in *Peristephanon* IV—and no
sooner followed than abandoned: "Prudentius thus assigns
great weight to the subject: love of golden names makes
light of poetical rules, and enthusiasm for discoursing about
holy men is never reprehensible or uncouth. The subject
(and the poet's dedication to it) take on the responsibility
for transgressing *carminis leges*."[22] As Witke suggests, the
violation is conscious, subtle, and recognizable by an audience attuned to the rules as a declaration of Christianity. I
should add that it is also a minor insult against the rules, a
critical jibe at the intrinsic worthlessness of the forms themselves. I think that Prudentius also intends to reveal the tensions between his form and content when he encloses the
eight central Horatian hymns of the *Liber Cathemerinon*
within a frame of Ambrosian hymns (in quatrains of iambic
dimeter), two on either side, as if to say: if the Christian
lyric, in essence inexpressible, be confined by poor and
faded measures, let these measures in turn be imprisoned by
those of St. Ambrose. Such tensions are more strongly contained in Prudentius' treatment of Vergil, to be discussed
later. And they are tacitly present where the many namings
of Christ as the origin and end of poetry are without reference to the Latin tradition, but instead to the moral and
intellectual functions of the mind itself. The question of
Prudentius' relation to the Latin tradition is so crucial to any
interpretation of his works, however, that I will present a

[22] *Numen Litterarum*, p. 137.

final illustration of my argument against his being a Christian humanist.

I quote the conclusion of the long narrative Passion of St. Romanus, where the poet characterizes two sorts of literature, worldly and heavenly, transitory and eternal. The distinction is of course moral, not just metaphysical (Platonic), for it culminates the hagiography's antagonism between the pagan persecutors and the faithful Christians. (It is worth noting that the author of the old Roman historical record is unnamed: he shares the same status as Vergil and Horace in the Prudentian corpus—obscurity.) Of major interest here is Prudentius' sense of the status of his own narrative in comparison with the two sorts of narratives he describes:

> gesta intimasse cuncta fertur principi
> praefectus addens ordinem voluminum
> seriemque tantae digerens tragoediae:
> laetatus omne crimen in fasces refert
> suum tyrannus chartulis vivacibus.
>
> illas sed aetas conficit diutina,
> fuligo fuscat, pulvis obducit situ,
> carpit senectus aut ruinis obruit:
> inscripta Christo pagina inmortalis est,
> nec obsolescit ullus in caelis apex.
>
> excepit adstans angelus coram Deo
> et quae locutus martyr et quae pertulit,
> nec verba solum disserentis condidit,
> sed ipsa pingens vulnera expressit stilo
> laterum, genarum pectorisque et faucium.
>
> . . . .
>
> hic in regestis est liber caelestibus,
> monumenta servans laudis indelebilis,
> relegendus olim sempiterno iudici,
> libramine aequo qui malorum pondera
> et praemiorum conparabit copias.
>
> vellem sinister inter haedorum greges,

ut sum futurus, eminus dinoscerer
atque hoc precante diceret rex optimus:
Romanus orat; transfer hunc haedum mihi;
sit dexter agnus, induatur vellere.   (*Per.* X, 1111-1140)

[They say the governor reported all the facts to the
emperor, with a series of scrolls in which he laid out in
order all the details of this great tragic drama, the oppres-
sor cheerfully entering all his own wickedness in packets
of records on sheets that were meant to last. But those the
long passage of time destroys, they are blackened with
grime or covered with dust where they lie undisturbed,
old age tatters them or buries them under ruins; whereas
the page that Christ has written upon is deathless and in
heaven not a letter fades away. An angel standing in the
presence of God took down all that the martyr said and
all he bore, and not only recorded the words of his discourse but with his pen drew exact pictures of the wounds
on his sides and cheeks and breast and throat. . . . This
book is in the heavenly register, preserving the records of
glory imperishable, and to be read again one day by the
everlasting Judge, who with just balance will match the
weight of woe and the abundance of reward. Would that
I, standing as I shall be on the left among the flocks of
goats, might be picked out from afar and at Romanus'
petition the King most excellent might say: "Romanus
prays for him. Bring this goat over to me; let him stand
on my right hand as a lamb and be clothed in a fleece."]

It is striking to come upon this passage after following Prudentius' own detailed narrative of the martyr's passion. The
Christan poet is discovered to have been imitating the
heavenly record in his pious concern to record every word
and every wound—as a reading through *Peristephanon* X
will bear out. If the old Roman record is lost to time (and
sinfulness), the implication of divine inspiration is clear; for
how otherwise can the poet have related the truth? Or he

59

may mean that he has gotten information from a pagan source even now being destroyed by time; but if so, he has radically transformed the old record into a new song glorifying God. Either way, Christian literature is set apart from non-Christian literature, and conforms to the literature of heaven.

There are, it seems, three levels of literature. Non-Christian literature is sinful and erroneous; composed without knowledge or love of God, its basis is entirely worldly and its condition is therefore perishable. Heavenly or angelic literature, by contrast, is an imagined ideal, yet its authority may be equated with Scripture's, for it is perfect in its intelligence and love of God, so is eternal. Actual Christian poetry would seem to occupy a middle position. It is imperfect, sinful, bound by the world and by time; yet it is occasioned by faith and love of God. Its worth is problematic, unknown to mortals, and must be judged by a higher power. By concluding the Passion of St. Romanus as he does, Prudentius implies that the problematic state of his own soul, expressed in his hope to be chosen from among the goats on the Day of Judgment, is shared by his poetry. Will it perish like the old Roman record? Or will it survive through history protected by the Church as a true imitation of heavenly narrative? Humility prevents the poet from stating outright that his celebration of the martyr is inspired by, or conforms with, the divine Word; but the unspoken hope is evident.

It does not follow from all this that Prudentius is a poet without a tradition worthy of emulation. In the *Praefatio* when he tells of his intent to honor God in voice and to sing of the Lord in hymns, he is following the tradition of David. "Give praise to the Lord on the harp: sing to him with the psaltery, the instrument of ten strings. Sing to him a new canticle [*Cantate ei canticum novum*]: sing well unto him with a loud voice. For the word of the Lord [*verbum Domini*] is right; and all his works are done with faithfulness."[23] Our poet usually names David as a type (pre-figuration) of Christ the King, not as a poet; but in one passage a dying martyr sings the sixth and seventh verses of Psalm 115. As these verses are quoted in the narrative, they are introduced by the term *hymnum*, which suggests that Prudentius identifies his own hymns with the genre of the Psalms: *hymnum canebat carminis Davitici* (*Per. X*, 838). As Augustine often explains in his *Ennarationes in Psalmos*, the *verbum Domini* is eternal, and all Christians in charity are singers of the *canticum novum*; so Ambrose argues in his commentaries on the Psalms. According to these Church Fathers, David sang the *canticum novum* to uncomprehending ears in his own times but in prophecy of Christ and for the delight and edification of future Christians. Himself living under the shadow of the Old Law, David could not completely comprehend his own music: David praised the *verbum Domini*, but through David the Holy Spirit sang and sings and will sing the *Verbum Domini* (Christ). Christians imitate this song by chanting Psalms in the liturgy.

The tradition of scriptural song is not a literary tradition per se; it is a spiritual or moral tradition in which literature can participate. The *canticum novum* is sung by any Christian whose soul glorifies God. St. Paul employs the metaphor in Ephesians 5:19 to describe the state of being filled by the Holy Spirit: "speaking to yourselves in psalms and hymns

---

[23] Psalm 32:2-4. The numbering of the Psalms will follow the Vulgate; translations of Scripture will be from the Douay version, with occasional words and phrases inserted from the Vulgate. We do not know which text of the Bible Prudentius had before him, if any—some allusions may well be from memory; but he would have had access to one of the old Latin versions reflecting the Septuagint. The exact text is of no import to my study, so far as I can tell; and I am hardly prepared to face the enormous textual problems associated with the *Vetus Latina*. I hope that where I do quote the Vulgate Latin, this will sufficiently approximate that of Prudentius' actual and unknown text.

and spiritual canticles, singing and making melody in your hearts to the Lord." Such activity, it is worth remembering, does not end at time present with the hymns of St. Ambrose or Prudentius. According to the Apocalypse of John (14:3), the scriptural book of future history, the *canticum novum* will be sung by the saved at the Last Judgment: "And they sung as it were a new canticle, before the throne, and before the four living creatures, and the ancients; and no man could say the canticle, but those hundred forty-four thousand who were purchased from the earth." We have seen in the Passion of St. Romanus and elsewhere Prudentius' concern with his own fate at the Last Judgment and his belief that this fate depends upon the conformity of his own poetry with the poetry of heaven. When the eschatological dimension of the tradition of scriptural song is apprised, this tradition is seen to parallel and to participate in the total span of salvation history. As a Christian poet, Prudentius is part of this tradition. His creative act participates in salvation history directly by its moral causes and effects; also by analogy: it begins by the gracious inspiration of God, it is embodied in the *canticum novum*, and it is completed in the Judgment of God.[24]

There is also a spiritual tradition behind the non-lyric compositions. From Moses and the prophets to the New Testament apostles runs a series of scriptural efforts to carry

[24] Prudentius' view of history is basically that set down in Scripture: a stream of time from Creation to Last Judgment, the Incarnation of Christ occurring between these events, time present being between Incarnation and Last Judgment. This scheme would eventually be systematized in the fourfold interpretation of Scripture. Prudentius does not quite systematize time accordingly, but he does have an outlook well characterized as a natural fourfold. Thus Old Testament events prefigure New Testament events, these in tandem prefigure the present, and present events gain their ultimate significance at the Last Judgment. St. John Cassian, who first presented the method of fourfold exegesis, flourished in the West a decade and a half after Prudentius' death. There is no relation between John Cassian and the St. Cassian celebrated in *Per.* IX.

God's mission to the people, and ecclesiastical history—the only history written by fourth-century Christians—continues this series. It goes without saying that the activism and the polemic characteristic of Prudentius' hexameter works are precedented.

If anyone doubts that Prudentius attaches himself to the apostolic tradition of energetic preaching, he should study the twin prefaces of the *Contra Orationem Symmachi*. In the "Praefatio" to Book I, St. Paul is described as a writer *contra paganos*: he is "the herald of God, who first with his holy pen subdued the wild hearts of the Gentiles" (*praeco Dei, qui fera gentium / primus corda sacro perdomuit stilo* [Prf. 1-2]). After some embellishment of this idea, a paraphrase and allegorization of Acts 27:14-28:6 occurs, the story of St. Paul's shipwreck, his safe landing, and his being bitten by the serpent out of the fire. The allegorization supplied by Prudentius speaks to current events. Paul's ship is the Church steering its course through Roman history, specifically the persecutions; his landing signifies the official recognition of Christianity by Constantine. Safe on shore, the Christians warm their souls by burning the barren shoots from the vine of Faith: they burn heresies. But out of this fire comes the snake with eloquent mouth (*oris rhetorici*, 77), or Symmachus. The Church, concludes this "Praefatio," will follow Paul's example by shaking off this serpent and casting it into the fire. Prudentius is not a "second Paul," for it is the Church who will destroy the snake; yet Prudentius, as the Church's mouthpiece, quite obviously follows the profession of St. Paul.

The next "Praefatio" paraphrases and allegorizes Matthew 14:24-33, the story of St. Peter's walking on water in imitation of Jesus, his subsequent self-doubt, and his being saved by (and also rebuked by) Jesus. Again Scripture is allegorized to refer to contemporary life, the raging waters prefiguring Symmachus' rhetoric. What is strikingly new is the intimacy of the typological link between apostle and poet. Here Prudentius rehearses in his own mind Peter's fear and trepidation during the tempest; Prudentius' invocation of Christ's aid as uniquely saving follows the moral precedent of Peter. We remember that in the hexameter section of Book II the poet dramatizes his spiritual conversion, which culminates in the direct aid of God. The story of Matthew 14 forms a perfect introduction to this conversion. As the all-too-imperfect man of faith, Peter prefigures Prudentius; and the hope that Peter's final status as "God's chief disciple" (*summus discipulus Dei* [II, Prf. 2]) may also be realized in the Christian poet is unexpressed but surely felt.

PRUDENTIUS IN ROME:
BIOGRAPHICAL DATA AND SPECULATIONS

The spiritual lineage from Peter and Paul traced in the *Contra Orationem Symmachi* represents a poetic claim of no little authority. By the close of the fourth century, the idea had become widespread that Peter and Paul were apostles of special status for the Roman Church.[25] Prudentius celebrates their dual martyrdoms in *Peristephanon* XII, where he characterizes their memorial churches as "two dowers of the faith, the gift of the Father supreme" (*duas fidei summo Patre conferente dotes* [*Per.* XII, 55]). Although only this brief composition deals with them, Prudentius mentions as a special category of poetry in his *Praefatio* the praise of the apostles (*laudet apostolos*). By setting the founders of the Roman Church in his *Contra Orationem Symmachi*, he can oppose his pagan antagonists' arguments from tradition with the authority of Christian tradition.

[25] Constantine had built the basilicas to St. Peter and St. Paul over the shrines associated with them since the second century. Under Pope Damasus, special attention was given the celebration of their festival, and the elaborate procession is alluded to in *Per.* XII. See José Ruysschaert, "Prudence l'espagnol poète des deux basiliques romaines de S. Pierre et de S. Paul," *Revista di archeologia cristiana*, 42 (1966), 267-286.

The specifically local Roman typology of the *Contra Orationem Symmachi*, the great stress throughout this poem on the traditions of the *urbs*, the tendency in other works to connect *Romanitas* with Rome rather than with Empire—these factors are biographically suggestive. Yet Prudentius is widely thought of as a Spanish poet, and he may have spent most of his days in Spain. *The Praefatio* tells that he governed two Spanish cities. The only ecclesiastical figure whom he addresses directly is also Spanish, one Bishop Valerian, now thought to have been attached to a see at Saragossa or Calahorra.[26] To this bishop, Prudentius composes what may be the first Christian verse epistle, *Peristephanon* XI, on the passion of Hippolytus.

The correspondence with Valerian is important for two reasons, but neither reason has, in the end, much to do with Prudentius' "Spanishness." First, the verse epistle is written from Rome. The poet spent an undetermined period of time in Rome, a period crucial in the formation of his poetic responsibilities. The Roman experience made possible his choice of some of his genres and may also have sharpened his literary response to classical authors and altered his sense of audience. Second, the correspondence with Valerian, along with other evidence, suggests that Prudentius was commissioned by this bishop to perform a specific task for the local church: to obtain the names and *vitae* of Spanish, Roman, and other martyrs. It may seem surprising that the aristocratic Prudentius, ex-governor of two cities, should find himself in a position of subservience to a bishop most likely his social equal or inferior. But this subservience is religious rather than social; Prudentius' lay humility in spiritual matters does not prevent him from expressing his accustomed authority.

[26] Cunningham (cited above, n. 2) argues convincingly for the city of Calahorra, for Valerian's being the first bishop to occupy this see, and for Prudentius' lyrics serving an important part in dignifying the cathedral by Valerian's request.

Prudentius' trip to Rome, thought to have been under-
taken around 402, may not have been only in response to
Valerian's request. Strong hints of spiritual autobiography
in the *Peristephanon Liber* characterize it as a religious pilgrimage. The poet refers to other non-Romans at the tomb
of Hippolytus as pilgrims (*peregrinos*) and seems to include
himself among them (*Per.* XI, 191-192). Whether actually
begun as a pilgrimage, the journey seems to have taken on
these associations. Thus Prudentius recounts a private devotional experience on the way, at Imola by the tomb of St.
Cassian.

hic mihi, cum peterem te, rerum maxima Roma
   spes est oborta prosperum Christum fore. (*Per.* IX, 3-4)

[Here when I was journeying towards thee, Rome, the
world's capital, there sprang up in my heart a hope of
Christ's favour.]

Bowed to the ground, he sees a painting of Cassian's passion—a scene personally meaningful: Cassian the Christian
rhetor pricked to death by the styluses of his pagan students
of literature. No need to doubt the sincerity of Prudentius'
reporting of his emotions; that he is moved by the painting
of Cassian is consistent with his piety and with his oft stated
view that both literature and the plastic arts can generate
great emotional power.[27] After reporting the verger's interpretation of the Cassian picture and admonition to pray to
this martyr, Prudentius concludes the poem:

pareo, conplector tumulum, lacrimas quoque fundo,
   altar tepescit ore, saxum pectore.

[27] See *Per.* X, 266-305, for the affective power of pagan sculpture:
sed pulchra res est forma in aere sculptilis (266). And: *ars seminandis
efficax erroribus* . . . (271). Also *C. Symm.* II, 45-48:

sic unum sectantur iter, sic inania rerum
somnia concipiunt et Homerus et acer Apelles
et Numa, cognantumque volunt pigmenta, Camenae,
idola, convaluit fallendi trina potestas.

tunc arcana mei percenseo cuncta laboris,
    tunc quod petebam, quod timebam murmuro,
et post terga domum dubia sub sorte relictam
    et spem futuri forte nutantem boni.
audior, urbem adeo, dextris successibus utor:
    domum revertor, Cassianum praedico. (*Per.* IX, 99-106)

[I obeyed, clasping the tomb and shedding tears, warm-
ing the altar with my lips, the stone with my breast. Then
I reviewed all my private distresses, and murmured my
desires and fears, with a prayer for the home I had left
behind me in the uncertainty of fortune, and my hope,
now faltering, of happiness to come. I was heard. I visited
Rome, and found all things issue happily. I returned home
and now proclaim the praise of Cassian.]

Do the words *domum revertor* and *spem futuri* relate only
to the return to Spain, or are they also metaphors of salvational desire? The poet does not explain why the trip to
Rome is successful, and it may be that his petitioning the
martyr's aid is a conventional expression of hope for a safe
journey in troubled times. But the context of heightened
spiritual experience itself, the hope for Christ's favor, indicates that another sort of journey is intended.

If Prudentius went to Rome on religious business and as
a pilgrim, what did he find there? And how did the Roman
experience influence his poetic output? During his lifetime,
the political center of the Empire was not so much Rome
as Constantinople. Yet Rome remained the key cultural center of the West and was fast becoming the religious center
of the Empire. Especially under the leadership of another
Spaniard, Pope Damasus (366-384), the see of Rome was
greatly strengthened.[28] For the development of Christian

---

[28] In defense of Damasus, a decree (382) of Gratian states that dis-
putes among bishops will be submitted to the judgment of the metro-
politan of their province, or, if the bishops themselves are met-
ropolitans, to the Bishop of Rome. Text in *Patrologia Latina*, 13, cols.
586-588.

culture, Damasus is perhaps best known by his having commissioned Jerome's Vulgate translation, but the pope also initiated a movement to expand Christian monumental art. The churches of Peter and Paul reflect this movement, as does the erection of new martyrs' tombs and cenotaphs, some of which are inscribed by Damasus' own hexameter epigrams and decorated with carvings by Filocalus.[29] Prudentius saw this monumental art when he arrived in Rome, and he probably saw as well its historical significance as an index of the Church's recently established power in the Empire. Did he envision an analogous role for his poetry? Like late fourth-century Christian art, his poetry is modeled on traditional Roman forms yet contains a new and alien (otherworldly) spirituality.

Be that as it may, Prudentius certainly read the inscriptions of Damasus when he visited the catacombs in his capacity of ecclesiastical research assistant for Bishop Valerian. The passion of Hippolytus is indebted to one of Damasus' epigrams. In a more general way, many of the celebrations of the martyrs are, like the *Contra Orationem Symmachi*, unthinkable outside an immediate Roman context.

It is a matter of historical import that a Spanish bishop and a Spanish poet would take an interest in the state of the martyrs' tombs in Rome. For the persistent local magnetism attached to saints and martyrs in the early Christian period is still evident in Prudentius' *Peristephanon Liber*. His sense of localness produces the statement that Cyprian "belongs" to Carthage (*est proprius partriae martyr* [*Per.* XIII, 3]) and that the martyrs of Tarraco will intercede for their city. This idea is recurrent; and it is implied in the formal integrity and hence isolation of each piece. Yet there is a countertendency to the sense of localness: the skeleton of an overall structure in the martyr poems—that is, the movement from Spain to Rome, from Rome to the Mediterranean world as a whole. The progress is from localness to catholicity. These

---

[29] Damasus' epigrams are collected in *Anthologia Latinae Supplementa*, Vol. 1, ed. Maximilian Ihm (Leipzig, 1895).

dual tendencies show the Roman Church in a state of transition, still very much urban yet reaching out to embrace the West and (so the hope is) even the whole Empire.

The centripetal power of Rome occasions these opening lines of *Peristephanon* XI:

Innumeros cineres sanctorum Romula in urbe
    vidimus, o Christi Valeriane sacer.   (*Per.* XI, 1-2)

[Countless are the graves of saints I have seen in the city of Romulus, Valerian, Christ's dedicated servant.]

After describing the varied conditions of the catacomb tombs in the city of Romulus, Prudentius recounts the *passio Hippolyti*. He then takes the liberty to suggest that the martyr's holy day as the Romans observe it be inserted into Bishop Valerian's calendar.

si bene commemini, colit hunc pulcherrima Roma
    Idibus Augusti mensis, ut ipsa vocat
prisco more diem, quem te quoque, sancte magister,
    annua festa inter dinumerare velim. (*Per.* XI, 231-234)

[If I remember aright, beauteous Rome honours this martyr on the Ides of August, as she herself names the day in the old fashion, and I should like you too, holy teacher, to count it among your yearly festivals.]

The Spanish bishop is being urged to accept Roman usage. His correspondent goes on to advise that the martyrdom of Hippolytus (a Roman) be honored along with those of Cyprian (an African) and Eulalia (who is Spanish). The poet's understanding of the religious authority of Rome is cosmopolitan rather than local.

What then is Prudentius' relation to his Spanish bishop? The subservient formula of address, *sancte magister*, must not mislead us. In its context of early Christian martyrology, which attached paramount value to the intercession of martyrs on behalf of petitioning Christians, the matter of Pru-

69

dentius' verse epistle is substantial indeed.[30] Both his reporting responsibility and liturgical recommendation concern
matters of salvation, for the interceding martyr must be
known and, once known, must be petitioned. In dealing
with this important subject, Prudentius, an aristocrat and
experienced administrator, speaks with the conviction of
authority.

Even granted the high spiritual importance of the *Peristephanon Liber*, the commissioning of this work cannot well
explain most of the Prudentian corpus. The poet's relation
with his bishop cannot explain how a work like the *Contra
Orationem Symmachi* came into being. Lacking biographical
facts but basing my explanation on the *Praefatio*, I specu-
late as follows: Prudentius suffers a crisis of conscience late
in life after having been a nominal Christian. Sometime prior
to his fifty-seventh year, he undergoes a conversion of spirit,
changes careers, transfers from the high ranks of imperial
organization to the lower ranks of the Church. He is already
an extraordinarily talented and cultivated layman, perhaps
a literary genius; and had he been devoted to the Church
earlier in life, he might have filled an important post in the
ecclesiastical order. Soon after his conversion of spirit, at any
rate, he journeys to Rome. He is a pilgrim motivated by
salvational desire and a commissioned man of letters in service to Bishop Valerian.

I surmise Prudentius' awareness of a more basic need of
the Church: the need for a first-rate poet like himself, one
well versed in the Roman literary tradition, able to imitate
its various forms and modes, already possessed of inventive
skill. These special literary qualifications cannot have

[30] Prior to the Last Judgment, Tertullian argues, only the martyrs'
souls are in heaven with Christ; the souls of all other virtuous Christians must await the end of time (*De Anima*, 55). This privileged
status of the martyrs, supported also by 1 Thess. 4:15-16, is commonly
accepted in early Christian literature and helps to explain the importance of martyrology during the period. Prudentius does not follow
Tertullian, but he does put great stress on the intercession of martyrs
at the Last Judgment.

prompted Bishop Valerian to request Prudentius' researches on the Roman martyrs—although the bishop may well have admired them. These researches would require an intensity of religious motivation, an ability to converse with the educated Christian aristocracy (such as it was), and some minimal literary sense. They would not require that he be a poet.

There is, however, one urgent task facing the Roman Church for which Prudentius is perfectly suited: the conversion of the aristocracy by means of the muse's persuasion. Whether or not he journeys to Rome in this professional capacity as a poet, having reached Rome, his special talent marks him for service in the Church's sensitive mission of cultural activity *contra paganos*.

In 402 and 403, the probable years of Prudentius' Roman sojourn, some of the best Roman families remain devoted to the old Roman and newer oriental divinities. It is not difficult to imagine that, given this spiritual recalcitrance on the part of the Roman aristocracy, the ecclesiastical authorities might commission the *Contra Orationem Symmachi*. At the same time, Hellenistic philosophy, particularly neo-Platonism, is still widely read and believed by non-Christians, and those most antagonistic to the Church can still refer to Porphyry's *Against the Christians* for respected intellectual support. A greater danger is that within the Church heretical views are still maintained, views often resulting from neo-Platonic manipulation of the Nicene formula. It is not difficult to imagine that, again, the ecclesiastical authorities might commission the *Apotheosis* or *Hamartigenia*. The hymns and celebrations of the martyrs do not respond to particular threats so much as contribute to the Church's efforts to establish a Christian Roman culture. Like the late fourth-century development of Christian monumental art (to which the *Dittochaeon* relates), these non-polemical writings respond indirectly to social turmoil. The *Liber Cathemerinon* and *Peristephanon* are positive rather than negative responses to an old and false culture, which they would destroy by creating a new one.

71

Prudentius' patron is the Church at large. As an aristocrat, he is not a professional poet per se, he does not write for financial remuneration. The patronage is instead spiritual. In exchange for his poems, the poet hopes for the reward of heaven, which he knows is obtainable only through fruitful service within the Church. From the Church's point of view, the work of a Prudentius is encouraged not because of any altruistic love of literature in the abstract, but because of a conviction of its usefulness. As a branch of rhetoric, poetry moves; it is useful, much as a sermon is, because it can persuade men spiritually. For the Church, the ultimate usefulness of poetry is as a means of saving souls—this aim distinguishes the Church from all other patrons. But a more practical, immediate, worldly usefulness is also at issue. For since the ultimate salvational purpose of the Church depends upon the Church's ability to win souls away from error and toward true faith, its patronage of poetry must be based on poetry's ability to fight error and encourage true faith in a timely and persuasive manner.

Pugnet Contra Hereses, Catholicam Discutiat Fidem

The defense of Nicene Christianity against heresy is one of the major poetic tasks accepted by Prudentius. He spends many hundreds of lines answering the question posed in the preface to the *Apotheosis*: "Is our doctrine true?" (*Est vera secta?*). The question is not one of abstract intellectual speculation. By the close of the fourth century, only a few decades had passed since the Church formulated and defended the fundamental doctrine of the Trinity. Given its importance and its recentness, we may appreciate Prudentius' sense of the urgency of conviction.

Such appreciation will permit a sympathetic reading of the hexameters beginning the *Psychomachia*. Modern editors have set in parentheses the poet's paratactic expansion of orthodox Christology. Some readers find these verses intru-

sive or extraneous, their "unpoetic" matter interruptive of
the epic quality of the invocation:

> Christe, graves hominum semper miserate labores,
> qui patria virtute cluis propriaque, sed una,
> (unum namque Deum colimus de nomine utroque,
> non tamen et solum, quia tu Deus ex Patre, Christe,)
> dissere, rex noster. . . .   (1-5)

> [Christ, who hast ever had compassion on the heavy dis-
> tresses of men, who art glorious in renown for thy
> Father's power and thine own—but one power, for it is
> one God that we worship under the two names; yet not
> *merely* one, since Thou, O Christ, art God born of the
> Father—say, our King. . . .]

But these doctrinal verses are *meant* to retard the invocation,
meant to intrude by their very importance. By means of
them, Prudentius announces that the epic about *anima* cannot be told unless its muse is the Christ of the Council of
Nicaea: truly God *and* truly man. If Christ were God only,
his human nature mere illusion, then the redemptive power
("compassion on the heavy distresses of men") of his Incarnation and Passion could not operate. If Christ were not
truly God but a creature, he could not create—much less
restore—man in the image of God. The formulation of
Christian doctrine against these heretical possibilities has
important consequences for literature and it affects our
interpretation of this poem. If Christ were God only, the
epic of the soul's salvation would be a mere fiction, for without Christ's atonement the virtues and vices would fight
perpetually, the vices would perpetually win, the temple of
Sapientia would never be built. If Christ were not truly
God, the epic would be more than fiction, but would be
evil, for then the temple of Sapientia would be built as
a pagan temple in honor of yet another hero or moral abstraction, and its worship would be idolatrous. The truth

73

and goodness of the *Psychomachia*, Prudentius claims, depends upon the Trinity.

The background of this claim is a century of controversy. Within the Church structure, the controversy was over the definition of the natures of Christ, divine and human, and of the persons of the Trinity. Known as the "Arian controversy," after the chief opponent of Nicene orthodoxy, the theological debate within the Church continued well after the defeat of Arius, and of the Arian party, into the fifth century. Meanwhile there continued the less subtle dispute between the Church and rival Manicheans over the relationship of matter and spirit.

Arianism is polytropic and so rather difficult to define, but at bottom it is rejection of the divinity of Christ. As such it can be viewed as a sophisticated theological version of the much older Manichean philosophy. Manicheanism proclaims an irreconcilable division between matter, which is evil, and spirit, which is good. Whereas a Jew or Christian would hold that Creation was good, a Manichean, with his harsh dualism, would argue that the God of Genesis is necessarily Satan, for matter must originate by the agency of an evil power. Similarly for the later Arians, the conception of Christ as both God and man, fully of two natures, is impossible, for no true God would willingly incarnate himself. Arians could accept the Gospel account in varying degrees, but they invariably denied that Christ is of the same essence as the Father; whence their quarrels with trinitarianism. Both Manicheanism and Arianism, in sum, are squeamish about matter, and an overview of late antiquity would ally them with the larger movements of neo-Platonism and oriental mystery cult. They posed grave threats to the fourth-century orthodox Church, and they influenced later heresies of different denominations. They were anathema to Prudentius: his *Hamartigenia* is primarily against Manichean ideas, his *Apotheosis* against Arianism.

Some critics have argued that these polemics are intellectual exercises composed well after the heat of the Arian

controversy had dissipated.[31] The same critics would presumably question the appropriateness of lines 3 and 4 of the
Psychomachia. Such an interpretation comes from mis-
estimating the historical persistence of heresy into the fifth
century as well as the seriousness with which the threat was
viewed at the time. On this latter point, it should be remembered that the formulation of the doctrine of the Trinity,
which characterizes all the scripturally attested manifestations of God's persons, is non-scriptural. The key language,
οὐσία (essence) and ὁμοούσιον (of one essence, consubstan-
tial), is revolutionary in having been created from the mind
of the Church rather than the revelation of the Holy Spirit
in Scripture. Or, if the Holy Spirit was thought to have
inspired the assembled bishops at Nicaea, the revelation was
a latter-day event, its authority different from that of Scripture. From its origin, then, Nicene orthodoxy was associated with the authority and unity of the Church.[32] The
primitive concept of the Church as a loose community of
"men of the Book" soon yielded to new concepts of catholicity and centralized power. Heretics, therefore, were more
than intellectual dissenters; they were (or were felt to be)
subversive of the authority and unity of the Church.

The persistence of heresy into Prudentius' period and
beyond is a matter of fact. In the first place, the creed signed
by all but a handful of the three hundred and eighteen bishops assembled[33] at Nicaea in 325 was tentative. Doctrinally

[31] E.g., Puech (cited Critical Introd., n. 18), pp. 172ff. Also Lavarenne, *Prudence* (cited Critical Introd., n. 1), Vol. 2 [*Apotheosis* and
Hamartigenia], pp. vii-viii, expresses astonishment that the poet, if
he wanted to fight heresies, concerned himself with old errors "and
did not even name the most formidable enemy, Arius."

[32] Constantine's conversion may itself have been motivated by
political considerations. One of his first acts after having subdued
the Eastern provinces was to call the Council of Nicaea. He had
Arian sympathies, but he nevertheless put pressure on the assembled
bishops to reach unanimity of faith in the trinitarian creed. He was
less concerned with the doctrine itself than with its concomitant
institutional strength for the Church, hence for the Empire.

[33] The number is significant—see p. 229.

75

CHAPTER I

so, in that it defined the natures of Christ completely, but
not the persons of God: the Holy Spirit was named but
not described (as it is described in the so-called "Nicene
Creed" of a later date). Politically so, in that the orthodox
party's fortunes were rapidly reversed. In 328, the exiled
heretical bishops, among them Eusebius of Nicomedia, were
allowed to return. That they then were able to intrigue
successfully against the Nicene bishops proves the existence
of a large centrist group of conservatives at the Council.
The orthodox Eustathius of Antioch was deposed and ban-
ished in 330, and Athanasius had to flee to the West in 335.
Arius himself was about to be declared orthodox and to
receive communion in the Church when he died in 336. And
the next several decades show the Arian parties (for they
are by now split among themselves) gaining strength politically. In 359 a double council of Eastern and Western bishops met, at Seleucia and Ariminum respectively, and passed
a semi-Arian position apparently aimed at preventing dogmatic precision. Jerome commented: "The whole world
groaned and marvelled to find itself Arian" (*Dial. adv.
Lucif.* 19). Henceforward the Nicene party began to make
headway, being favored morally (the Arian bishops were
scoundrels and sycophants) and intellectually (through the
theological exposition of Basil, Gregory of Nyssa, and
Gregory of Nazianzus), as well as by the factionalism
among the Arians.[34] Not until 381, however, was the official
victory of the Nicene faith won under the Emperor Theodosius at the Council of Constantinople. Once again Arianism was anathematized and outlawed, the heretical bishops
driven from the Empire. This second general council confirmed the dogmas of the first; and advanced them—the
Holy Spirit was now described, and the Trinity thereby
defined.

[34] Prudentius is fond of contrasting the splitting tendencies of
heretics with the unity of the Church; a recurrent simile is that of
two paths, the one straight and narrow, the other broad with a confusion of branches. See *Ham.* 789ff.; *C. Symm.* II, 851ff.

So the doctrines of Nicene Christianity were recent and vulnerable when Prudentius knew them. During much of his lifetime the Empire had been Arian or of doubtful faith, and the doctrines of the Church were certainly obscure to the majority of her members. One can sense the poet's relief at everything finally being settled in these lines of exuberant idealism:

en ades, Omnipotens, concordibus influe terris
iam mundus te, Christe, capit, quem congrege nexu
pax et Roma tenent.   (*C. Symm.* II, 634-636)

[Come then, Almighty; here is a world in harmony; do Thou enter it. An earth receives Thee now, O Christ, which peace and Rome hold in a bond of union.]

But of course there was no such harmony. Civil strife was increasing, and the Roman armies were suffering defeats at the hands of the barbarians. Not only had many of the barbarians been converted to Arianism (including the federated Goths who formed the manpower reserve of the Roman legions), new and subtler versions of heresy were virulent among Christians of the Empire.

Modern historians can scan the centuries and see that at such and such a time a movement or ideology is in a period of decline, has lost its momentum, is no longer a serious threat to the system. Such statements are generally made about Arianism and Manicheanism at the end of the fourth century, and it is not our purpose here to dispute their objective truth. We should remember, though, that the subjective impression of people at the end of the fourth century did not benefit from our own distanced viewpoint. Aside from the evidence of the *Hamartigenia* itself and of Augustine's account of Manicheanism in the *Confessions*, we know that in 372 the emperors Valens and Valentinian I felt it necessary to issue this edict:

Wherever an assembly of Manichaeans or such a throng is found, their teachers shall be punished with a heavy penalty. Those who assemble shall also be segregated from the company of men as infamous and ignominious, and the houses and habitations in which the profane doctrine is taught shall undoubtedly be appropriated to the resources of the fisc. (*Cod. Theod.* XVI, 5.3)[35]

Such measures, if enforced, did not halt the movement. The fifth-century historian Sulpicius Severus (*Chronica*, 46) reports that around 370, Priscillian, an educated Spanish layman, began to propagate a kind of Gnosticism introduced into Spain by a certain Marcus from Egypt. By 380, the doctrines attributed to him were condemned at a synod at Saragossa, Priscillian himself having already recruited a large following, including two bishops, to his party. Despite the synod's condemnation, Priscillian was elected Bishop of Avila. This was a serious threat, and was so treated: Priscillian and his followers (now labeled Manicheans) were exiled from Spain in 381; and in 385, in the first case of capital punishment for heresy, Priscillian was executed by the Emperor Maximus. After the fall of Maximus in 388, the province of Galicia had become almost entirely Priscillianist. A council at Toledo in 400 was still dealing with the problem—they deposed all bishops who would not give up the heresy but allowed those who submitted to be confirmed in office. Apparently this rather more conciliatory move was also unsuccessful, for the heresy continued through the fifth century in Spain and was condemned by the Council of Braga in 563. If Manicheanism was on the wane when Prudentius flourished, it was nevertheless a force to be reckoned with.

The Priscillianist version of Manicheanism seems much on Prudentius' mind even though it is unnamed in his works.

[35] *The Theodosian Code*, trans. Clyde Pharr (Princeton, 1952), p. 450. All of Book XVI, Title 5 (*De Haereticis*), is illuminating for the continuity of heretical and Manichean belief during Prudentius' period of literary activity. All subsequent references to the Codex Theodosianus are made from Pharr's edition and will be cited by book, title, and article.

According to this eclectic heresy, Satan is not a fallen angel but the principle of evil, and the human body is his creation; human souls are essentially divine and their existence in bodies is a kind of punishment or imprisonment. Prudentius refutes these concepts. Creation is originally good, he argues, and it is the sin of creatures rather than an evil principle which causes disorder. Thus Satan's willful sin:

> inventor vitii non est Deus: angelus illud
> degener infami conceptum mente creavit. (*Ham.* 159-160)

[The contriver of evil is no God. It was a debased angel that conceived it in his foul mind and brought it into being.]

And man's:

> nec mirum si membra orbis concussa rotantur,
> si vitiis agitata suis mundana laborat
> machina, si terras luis incentiva fatigat:
> exemplum dat vita hominum, quo cetera peccent.
> (*Ham.* 247-250)

[And no wonder if the world's parts are shaken and tossed, if the machinery of the universe fails to work smoothly because it is thrown out of order by faults in itself, and the urge that plagues it gives the earth no rest; for the life of man sets an example for all else to sin.]

Other Priscillianist tenets are modalist trinitarianism and docetic Christology. Modalism denies the permanence if not the existence of the three Persons of God: God is one and as such assumes different transitory modes. Docetism (from δοκέω, "to seem") is the related doctrine that Christ's Incarnation is mere appearance, that Christ has no real human nature. Prudentius undoubtedly met people in Spain who believed that Christ had no prior existence before his birth from the Virgin Mary, that as such Christ was a tem-

79

porary "mode" of the Father. He combats this idea in his works. The Old Testament revelations of God to man were revelations not of the Father but of the Son; thus Abraham saw Christ, and Jacob wrestled with him (*Apo.* 28-30) and Moses saw the Word in the likeness of Christ (*Apo.* 33-54).[36] *Apotheosis* 6-27 is a theoretical rebuttal of modalism, ending as follows:

> quisque hominum vidisse Deum memoratur, ab ipso
> infusum vidit Gnatum; nam Filius hoc est,
> quos de Patre micans se praestitit inspiciendum
> per species quas possit homo conprendere visu.
> nam mera maiestas est infinita, nec intrat
> obtutus, aliquo ni se moderamine formet.   (*Apo.* 22-27)

[Whosoever of men is said to have seen God has seen the Son whom He imparted; for it is the Son who, issuing from the Father, has manifested himself to our eyes in forms which man can grasp with his sight; the pure majesty is infinite, and comes not within our vision unless it takes some tempering shape.]

The passage also counters docetism by emphasizing that the Father cannot suffer: therefore the Son can and in fact has.

Priscillianism was not the only heresy vigorous in 400. A new version of docetic Christology arose in mid-century in the course of the anti-Arian struggle. Called Apollinarianism after Apollinarius, Bishop of Laodicea, the doctrine was a radical refutation of Arianism. It asserted (with orthodox Christianity) the unity of divine and human natures in Christ and countered the Arian views that Christ was not fully God and that there was a moral development in Christ's life. Apollinarius followed Origen's teaching that the parts of man were three: body, spirit, and soul. He believed, however, that Christ's human nature consisted of

---

[36] See also *Cath.* VIII, 147.

body and soul but not of spirit. Therefore, Christ's humanity was unique, for in Christ alone the Logos replaced the
human spirit. Christ was therefore not completely human,
but only seemed so. Arian doceticism was turned upside
down.

Partly because Apollinarianism originated as staunchly pro-
Nicene and partly because it represented a new theological
departure, it found adherents at a time when straight Arianism was exposed as false. The new heresy was condemned
by synods at Rome in 374 and 380, and by the Council of
Constantinople. It continued to flourish nonetheless, and its
position of "first-mention" in the following edict of 388
issued by Gratian, Valentinian II, and Theodosius suggests
its status as a clear and present danger to the Church.

We command that the Apollinarians and all other followers of diverse heresies shall be prohibited from all places,
from the walls of the cities, from the congregation of
honorable men, from the communion of the saints. They
shall not have the right to ordain clerics. . . . They shall
go to places which will seclude them most effectively, as
though by a wall, from human association. Moreover,
We subjoin to the foregoing provisions that to all the
aforesaid persons the opportunity to approach and address Our Serenity shall be denied. (*Cod. Theod.* XVI,
5. 14)

These measures were not effective against the Apollinarians,
similar edicts being required in 397 and 435.

As with Priscillianism, there is no passage in Prudentius'
opera explicitly against Apollinarianism. But it is suggestive
that along with metaphors of Christ's assuming "human
clay," more theologically worded passages refer to Christ's
assumption of human nature (which must include body and
soul) rather than of flesh (which might be interpreted as
just body or, figuratively, as human nature). Thus in the
"Hymnus de Trinitate":

81

edere sed Verbum Patris est, at cetera Verbi,
adsumptum gestare *hominem*, reparare peremptum,
conciliare Patri, dextraque in sede locare.

(*Apo*. Hymn, 7-9)

[But while to give forth the Word belongs to the Father,
all else is of the Word, to take on and wear *the nature
of man* and restore him from destruction, to reconcile
him to the Father and set him at His right hand.]

These lines may show a careful avoidance of Apollinarianism, but this possibility remains a matter of speculation.

A subject closely connected with the Apollinarian heresy
certainly was on Prudentius' mind: the formation of a Christian psychology. Augustine's theories of Original Sin, of
caritas and *cupiditas*, of the dynamic movement of the soul
in *amor*—these were only in the process of formulation at
the end of the fourth century. The Church had not yet
developed a Christian psychology clearly differentiated
from the ancient Platonic and Aristotelian conceptions. The
structure of the soul, not earlier a subject of great urgency,
became so with the growth of Apollinarianism. For the
Apollinarian concept of Christ's mutilated humanity depends logically upon the trichotomy of human nature into
body, spirit, and soul. Since this arrangement had been a
basic tenet of Platonic psychology well before the Christian
era, not merely the prestige of Platonism had convinced
many early Fathers—especially Greek Fathers, and notably
Origen—of its verity. The Greek Fathers looked to Paul's
first Epistle to the Thessalonians (5:23): "And may the God
of peace himself sanctify you in all things; that your whole
spirit and soul and body may be preserved blameless in the
coming of our Lord Jesus Christ." This trichotomy has
never been declared heretical, for it does not deny essential
Christian doctrine: it denies neither the basic distinction between body and soul, the creation of the soul of Adam by
God, nor the immortality of the soul. But at certain periods

82

of Church history the structure of the soul has become a matter of debate, and the end of the fourth century was one such period. Indeed, the interest in psychology was rather sudden. Since Origen believed in the trichotomy, the flaring up of a controversy over Origen's orthodoxy around 400 all over the Mediterranean world is perhaps not un-related to the Apollinarian controversy.

An intellectual achievement of the post-Nicene period in the West was general consensus, if not dogma, on the soul's structure: the two-part division into body and soul is basic. The advanced solution worked out by Augustine in his *De Trinitate* (A.D. 416) is to support the simple body-soul dichotomy as probably correct while at the same time dis-covering in the unitary soul (*anima*) the image of the Trinity: thus the Father, Son, and Spirit have their mystic counterparts in the soul's activities of memory, intellect, and will. Note that the three faculties are *within* the soul, bear-ing only a numerological likeness to the Greek body-spirit-soul.

Ambrose of Milan, writing a few years before Pruden-tius, is outside the basic consensus. He continues the Origen-ist trichotomy in the West. St. Ambrose is indebted to both Origen and Philo for much in his exegetical writings, includ-ing the *De Abraham*, which Prudentius read and used in the composition of the *Psychomachia*. Many of the typological details in the "Praefatio" of the *Psychomachia* derive from Ambrose's commentary, as does its basic assumption that scriptural exegesis reveals profound psychological truths. Amidst this significant influence, however, Prudentius in-sists on altering the Greek trichotomy. That Prudentius, a layman and no theologian, should revise Ambrose's think-ing in this respect suggests not so much willfulness on his part as willingness to voice the dominant thought of the Church. Elsewhere we discover him consciously advocating a theory of the soul's structure. Thus the hymn "On the Burial of the Dead" begins,

83

Deus, ignee fons animarum,
duo qui socians elementa,
vivum simul ac moribundum,
hominem, Pater, effigiasti,
    tua sunt, tua, rector, utraque,
tibi copula iungitur horum,
tibi dum vegetata cohaerent
et spiritus et caro servit.
    recissa sed ista seorsum
solvunt hominem perimuntque;
humus excipit arida corpus,
animae rapit aura liquorem.   (*Cath.* X, 1-12)

[God, the burning source of spirits, who, by uniting two
elements, one living and one dying, together, didst in Thy
Fatherhood create man, Thine, O Ruler, Thine are both;
it is for Thee the bond is drawn between them; Thee,
while they cleave together in quickening life, both soul
and flesh serve. But their sundering apart is the dissolution
and the end of man: the dry earth receives his body, the
breath of air carries off the pure spirit.]

And the hymn ends with reunification of body and soul
when the resurrection of the body occurs at the Last
Judgment.[37]

But the structure and nature of the body-soul relationship
is not a question of orthodoxy for Prudentius. Despite
noticeable vigor in support of the dichotomy, he never
attacks the theory of trichotomy as *error*. Yet he does treat
other questions about the nature of the soul as matters of
orthodoxy. Amidst the theology of the *Apotheosis* are nearly two hundred lines on the nature of the soul. Two enemies
are singled out, emanationism and traducianism; and against
these is set the theory of creationism.

[37] See also Prudentius' most authoritative statement on the body
and soul relationship: that in God's speech, *C. Symm.* II, 212-217.

Emanationism, with obvious affinities to neo-Platonism, claims that souls partake of the divine nature, that they are, so to speak, particles of divinity. Origen's belief in the pre-existence of souls is emanationist. The seriousness of the debate over yet another psychological question in Pruden-tius' time can be guessed by the fact that in 396 St. Jerome accused John of Jerusalem (one of the most elevated mem-bers of the ecclesiastical hierarchy) of belief in a form of emanationism contained in Origen's *On First Principles*: "that souls are tied up in the body as in a prison; and that, before man was made in Paradise, they dwelt among rational creatures in the heavens."[38] Circulating in *On First Princi-ples* during the fourth century, this tenet naturally found favor with Manicheans and Priscillianists. In the *Apotheosis*, Prudentius may be facing off against either sort of heretic when he takes as his subject the nature of the soul. This opponent has asked: does the Church admit that the soul inbreathed by God (*substantia . . . inspirata Deo*) can suffer in hell? The poet replies:

crede animam non esse Deum, sed crede creatis
maiorem cunctis, ipsam quoque crede creatam.
formata est namque ore Dei, quae non erat ante,
sed formata habitu pulcherrima pictaque rebus
divinis, et plena Deo similisque creanti,
non tamen ipsa Deus, quoniam generatio non est,
sed factura Dei est; solus de corde Parentis
Filius emicuit; verus, verus Deus ille.   (*Apo.* 786-793)

[You must believe that the soul is not God, but that, while it is greater than all created things, it too was created. For it was made by the mouth of God; it did not exist before, but was made, beauteous in form, adorned with qualities divine, filled with God, and like its creator, yet not itself

[38] Jerome, *Adv. Ioann. Hier.* 7. Trans. in *Creeds, Councils and Controversies: Documents Illustrative of the History of the Church A.D. 337-461*, ed. J. Stevenson (London, 1966), p. 174.

God, since it is not a begetting but a creation of God. The Son alone came forth from the Father's heart; He, He is true God.]

Note that orthodoxy on the nature of Christ is closely related to orthodoxy on the nature of the soul. This is to be expected. The fourth-century creed's "begotten not made" clause implies by its characterization of Christ's divinity the creationist doctrine of the human soul: Only Christ is an emanation of the Father; the soul in the image of God is created.[39]

The other main psychological error, traducianism (from Latin *tradux*, "shoot, sprout"), claims that the soul is transmitted by the human parents to their children. In contrast to emanationism, it emphasizes the total depravity of man by the absence of any divine infusion into man's nature. This theory was not in fact heretical in Prudentius' day; it was not condemned until 498, by Pope Anastasius II. Tertullian had advocated it in his *De Anima* in a materialist form: the soul as matter transmitted in the physical act of generation. But there was also a theory of spiritual traducianism current in Prudentius' time, especially among the Apollinarians.

Augustine himself considered the transmission of Original Sin too difficult to understand with certainty, and he seems to have favored a spiritual traducianism. Prudentius attacks only the materialist viewpoint directly:

vitandus tamen error erit, ne *traduce* carnis
transfundi in subolem credatur fons animarum
sanguinis exemplo, cui texta propagine vena est.

(*Apo.* 915-917)

[But we shall have to shun the error of supposing that the germ of the soul is transmitted to offspring by propagation of the flesh after the manner of the blood, for which the vessel is made by generation from the parent stock.]

[39] For another passage against emanationism, see *Apo.* 878-882.

86

Yet as this argument continues, the poet seems to deny also
the theory of spiritual traducianism held by the Apollinarians: *non animas animae pariunt* (souls do not give birth to
souls). Instead, a certain mysterious natural law (*lege latenti
... opus natura*) operates to give the souls power to breathe.
While Prudentius often mentions the creation of the first
soul by God, he does not state that God creates each subsequent soul; yet he is constantly referring to the soul as
creatam, created. On this whole topic Prudentius' own
thinking reflects the Church's uncertainty—it is creationist
without being exactly sure of its justification.

If Prudentius has a theory of the soul, it is this: that the
soul is the highest creation of God; that its first breath is,
according to an unknown process of nature, already tainted
by Original Sin—*vetus illa tamen de crimine avorum / dici-
tur*; that at baptism it is washed utterly clean by divine
grace; and, that nonetheless it continues to be subject to
Original Sin. Here is the process from baptism onward:

> inde secunda redit generatio et inde lavatur
> naturae inluvies, iterumque renascimur intus
> perfusi, ut veterem splendens anima exuat Adam.
> quae quia materiam peccati ex fomite carnis
> consociata trahit, nec non simul ipsa sodali
> est incentivum peccaminis, inplicat ambas
> vindex poena reas peccantes mente sub una,
> peccandique cremat socias cruciatibus aequis.
> his crucibus Christus nos liberat incorruptae
> matris et innocui gestator corporis unus. (*Apo.* 924-933)

[Then comes the second birth and the natural filth is
washed away; our inner being is born again when we are
baptised, so that the soul shines bright and puts off the
old Adam. But as in its fellowship with the body it draws
occasion to sin from the incitements of the flesh, and itself
also at the same time provokes sin in its comrade, aveng-
ing punishment lays hold of both wrongdoers together
since they sin with one mind, and burns the partners in

sin with like torments. From these torments Christ sets us free, for He alone had a mother immaculate and wore a sinless body.]

Again we note some confusion about the nature of Original Sin. The body seems implicated in an almost Manichean way, yet the soul is also implicated. The conclusion, however awkwardly reached, is orthodox: sin involves a partnership or collaboration between body and soul, both of which are tainted by Original Sin, but each of which has its own motion and character as created by God.

Such incursions into the new field of Christian psychology prepare for the *Psychomachia*. When a long poem appears on the subject of the human soul divided against itself, pursuing contrary motions toward God and against God and, with the grace of God, moving at last toward its true goal of salvation—this is an important event in the history of Christian spirituality. My purpose has been to demonstrate that such a poem is not produced in a historical vacuum, but is occasioned by, among other things, the Church's struggle versus heretics, and specifically by the Church's need to persuade the aristocracy of Nicene orthodoxy.[40] The fourth-century Church had successfully carried through its effort to define the nature of the Trinity, but had not yet solved complementary problems concerning the nature of the soul. The flourishing of interest in psychology after the Council of Constantinople is not random in its timing. Heretical sects posing a continued threat to the Church's claim of orthodoxy, the Priscillianists and the Apollinarians especially, were well aware of the Church's

[40] Except for the scribe's use of Rustic Capitals, mentioned Critical Introd., n. 5, no hard evidence exists for the circulation of Prudentius' works amongst this class. But Alan Cameron has put forward for consideration the possibility that Claudian borrowed from Prudentius: that *Apo.* 111-112 influence *Gigantomachia* 106-107. This, if true, is good circumstantial evidence. See discussion in *Claudian* (cited Critical Introd., n. 4), pp. 469-473.

uncertainty about the nature of the soul; consequently they rephrased the old, exposed errors in psychological terms. Prudentius participated in the general Church interest in the nature of the soul and in specific Church campaigns against these heretical groups.

Conculcet Sacra Gentium, Labem, Roma, Tuis Inferat Idolis

The second major danger against which Prudentius hurled his public voice was paganism. It was not dead. Our modern historical objectivity allows us to perceive that, like Arianism and its offspring, paganism was on the wane by the close of the fourth century. But neither had pagan ritual been utterly crushed, nor did the Christians believe it to have been—and this ritual was only the outward and visible form of pagan ideology and culture. The subjective reaction of the Church at this time is of importance in determining Prudentius' own attitude toward pagan ritual and pagan culture.

Well into the fifth century, books circulated around the Empire bearing the accusation that the barbarian invasions and (after 410) the sack of Rome were punishments sent by the old gods against the impiety of the Christians. The seriousness of these charges and their wide acceptance can be gauged by such refutations as Augustine's *De Civitate Dei contra Paganos* (begun in 413, completed in 426) and Paulus Orosius' *Historia adversus Paganos* (417). The number of such titles "against the pagans" proves that the Church was worried about paganism. This worry was not baseless.

When Constantine granted the Church a special religious status in the Empire, he did not try to eliminate paganism. On the contrary, a series of edicts issued by him and by his sons repeated the basic Roman principle of religious tolerance while merely increasing the privileges (state funding, tax exemptions, etc.) of the Church. Roman emperors continued to possess the official title of *pontifex maximus*,

89

Gratian, in 375, being the first to refuse this office. Until 383 paganism was the official state religion of Rome. Admittedly there was a series of anti-pagan pronouncements by Constantius II, such as this in 341:

> Superstition shall cease; the madness of sacrifices shall be abolished. For if any man in violation of the law of the sainted Emperor, Our father, and in violation of this command of Our Clemency, should dare to perform sacrifices, he shall suffer the infliction of a suitable punishment and the effect of an immediate sentence. (*Cod. Theod.* XVI, 10.2)

But no such law of Constantine survives, and we know of no evidence that the father of Constantius broke his promises of toleration (313 and 324). In the words of Libanus, "Constantine used the temple treasures, but altered not a single item of the accustomed worship: there was poverty in the temples, but one could see all the rites being carried out" (*Pro Templis*, 6). This situation probably prevailed under Constantius as well. (An edict addressed to the prefect of Rome in 342 directs that the temple buildings outside the walls of the city be left intact; and there is no evidence of temples inside the walls being torn down at this time.) Until the eighties, when anti-pagan laws began to be enforced in earnest, the principle of toleration seems to have been regarded by Christian emperors as an adjunct of wise rule. Julian the Apostate (355-363), in his attempted reformation of the pagan imperial priesthood, draws the line at outlawing Christian worship; he is content to deny to Christians a teaching role in the Roman educational system.

Perhaps shaken by the attempted revitalization of paganism under Julian, emperors following him were more anxious to see the ancient religious rites irrevocably destroyed. Under Gratian and then Theodosius the laws become aggressively anti-pagan. Thus in 382 funds to defray the costs of sacrifices were no longer allowed to leave the imperial treasury. In 383 Gratian ordered the altar of the Goddess Victoria removed from the Senate and initiated a major political battle. Two representatives of old Roman patrician families, the pagan Symmachus and the Christian Ambrose, debated the justice of this anti-pagan legislation, and their arguments lived on for years (and inspired the *Contra Orationem Symmachi*). The position of Symmachus in this controversy was dignified and defensive; without great religious fervor, he argued for preservation of the last tokens of civil ritual as symbols of *Romanitas*. Other pagans of the Roman aristocracy were rather more vigorous. Praetextatus, who once quipped to Pope Damasus that he would immediately become a Christian if he were made Bishop of Rome, is known to have publicly restored temples in defiance of Gratian's decree. Praetextatus, not Symmachus, was the leader of the pagan party until his death in 385, and he was a deeply religious man. A member of three of the four ancient priesthoods (he was *augur, pontifex Vestae, quindecimvir*), he was of the priesthood of Sol, and he had been initiated into the rites of Sarapis, Magna Mater, and Mithras. It is probably not accidental that no writings of this man survive, whereas later Christian copyists preserved the letters of Symmachus. Judged solely from Symmachus' testimony, the pagan party appears to have been all but defeated by 385. Had this been so, Prudentius' *Contra Orationem Symmachi* would indeed be an academic exercise. But this was not so in fact.[41] The following edict (391)

[41] See the remarks of Thomson (cited Critical Introd., n. 1), pp. x-xii, on the persistence of paganism in relation to the *C. Symm.* It is hardly necessary to posit a renewed attempt to restore the altar to Victory in order to interpret Prudentius' polemic as responding to an actual pagan threat. Alan Cameron, *Claudian* (cited Critical Introd., n. 4), p. 240, correctly opposes critics (Romano; W. Schmidt) who have argued that Prudentius was directly inspired by such a fresh attempt. But Cameron misleadingly writes, "He is fighting again the battle of 384 [over altar]—won for him when the pagan senators tear off their fillets and bow to Christ after Theodosius' appeal to them in 394 [after battle of Frigidus]. There is no suggestion that the

shows Christian authorities dealing with a concrete situation
of pagan practice.

> No person shall pollute himself with sacrificial animals;
> no person shall slaughter an innocent victim; no person
> shall approach the shrines, shall wander through the tem-
> ples, or revere the images formed by mortal labor, lest
> he become guilty by divine and human laws. Judges also
> shall be bound by the general rule that if any of them
> should be devoted to profane rites and should enter a
> temple for the purpose of worship anywhere, either on a
> journey or in the city, he shall immediately be compelled
> to pay fifteen pounds of gold, and his office staff shall pay
> a like sum with similar haste, unless they resist the judge
> and immediately report him by a public attestation. Gov-
> ernors and the rank of consular shall pay six pounds of
> gold each, their office staffs a like amount; those with the
> rank of corrector or of praeses shall pay four pounds each,
> and their apparitors, by equal lot, a like amount. (*Cod.
> Theod.* XVI, 10. 10)

In other words, the Roman administrative apparatus was so
far from being Christianized that at all levels of rank material incentives for informers were necessary. If this was the
case in 391, it is quite unlikely that the situation was totally
reversed by the time Prudentius began writing.

The nineties did witness considerable change in the
pagans' position, and one event, the battle at the Frigidus

---

old danger has recurred in Prudentius' own day." Cameron here uses
the words "old danger" to refer to the struggle over the altar (or does
he include events of the nineties?); but his implications are larger, to
wit, that the danger of paganism itself has declined, that the C. *Symm.*
is indeed an academic exercise. Perhaps the oddest formulation of
this theory is by François Paschoud, *Roma Aeterna* (cited Critical
Introd., n. 4), p. 224: "Why not suppose that Prudentius, little convinced by Ambrose's arguments, wrote the *Contra Symmachum* to
persuade himself, and perhaps certain rigorists in his circle, that there
was no incompatibility between patriotism and Christianity?"

(394), could be termed a reversal of fortune. It was a contest of faiths. Here the two armies were headed by the Christian Theodosius and the nominally Christian Eugenius, a cultivated man of letters who favored the pagan party and who probably intended to emulate Julian's restoration. The Roman aristocracy at this time was solidly behind Eugenius. On their side of the battlefield, statues of Jupiter with thunderbolts of pure gold had been erected and standards bearing the picture of Hercules were advanced ahead of the army. On the Christian side was held the sign of the cross. According to all accounts, Theodosius was on the verge of losing (he had already lost 10,000 men) when a violent dust storm turned the pagans' lances against themselves. The event was interpreted as a miracle. The last substantial hope of the pagan party for control of the state was destroyed at this battle, and the main leader of this movement committed suicide in the tradition of Cato. This was Flavianus, who, as Praetextatus had done a decade earlier, attempted a revival of the worship of Jupiter, Saturn, Mercury, and Vulcan, as well as the oriental divinities Isis and Magna Mater, Attis and Sarapis.

The pagan revival of the nineties was, as its near military success suggests, a vigorous and far-reaching movement. Others besides Prudentius reacted to it in verse. Preserved in the earliest Prudentius manuscript (Paris 8084) is an anonymous *Carmen adversus Flavianum*, a fierce invective against the very Flavianus who died at Frigidus. The author combines scornful ridicule of Flavianus' mystic rites with exultation at his death. He asks: what use were these incestuous gods and goddesses to you? and why did you waste all your days on degrading sacrifices and magic charms? The satiric tone is so bitter that one senses beneath it a genuine appreciation of the danger embodied in Flavianus. At one point the pagan leader is accused of having attempted to corrupt Christians by bribes of administrative posts. Assuming the truth of the accusation, one suspects that Flavianus was able to corrupt more than a few Christians. A second

93

anonymous satire of the period, the so-called *Carmen ad Senatorem ex Christiana Religone ad Idolorum Servitutem Conversum*, may reflect the general success of the pagan party in winning Christians to apostatize. As its manuscript title explains, this poem is addressed to an unnamed senator who has renounced Christianity (the official, legal religion at this time) in favor of Isis and Magna Mater. The author of this satire, which is rather less acrid than the one against Flavianus, explains with an urbane irony that he is using verse because the senator himself has always maintained a fondness for poetry; later he remarks that it is better to be a simple Christian than a philosophical pagan. Such statements are indicative of the cultural milieu of the controversy. The representatives of civilization are dignified, elegant, somewhat given to pedantry, holding on to antique forms of life and literature (and such is the delightful yet pathetic view of polite pagan society in Macrobius' *Saturnalia*) in contrast to the relatively uncultured, upstart Christians. Like the character "Evangelus" in the *Saturnalia*, the two Christian satirists of the nineties must have appeared fantastically gauche to the Roman aristocracy. Such extant Christian apologetics provide a good view of the cultural gap Prudentius was to fill.[42]

What happened to the pagan party in Rome after the battle at Frigidus? It was certainly suppressed as an active and open force under the strong rule of Theodosius. So recently silenced, it would easily have been viewed by Prudentius and the Church as still potentially dangerous and deserving of continuous attack. But was the threat of paganism merely subjectively felt? Little imagination is needed to picture the defeated party maintaining their beliefs in

[42] The *Carmen adversus Flavianum* is edited by Baehrens, *Poetae Latini Minores*, Vol. 3 (Leipzig, 1886), pp. 287f. The *Carmen ad Senatorem* is edited by Peiper in *CSEL*, Vol. 23 (Vienna, 1881), pp. 227f. An excellent recent article is J. F. Matthews, "The Historical Setting of the '*Carmen contra paganos*' (Cod. Par. Lat. 8084)," *Historia*, 19 (1970), 464-479.

spite of a perfunctory public observance of Christian worship. There is no evidence that members of the important
families were dispossessed or punished, so that in all probability they continued to have some hope for eventual restoration of paganism. Meanwhile pagan ritual went under-
ground. Herbert Bloch so intimates in commenting on a
recent archaeological finding of "a large group of coin-like
monuments, the so-called contorniates . . . which seem to
belong to this period, that is to the years from about 355-60
to 410. Emphatically pagan in content, they served in
Alföldi's opinion as new year's gifts and, of course, as pagan
propaganda. It is interesting that they continue to be produced after the catastrophe of 394. Among the subjects represented may be mentioned on the obverse: Alexander the
Great and emperors of the past, especially Nero and Trajan;
and on the reverse; scenes from the Alexander romance, the
pagan religions, including the cults of Magna Mater, Attis,
and Isis, classical mythology, Roman legends, the races and
games in the circus."[43]

The literary equivalent of this evidence is perhaps the
Saturnalia of Macrobius. Modeled after the *Symposium*, the
Saturnalia is a collection of miscellaneous bits of wisdom
and *nugae* presented in the form of an extended conversation about the merits of Vergil. Significantly, the literary
discussion is an actual religious observance, during which
religious antiquities of all sorts are presented under the cultural aegis of Vergil. What one encounters in the course of
this conversation is a whole series of "commemorative
medallions" of paganism—paganism here embracing civil

---

[43] Herbert Bloch, "The Pagan Revival in the West at the End of
the Fourth Century," in Momigliano, ed. (cited Critical Introd., n.
4), p. 202. The study to which Bloch refers is A. Alföldi, *Die
Kontorniaten. Ein verkanntes Propagandamittel der Stadrömischen
Heidnischen Aristokratie in ihrem Kampfe gegen das christliche
Kaisertum*, 2 vols. (Budapest, 1942-1943). I am generally indebted to
Bloch for his differentiation of Symmachus from Praetextatus and
for his perceptive remarks on the importance of Macrobius' *Saturnalia*
in the context of anti-Christian cultural resistance.

CHAPTER I

religion and, indeed, Roman civilization in all its aspects.
The *Saturnalia* dates from a period well after 394, and may
be as late as 430.[44] Its author certainly was wellborn and
certainly a pagan, though he doubtless did not celebrate
pagan rites, at least not openly; he probably was praetorian
prefect of Italy, a position of no little power for a pagan in
Christian society! Proof of the intact—if by now nostalgic
and sentimentalized—idealism of the pagan aristocracy is
that the prominent speakers in the *Saturnalia* are the heroes
of the previous generation: Praetextatus, Symmachus, and
Flavianus. Given the continuity of the pagan tradition,[45] it

[44] The dating c. 430 has been suggested by Alan Cameron, "The
Date and Identity of Macrobius," *Journal of Roman Studies*, 56
(1966), 25-38. His arguments for a later (and different) Macrobius
seem incontrovertible. But his literary judgment is puzzling. "That
the *Saturnalia* is a pagan work is undeniable" (34), but what does
"pagan" mean? In arguing against an early date, Cameron writes:
". . . it would be a very curious sort of propaganda for this period
of crisis [c. 395], when the tension between paganism and Christianity
was crystallized as never before. Macrobius could so easily (say)
have assigned Symmachus a speech on the history and significance of
the cult of Victoria. But what do we find instead? The first subject
discussed by this notorious band of die-hard pagans is the genitive
plural of the word *Saturnalia*" (34-35). Macrobius chose these inter-
locutors "not (or at any rate not primarily) for their paganism, but
for their erudition. . . ." (35); and again, "The pagan past is idealized
on every page: but because it is *past*, not because it is pagan" (36).
But surely Cameron has missed the sincere pagan piety of the work,
however non-militant and sentimental its atmosphere. Why, we must
wonder, did Macrobius not include any erudite Christians in the
Saturnalia? Was Macrobius' memory of Frigidus really so short?
More discussion of the *Saturnalia* in Chapter IV.
[45] Sophisticated pagan expression can be located in the contemporary Claudian's works. *In Rufinum* begins with a coy suggestion that
because of the horrendous evils found in the world the poet may
abandon his former belief in God in favor of "that other philosophy,"
Epicurianism. Claudian's epic (or mock-epic) world is enthusiastically pagan; from within this environment he is able to hurl a few
witty, anti-Christian jibes. Thus the divinity is addressed, "Oh thou,
whosoe'er thou art, that holdest sway in Olympus. . . ." (*pro quisquis
Olympi / summa tenes*) [*In Eutropium*, I, 140-141]. Of Claudian's

96

is not surprising that Prudentius would consider the anti-pagan darts of *Contra Orationem Symmachi* necessary, even after Frigidus.

As in Rome, paganism was well entrenched throughout the Empire. Thus Augustine writes in 408 to Nectarius, decurian of Calama and a pagan (though of Christian parentage), complaining that the citizens of Calama had held forbidden pagan celebrations. During these, a group of pagan dancers stoned the church, whereupon the bishop had to remind the magistrate of the well-known laws (*leges notissimas*) covering such occasions. One week later the church was stoned again and, though full of people, its roof was fired. The pagans rioted: "In the meantime the bishop was hiding in a certain spot into which he had thrust himself to lie all cramped, and from which he kept hearing the voices of those who were seeking to put him to death and were reproaching themselves for letting him escape and so for perpetrating such a heinous crime to no effect. This went on from almost four o'clock until a late hour of night. No attempt at repression, no attempt at rescue was made

---

short poems, two are superficially Christian. *De Salvatore* (32) is orthodox but without conviction. *In Iacobum Magistrum Equitum* (50) is of course a jest, yet its context, as I take it, is serious: the Christian suppression of pagan art and literature.

> Per cineres Pauli, per cani limina Petri,
>   ne laceres versus, dux Iacobe, meos. (1-2)

Quoted from *Claudian* (Loeb Classical Library), ed. and trans. Maurice Platnauer, 2 vols. (London, 1963), Vol. 2, p. 278. Alan Cameron, *Claudian*, minimizes his paganism, arguing that the poet in a Christian court "considered himself, or at any rate wished to be considered, among the number of the faithful" (p. 216). Yet Cameron acknowledges of the *De Salvatore*, "The poem as a whole is more notable for its verbal conceits than for its depths of piety" (p. 216). *In Iacobum*, he believes, does not have an overriding anti-Christian sense: the poem responds to Jacob's criticism of Claudian's *De Bello Getico*, in which Jacob's ineffectiveness in the war is described; and, "Claudian did not attack the cult of saints as such: he attacked Jacob's excessive and untimely devotion to it" (p. 236).

by any of those who could have exercised some weight of authority."[46] Earlier in this letter Augustine develops the theme that by imitation of the pagan gods the most depraved of men become still worse. But he is not concerned only with the mob; he alludes to the allegorization of pagan mythology, received by the *sapientes* as well as by the common people, and expounded in a pagan temple. That temple worship is not unusual at this date is proven by the matter-of-factness with which Augustine describes those illegal circumstances: "But it may be objected that all those ancient tales about the life and character of the gods are to be understood and interpreted far differently by men of wisdom. Thus, in fact, we heard just the other day harmless interpretations of this kind read to the people gathered in the temples."[47] Thus Augustine here attacks the paganism of the educated as well as the paganism of the mob. Both groups put their faith in lies and fables; but the educated at least should know better. Much of the letter is patient and restrained argument meant to lead Nectarius back to the way of truth. We can see from Augustine's attitude, from the pagan identity of his correspondent, and from the practices described that the old religion was still flourishing in the fifth century. This letter is one of several reports of religious riots at this time. Despite a whole series of imperial edicts, the civil authorities still could not enforce religious peace; what is more, belief in the pagan gods continued among men of authority.

As a poet *contra paganos*, Prudentius aims his arguments

[46] Letter 24 [91]. 8. Trans. in *St. Augustine: Select Letters* (Loeb Classical Library), ed. James H. Baxter (London, 1930), p. 165. It is noteworthy that the rioting occurred in Africa, where not just the urban but the village and rural population was converted to Christianity much earlier than elsewhere in the Empire, probably by the end of the third century. See A.H.M. Jones, "The Social Background of the Struggle between Paganism and Christianity," in Momigliano, ed. (cited Critical Introd., n. 4), pp. 17-37.

[47] Letter 24 [91]. 5. *Select Letters*, p. 159.

to pierce the hearts of these educated pagans. In *Contra Orationem Symmachi* he offers Christian apologetic according to conventions of prose writers like Tertullian and poets like Commodian or the anonymous authors of the *Carmen ad senatorem* and *Carmen adversus Flavianum*. These conventions include: the denial of the true divinity of the pagan gods by euhemeristic argument (that is, the gods were originally heroes falsely elevated by superstitious men) or by identification of them with devils; the charge of the gods' immorality; and the argument that worship of these gods is simply ineffective, self-degrading according to natural law, or idolatrous and therefore sinful. Prudentius often combines the euhemeristic and ethical attacks, as in this tableau of Bacchus:

> Thebanus iuvenis superatis fit deus Indis,
> successu dum victor ovans lascivit et aurum
> captivae gentis revehit spoliisque superbus
> diffluit in luxum cum semiviro comitatu
> atque avidus vini multo se proluit haustu,
> gemmantis paterae spumis mustoque Falerno
> perfundens biiugum rorantia terga ferarum.
>
> (*C. Symm.* I, 122-128)

[A young man of Thebes becomes a god because he has conquered India and comes wantoning in triumph for his victory, bringing home the gold of the vanquished nation, and in the pride of his spoils abandoning himself to indulgence in company with his emasculate following, in his lust for wine soaking himself with many a draught and with the Falernian juice that foams from his jewelled cup besprinkling the dripping backs of the wild beasts that draw his chariot.]

Here the comparison with other and cruder Christian apologetic ends. Prudentius is outstanding in being able to sustain his hexameters' movement through long periods, thus ironically masking the ridiculous in sonority. Note the skillful sinking achieved in the next sentence, where the worship of such a god *pro meritis* must be the activity of fools.

his nunc pro meritis Baccho caper omnibus aris
caeditur. . . .   (*C. Symm*. I, 129-130)

[In recognition of these merits a goat is now sacrificed to Bacchus on every altar. . . .]

The anti-pagan satire is controlled, rhetorically subtle; though not without its Juvenalian venom, it manages to sustain a certain elegance and urbanity.

And Prudentius' polemic usually avoids the tastelessness of the poet who attacks Flavianus' religion by exulting over his death (which the gods could not prevent). Prudentius possesses some tact. He does not attack the Roman aristocracy itself; instead, he employs arguments developed many centuries earlier by educated pagans. Many of his pagan contemporaries would endorse a euhemeristic interpretation of the old Olympian gods, if not of the new oriental divinities. Many would also acknowledge the immorality contained in myths about the Olympians, arguing that their true religious meaning emerges only after an allegorization. Prudentius tries to occupy common ground, from which he can appeal to the best instincts of the Roman aristocracy. Thus the martyrdom of Lawrence is introduced in a context of patriotism:

Antiqua fanorum parens,
iam Roma Christo dedita,
Laurentio victrix duce
ritum triumphas barbarum.
  reges superbos viceras
populosque frenis presseras,
nunc monstruosis idolis
inponis imperii iugum.

100

    haec sola derat gloria
urbis togatae insignibus,
feritate capta gentium
domaret ut spurcum Iovem. . . .   (*Per.* II, 1-12)

[Rome, thou ancient mother of temples, but now given
up to Christ, Lawrence has led thee to victory and triumph over barbarous worship. Thou hadst already conquered haughty kings and held the nations in check; now
thou dost lay the yoke of thy power on unnatural idols.
This was the one glory lacking to the honours of the city
of the toga, that it should take savage paganism captive
and subdue its unclean Jupiter. . . .]

The struggle against paganism is seen as a grand continuation of Roman tradition. The martyr, his body being roasted
on a gridiron, prays to Christ—

    qui sceptra Romae in vertice
rerum locasti, sanciens
mundum Quirinali togae
servire et armis cedere. . . .   (*Per.* II, 417-420)

[who hast set the sceptre of the world on Rome's high
citadel, ordaining that the world obey the toga of Qui-
rinus and yield to his arms. . . .]

—and asks that the "superstition which came from Troy"
and that "still confounds a senate of Catos" (*confundit error
Troicus / adhuc Catonum curiam*, 445-446) be wiped
away. Lawrence dies, having argued his case well: the senators bear his body away, the new sentiments turning their
hearts to Christ.

This timely propaganda is all for Christ, of course, but its
patriotism is not bogus. Prudentius' role as missionary to the
Roman aristocracy requires some identification with their
values and the history of their city. When he addresses "the
noble order of senators (*senatorum . . . clarissimus ordo*

101

[*C. Symm.* I, 489]), he does not have to strain to do so; his own aristocratic class outlook is sincere. But this outlook is somewhat tempered by the Christian democratic understanding that each person's soul, whatever his place in society, is a worthy component of the Church. In its extreme form, the morality of the Beatitudes can be discovered in *Peristephanon* II, 113-114, where the beggars and cripples are termed the treasure of the Church. More typically Prudentian is the following passage, where the converted senators literally represent Rome but are denied the exclusiveness and isolation characteristic of the aristocracy. The higher order are only really noble when joined by the plebs.

> sescentas numerare domos de sanguine prisco
> nobilium licet ad Christi signacula versas
> turpis ab idolii vasto emersisse profundo.
> si persona aliqua est aut si status urbis, in his est;
> si formam patriae facit excellentior ordo,
> hi faciunt iuncta est quotiens sententia plebis
> atque unum sapiunt plures simul et potiores.
>
> (*C. Symm.* I, 566-572)

[We may count hundreds of families of old noble blood who turned to the sign of Christ and raised themselves out of the vast abyss of base idolatry. If there is any embodiment of the city and its being, it is in these. If it is the higher order of men that give their country its character, these do so, when the people's will unites with theirs and the majority and the better are of one mind.]

This passage, though mediocre, helps explain the literary qualities that make Prudentius an outstanding poet, for it puts Christian doctrine into an aristocratic milieu. The audience requires civilized statement before it will grant attention; it requires sustained elevation of tone, fluency in classical meters, emulation of Augustan models. As Charles Witke has put the matter, "Before a poem can be a cultural weapon or can defuse the 'other side's' weapon, it must first be a poem."[48] Prudentius' audience will not tolerate Ambrose's hymns, good as they are, much less chant them; they are too biblical perhaps, too short, not elegant enough. It will listen to Prudentius' fine hymns, with their surface emulation of Horace, their complexity of movement, their sustained expression. Modern hesitancy toward their subject matter notwithstanding, Prudentius' martyr poems in the *Peristephanon Liber* display considerable rhetorical skill, such as is not to be found in their counterparts in the catacombs. Similar comparisons could be drawn for the hexameter works. In all cases there is genre invention and renovation: we find not merely a high quality of poetry but poetry of a new type, the fruit of a creative use of tradition. In this respect, Prudentius is a classical Latin poet. But with a radical difference. His creativity is due not simply to poetic "genius," and not at all to a love of the literary tradition, but to the cultural demands of his audience as these intersect with the needs of the Church.

Let us not forget that the Church at the close of the fourth century still had to wage a concerted campaign to win the upper classes. This was a matter of high priority, as can be judged by the efforts of Jerome and Augustine directed toward conversion of these classes. In particular, the Church lacked a Christian culture that could compete with pagan culture.

This lack can be detected in St. Jerome's defensive overassessment of Christian letters. Jerome writes in 397 to Magnus, a pagan Roman orator, on the subject of his own quotations of profane writers, and the letter contains the famous allegorization of the beautiful captive purified (Deut. 21:10-14) in justification of the use of pagan literature. What concerns us now is that when the Church Father makes an overall assessment of Christian writers his standards of literary *imitatio* relate not to Scripture but to the Greek and Roman traditions: "Can anything be more learned or more pointed

[48] *Numen Litterarum*, p. 103.

than the style of Tertullian? His *Apology* and his books *Against the Gentiles* contain all the wisdom of the world. Minucius Felix, a pleader in the Roman courts, has ransacked all heathen literature to adorn the pages of his *Octavius* and of his treatise *Against the Astrologers*. Arnobius has published seven books against the Gentiles, and his pupil Lactantius as many, besides two volumes, one *On Anger* and the other *On the Creative Activity of God*. If you read any of these you will find in them an epitome of Cicero's dialogues. . . . Then there is Cyprian. With what terseness, with what knowledge of all history, with what splendid rhetoric and argument has he touched the theme that idols are no Gods! Hilary too . . . has imitated Quintilian's twelve books both in number and in style. . . . In the reign of Constantine, the presbyter Juvencus set forth in verse the story of our Lord and Saviour, and did not shrink from forcing into metre the majestic phrases of the Gospel."[49] Despite Jerome's praise of these Christian writers, his correspondent Magnus—if he was a person with literary judgment—probably continued to prefer Quintilian to Hilary, and Vergil (here Jerome does not dare the comparison) to Juvencus. At the turn of the century, the Christians quite clearly had no culture to rival that of the pagans, and their arsenal in the religious struggle was therefore inadequately equipped. Had Jerome known Prudentius' work, he might, with at least some justification, have named a lyric poet with Horace, a philosophical poet with Lucretius, an epic poet with Vergil.

Such a comparison, however, would be correct only as it revealed Prudentius as the first Christian poet with the sophistication to produce top-quality imitations of the Roman classics. His achievement has nothing to do with any Christian humanism, as has that of Juvencus, whose historical context was far different. Under the rule of Constantine,

[49] Letter 70. Trans. W. H. Freimantle, *St. Jerome: Letters and Select Works*. Select Library of Nicene and Post-Nicene Fathers, Series 2, Vol. 6 (New York, 1893), p. 150.

the Church's struggle against paganism had emerged from the period of fervent defensiveness in the face of the persecutions. The Church had survived the holocaust and had gained sudden prestige and political power, but pagan institutions were merely neutralized, not smashed. The struggle in earnest would not begin till the eighties; meanwhile there were decades of genuine religious tolerance. The cultural climate of the Constantine era was such that awareness of an antagonism between Christ and the old Roman traditions was either non-existent or well concealed. Indeed, their compatibility was asserted, probably by political design. The court-poet Juvencus composed a religious epic in which Vergil is imitated and quoted with aplomb. The poetic effort was approved. The classics gave rhetorical polish to the Gospel narrative: the life of Christ was at long last heroic, and no clash of contrasts could be detected.

Prudentius also works the Egyptian gold, but without drooling over its preciousness. He and Juvencus are worlds apart. The struggle against paganism, then resolved into peaceful coexistence, now was resumed—and resumed on cultural grounds. The antagonists also were much changed. Christianity, then theologically weak, had developed a coherent and all-encompassing ideology, the Nicene faith. Paganism had grown more otherworldly by merging with oriental mystery cults, and it had become further enfeebled by philosophical eclecticism. And the terms of the struggle were changed. The pagan aristocrats were now on the defensive, fighting for the preservation of their cults and for their continued existence as a class. The Christians were fighting for nothing less than total control of spiritual and political life. At the close of the fourth century, the easy balancing of traditions, classical and scriptural, was no longer possible, and so we discover the intriguing phenomenon of Prudentius: the best Christian master of classical poetry cynically using his craft against its past origins and against its future life. Unlike Juvencus, Prudentius does not compose epic; he uses epic to compose allegory. The history

105

of medieval literature will verify that while allegory grew
to vigorous life, epic never fully recovered from Prudentius'
treatment of it.

Prudentius, then, is a Christian humanist only precarious-
ly, in a tactical sense, as a servant of the Church *contra
paganos*. When he offers the humanist compromise to the
Roman aristocracy, it is a false offering. The Latin language
is only an addendum to the sacred revelation of the Old
Testament, and no sooner is it heard than its independent
voice is assimilated, even obliterated, by the greater revelation. In the end, the only writings are Christian, the only
music is Christian: the pagan gods are swept aside and Christ
is truly God and glorious.

> nam quae iam littera Christum
> non habet, aut quae non scriptorum armaria Christi
> laude referta novis celebrant miracula libris?
> Hebraeus pangit stilus, Attica copia pangit,
> pangit et Ausoniae facundia tertia linguae.
> Pilatus iubet ignorans: I, scriba, tripictis
> digere versiculis quae sit subfixa potestas,
> fronte crucis titulus sit triplex, triplice lingua
> agnoscat Iudaea legens et Graecia norit
> et venerata Deum percensoat aurea Roma.
> quidquid in aere cavo reboans tuba curva remugit,
> quidquid ab arcano vomit ingens spiritus haustu,
> quidquid casta chelys, quidquid testudo resultat,
> organa disparibus calamis quod consona miscent,
> aemula pastorum quod reddunt vocibus antra,
> Christum concelebrat, Christum sonat, omnia Christum
> muta etiam fidibus sanctis animata loquuntur.
>
> . . . .
>
> si gens surda negat sibi tot praeconia de te,
> tam multas rerum voces elementaque tantae
> nuntia laetitiae stolidas interare per aures,
> audiat insanum bacchantis energima monstri,
> quod rabidus clamat capta inter viscera daemon,

106

et credat miseranda suis. torquetur Apollo
nomine percussus Christi, nec fulmina Verbi
ferre potest; agitant miserum tot verbera linguae,
quot laudata Dei resonant miracula Christi.

(Apo. 376-405)

[For what literature now does not contain Christ? What
bookcase is not filled with the praise of Christ, celebrating
his wonderful works in new books? The Hebrew pen,
the fulness of Athens, and third the eloquent tongue of
Italy are all composing them. Pilate in his ignorance gives
command: "Go, scribe, set out in lines thrice inscribed
what power it is that is crucified. On the head of the cross
let there be a threefold superscription; in the three
tongues, as they read, let Judaea recognise and Greece
know God, and golden Rome worship Him while she
scans the words." All the loud music that sounds in the
curved trumpet's hollow metal, all that the great deep-
drawn breath pours forth, all the ringing notes of holy
harp and lyre, all the mingled harmony of unequal organ-
pipes, all the songs that grottos in rivalry re-echo to the
shepherds' voices, proclaim Christ and sound Christ's
name; even all dumb things are quickened by the holy
music and speak of Christ. . . . If a race that is deaf says
that all this proclaiming of Thee, all these voices of nature,
these elements that bring tidings of joy so great, enter
not its dull ears, then let it hear the wild monster's
demoniacal raving, the cries of the raging devil in the
flesh he has taken captive, and let it, poor creature, believe
its own! Apollo writhes when the name of Christ smites
him, he cannot bear the lightnings of the Word, the lashing tongue torments him sorely whenever the praises of
the God Christ's wonderful works are sounded.]

The passage summarizes Prudentius' understanding of literary history. After a long line of prophetic Hebrew testament begun by father Abraham, Latin literature begins with

107

Pilate's unwitting inscription, the first Latin naming of Christ. At the name of Christ, Apollo writhes and the entire classical tradition writhes with him. Unlike other poets of different temperament or times, Prudentius does not claim that Christian truth lies hidden in Plato or in Vergil; nor that the recognition of God, albeit partial and imperfect, existed among the Gentiles. He is far less eligible to be called a Christian humanist than his contemporary St. Jerome (who taught classical literature in Jerusalem) or the young St. Augustine. For Prudentius, the hostility between Christ and Apollo is unmitigated. True, he appropriates much of Apollo's craft, but he believes that true poetry originates in the inner music of the soul devoted to God. He would not be pleased with Sidonius' classification of his works because his view of literary history ignores matters of style and ignores the pagan counter-culture: it reads literary history as a branch of spirituality. In Prudentius' ideal library, all the books are new, and all are Christian; those not containing the *canticum novum* are excluded. In sum, the humanist compromise of Prudentius is uncompromising, for it is only through their inclusion in this Christian literature that civilization's tongues can glory.

Psychic Warfare and Worship: The Form and Mode of Conversion

THE *Psychomachia* is an allegorical history of Christian conversion. Allegory, by nature, typifies, enlarges, and clarifies. This poem's personification allegory peoples a new, heretofore invisible world with animate moral ideas, and its scriptural allegory establishes real connections between this inner world and the higher order of divinely ordained salvation history. From Prudentius' standpoint, the *Psychomachia*'s representation of a complete, victorious moral struggle for—and within—the typical Christian mind is a statement of universal psychology. It is, he believes, true and applicable to all Christian souls. It can convert others to Christ.

Such a statement must be clear. It can be compounded by subordinates so that its final form is very complex, but its main predicate must be neither arbitrary nor ambiguous. This is so because the ideal Christian psyche is beautiful (reflective of divine order), illuminated (by grace), and knowable. A Christian psychology, even as it dramatizes the attainment of this ideal state by the defeat of sin, will require literary qualities of clarity and order. Other statements of a darker, mysterious psychology—be they primitive Greek, Vergilian, or twentieth-century—exist as myth, which expresses the inexpressible and proclaims the limits of human understanding. A Christian psychology, depending as it does upon the illumination of human understanding by God's grace, will exist as allegory. "For allegory . . . need not be allegorized. The author has done it for us."[1]

[1] The conclusion of W.T.H. Jackson, "Allegory and Allegorization," *Research Studies*, 32 (1964), 161-175. Jackson's theory on the

Prudentius has indeed created a narrative in its main lines self-interpreting. Most obviously, the moral personifications are known by name, their attributes and acts therefore immediately discernible. Secondary attributes, as contributed by costume and accoutrement, are usually conventional; characterization by speech follows standard rhetorical lines and works to elaborate the primary characterization by name. These personifications are rarely mingled in the course of the narrative, even though they compose moral armies and might be imagined as fighting (in the manner of the legions) in formation; instead, each virtue or vice performs her part (single combat) seriatim, thus permitting individual scrutiny. And this action is performed in daylight, or, to be more accurate, in artificial illumination. Despite the obscure origin and fate of the vices, the *Psychomachia* has no nighttime scenes, no mist-shrouded forays, no dreams, no enigmatic prophesies. The introductory mystery of Abraham's prophetic warfare has been revealed to all who know Christ; the final beatific vision is revealed in jewel-like hardness and brilliance; and the way from that beginning to this end is well controlled.

The narrative's progress is shaped and controlled by structural symmetry. Symmetry in the *Psychomachia* is both concentric and incremental; it emphasizes typological as well as thematic parallels. At its simplest, it delineates the conversionary plot, a two-part sequence of warfare and holy peace. Minor tensions, suspense, and reversals may lend added interest to this plot, periodic digressions into the areas of scriptural and ecclesiastical history may expand its meaning, but this plot is always visible. During the warfare section, the speeches of the virtues refer to the goal of peace. During the section of peace, similar speeches refer to the necessity of prior warfare. In opening and concluding hexameter prayers, the poet himself links the two themes. Now

role of Vergilian epic in Prudentius' allegory will be noted in Chapter IV.

these complementary themes and their arrangement in the two-part plot are such obvious features of the *Psychomachia* that they are easily taken for granted, but we should ponder their importance. Probably the main guarantee of the allegory's clarity is that its personifications' major actions are of already established significance in Christian thought.

Warfare and worship are important scriptural metaphors, originating from Old Testament history and applied, especially by St. Paul, in New Testament moral theology. Their capacity is large, and a range of moral applications can be discovered in the Psalms, the Sapiential literature, and the prophetic books; but they devolve as metaphors for the contrasting Christian moral states, sinful and enlightened, whose sequence may be described as a conversionary leap. This sequence also is precedented in scriptural history. In the development of patristic commentary, the metaphors of warfare and worship are sporadically, incompletely psychologized until, at the close of the fourth century, they can refer unambiguously to inner mental states. But this shift, signaled by the *Psychomachia* and by the writings of St. Augustine, marks no decisive break with the past. Revealed Scripture is accorded a new area of applicability, the inner world of the soul; but the principles of scriptural interpretation, and therefore the meaning of scriptural metaphor, remain intact.

If Prudentius has in fact transformed scriptural metaphor into allegory (by employing personifications to act out what otherwise would remain only conceptualized action),[2] the transformation tells much about the psychology produced. The source of the psychology is not the poet's own mental experience, as C. S. Lewis believes, but an idea or system of ideas existing independently of the poet's particular thoughts and feelings.[3] Not arising from familiarity with

[2] Explained by Bloomfield, "A Grammatical Approach to Personification Allegory" (cited Critical Introd., n. 2).

[3] Bloomfield also objects to C. S. Lewis' theory that the allegory translates mental experience directly (and therefore fails).

the features of what we moderns conceive as the personality, the psychology is abstract, general, universal. Prudentius considers it to be objectively real, of course, but it has little to do with psychological realism. We have already seen that in the *Contra Orationem Symmachi* an elemental soul-struggle is dramatized in order to make manifest a real but invisible condition within the poet.[4] This representation, however lively, is hypothetical and generalized: it stands for the poet's moral conversion by typifying its action, not by denoting a particular sequence of mental occurrences. The *Psychomachia* works similarly. In both poems, Prudentian introspection is rhetorical: it depends utterly upon external data.

The psychic actualization of St. Augustine's *Confessions* is simply not capable of achievement by Prudentius—unless it be felt in the *Praefatio*. On this score, however, it must be admitted that even Augustine's language is not truly analytic: more than denotive of autopsychology, his words move toward God. The *Confessions* describe the soul's search for God and they offer the soul to God, but they are not written down for this purpose. As literature, the *Confessions* mediate other men's conversions: they make known a soul, and that soul's finding God, in order that the experience may be emulated. And the experience is not unique either, it appears. Augustine's conversion under the fig tree in the Milanese garden occurs, it is true, within him alone; but it depends for its full meaning on scriptural fig trees, gardens, conversions. With even its high degree of psychic actualization, the conversion is in part archetypical. In comparison, that narrated in the allegory of the *Psychomachia* is exclusively so. Prudentius openly traces the exegetical circle in the *Psychomachia*: he creates his psyche out of scriptural metaphor, allows its career to be patterned on the archetypical career of Father Abraham, and sets its final significance in the context of prophetic scriptural history. The

---

[4] See pp. 43-46.

psychology of the *Psychomachia*, then, amounts to a psychological exegesis of Scripture or, more simply, a version of Christian moral philosophy.

This is not to nullify the importance of the allegory's psychological locus. Christian history arises from a radical disjuncture, willed sinfully by Adam, in man's heretofore perfect relation to God. Since that time, every man's soul has continually borne the sin experienced in Adam's soul. Because of his carnal condition of alienation from God, man feels a sense of lack, and therefore he desires. His faculty of desire is his soul. Man's fulfillment depends upon what he desires, the things of the world (which can never satisfy) or God (who alone can make blessed). The conflict between these desires is a normal experience of post-lapsarian man. The intervention of God directly in salvation history and God's revelation in Scripture have aided man in his effort to direct his desires toward God. But the conflict remains; the will must continually fight to affirm the aid offered by God. The significance of conversion is that, in the midst of this permanent condition of sinfulness, man's will has by the grace of God come to desire God only.

The allegory's Greek title captures some of this meaning.[5]

[5] Prudentius is but one author affected by the fourth-century vogue for Greek titles; Claudian is another. A full discussion of the meaning of the word *psychomachia* is in Gnilka, *Studien zur Psychomachie des Prudentius* (cited Critical Introd., n. 36), pp. 19-26. Gnilka summarizes earlier modern interpretations as well as the ancient evidence, and he poses three possibilities: the *psychomachia* is *in* the soul, *on behalf of* the soul, or *of* the soul. He favors the last possibility, arguing for the soul's expeditionary campaign against the *bodily* vices. This interpretation he qualifies somewhat by quoting Augustine's *Confessions* VIII—*ista controversia in corde meo non nisi de me ipso adversus me ipsum*—to illustrate that Prudentius' title may carry greater complexities of meaning. Against Gnilka, I argue for a basically psychological definition. Regarding Prudentius' Greek titles in general, that his knowledge of Greek is negligible is argued by Carmelo Rapisarda, "Prudenzio e la lingua Greca," *Miscellanea di studi di letteratura cristiana antica*, 2 (1948), [Estratto]. But the title

113

The component *machia*, "a fight," introduces the first major scriptural metaphor. By joining this to *psyche*, Prudentius characterizes the soul's normative state as one of struggle. That the title contains no hint of the second major metaphor is of some interest. Since the soul's condition of warfare, rather than its aim or end, is announced, the stress is put on the problematic nature of the warfare. Will the virtues prevail, and will the soul find rest in a stasis of worship? Or will the struggle be resolved less happily? The title contributes to the orthodox moral idea that the plot's outcome is not predetermined. And although the title is certainly Prudentius' literary coinage, we observe that the verb ψυχομαχεῖν, attested in Polybios, seems to mean "to fight for one's life" in the context of a death-bed struggle.[6] The fight for life is, paradoxically, not for the continuation of life— and yet it is just that. Since *psyche* means both "soul" and "life," a *psychomachia* can be a soul's struggle for eternal life as well as a soul's struggle in this world for the clarity of Christian self-perfection. The two are obviously one and the same.

THE SHAPE OF CONVERSION

Taking up the key ideas contained in its title, the "Praefatio" of the *Psychomachia* relates and then supplies the exegesis for several episodes in the life of Abraham. The first is the battle waged against the gentile kings by Abraham in order to rescue Lot. This battle ends in victory, an example for all Christians knowing the spiritual significance of the righteous warriors. Abraham, the poet explains, is an exemplum of the Christian soul, and the army that comes to his

---

Apotheosis, which makes little sense according to the major meaning of the word in Latin, may evidence a sophisticated understanding of Greek patristics; see Christian Gnilka, "Notizen zu Prudentius," *Rheinisches Museum für Philologie*, 109 (1966), 92-94.

[6] For full lexicological notes on this definition, see Gnilka, *Studien zur Psychomachie des Prudentius*, pp. 21-23, nn. 17-21.

aid is Christ. Some later events in the life of Abraham are paraphrased in this typological "Praefatio": the blessing of Melchisedech, the entertainment of the three angels, and Sarah's fruitfulness. These are alluded to in its concluding passage, the allegorization in which illustrates how thematically close are the conversion experience and salvation. Following the Genesis story, the one generates the other:

mox ipse Christus, qui sacerdos verus est,
parente inenarrabili atque uno satus,
cibum beatis offerens victoribus
parvam pudici cordis intrabit casam,
monstrans honorem Trinitatis hospitae.
animam deinde Spiritus conplexibus
pie maritam, prolis expertem diu,
faciet perenni fertilem de semine,
tunc sera dotem possidens puerpera
herede digno Patris inplebit domum.   (Prf. 59-68)

[Then Christ himself, who is the true priest, born of a Father unutterable and one, bringing food for the blessed victors, will enter the humble abode of the pure heart and give it the privilege of entertaining the Trinity; and then the Spirit, embracing in holy marriage the soul that has long been childless, will make her fertile by the seed eternal, and the dowered bride will become a mother late in life and give the Father's household a worthy heir.]

This is the ideal, victorious *psychomachia*. Its authority as a model for other soul-struggles derives from Scripture, the authority of which is enlarged by the masterful exegetical connections with the persons of the Trinity. The soul, Prudentius proclaims at the outset, can know God; God is involved in the soul's progress on earth through the persons of Christ and the Holy Spirit, in the soul's stasis in heaven through the person of the Father. This Nicene typology of Genesis continues to be felt as an ideal foil to the allegorical action presently unfolding.

115

When the hexameters start forth, the reader is returned squarely to the problematic world of moral struggle which he, an individual Christian, inhabits. The personification allegory defines the worldly reality of the *Psychomachia*, a reality in which virtues are continuously beset by the forces of sin. At its outset, no moral progress has been made: the virtues and vices are counterpoised, the outcome of their contest uncertain. Yet the battle is invoked hopefully, even enthusiastically, so as to suggest that great benefit will accrue to its witnesses. The reason for this tone is of course that the muse of the allegory is Christ. Christ is the one person of God directly operative in this section of the *Psychomachia*, and his mode of existence is different here from what it is in the "Praefatio." Rather than a signification of something else, of an Old Testament figure (the 318 soldiers; Melchisedech), Christ is actually present in the believer's soul as dispenser of grace. This new mode of existence answers and resolves the worldly reality as it is defined by the personification allegory. Indeed, the poet invokes Christ to make that reality intelligible by revealing the allegory:

> dissere, rex noster, quo milite pellere culpas
> mens armata queat nostri de pectoris antro,
> exoritur quotiens turbatis sensibus intus
>
> . . . .
>
> quaeve acies furiis inter praecordia mixtis
> obsistat meliore manu. (5-11)

[Say, our King, with what fighting force the soul is furnished and enabled to expel the sins from within our breast; when there is disorder among our thoughts and rebellion arises within us . . . what array with superior force withstands the fiendish raging in our heart.]

For Christ (the apostrophe continues) has not exposed his followers to the sins without the aid of mighty virtues. And this moral strength comes from Christ not only in a general sense. In the context of the *Psychomachia*, Christ may gra-

116

ciously permit (*liceat*) us to perceive a true representation of saving virtues (*salutiferas*, 14) within the personification allegory, where there is no distinction between poetic and non-poetic psychology. The allegory itself is a gift of grace.

> vincendi praesens ratio est, si comminus ipsas
> Virtutum facies et conluctantia contra
> viribus infestis liceat portenta notare.   (18-20)

[The way of victory is before our eyes if we may mark at close quarters the very features of the Virtues, and the monsters that close with them in deadly struggle.][7]

The personification allegory proper begins on the next line. The pivotal *liceat* (in the subjunctive) is immediately fulfilled: we *shall* mark at close quarters these combatants. The poet's prayer has been efficacious. For all this promise and hope of victory, however, the salvational aim is only vaguely alluded to, while a great multitude of images have stressed the theme of contention as the basic human condition. If Christ bestows the allegory for our salvation and if he participates within the allegory as commander of the virtues, the fight itself must be waged in our minds, and we are responsible for its outcome.

Now the battles commence. Most but not all are single combats, and these follow one upon the other as would tableaux in a Roman procession. Their arrangement is this:

1. Fides versus Cultura Deorum Veterum
2. Pudicitia versus Sodomita Libido
3. Patientia versus Ira

[7] Thomson's text consistently capitalizes the words "Virtues" and "Vices" and the names of the personifications. This editorial practice aids our recognition of the personifications as characters in the fictive mental action; but it overstresses the fictiveness of the allegory by segregating these personifications from the general language of morality (non-capitalized)—that is, by creating, erroneously in my opinion, two classes of experience, where the poet would recognize their essential unity.

117

4. Mens Humilis and Spes versus Superbia
5. Sobrietas versus Luxuria
6. Ratio versus Avaritia
7. Fides versus Discordia cognomento Hereses.

That Faith must fight twice, her action framing the battle order, is suggestive in several ways. First, it underscores the essential Christianity of the virtues, some of whom are notably Christian anyhow (as Humility), but some of whom could find homes in other ancient ethical systems. Second, it points to the recurring necessity of militance, or at least vigilance against dogmatic error. The seventh battle begins after the army of virtues have retired from the battle field, believing themselves victorious; but a new foe, heresy, has insinuated herself amongst them. Third, it establishes a plausible parallel between ecclesiastical and psychological history. Faith's enemies are exactly those of the poet Prudentius in his public hexameter orations; as in those poems, she has an internal and an external existence, and her struggles are carried forth into time present.

It is worth noting that despite the terms of the invocation, Christ is not actually present in the allegory as a character. There are a number of symbolic references to, and namings of, Christ, but Christ does not in any positive sense "appear" in the allegory until he is worshipped as Sapientia. Meanwhile, it seems, Faith is the moral heroine of the *Psychomachia*. She leads the army of the virtues. After all the known vices have been defeated, she advises the virtues not to rest, to remain on guard against future attacks. The virtues then, directed by Fides and Concordia, busy themselves in constructing their city. The city's plan resembles that of an important scriptural city, its building executed with exactitude of symbolic detail. At the end of the allegory, the army of virtues has constructed on its citadel a holy temple in whose shrine sits Sapientia enthroned. The mind's image conforms with the model of the Heavenly Jerusalem.

118

Yet this moment of stasis, the poet reminds his audience in a concluding prayer to Christ, is provisional. It is a vision of eternal bliss, a reflection of the poet's and his audience's hope; but as a moral goal, its future attainment depends upon the soul's continued willingness to engage in *psychomachia*.

Looking back over the *Psychomachia*, we can see that Prudentius has twice refrained from awed silence after visions of perfection. The ideal end of the "Praefatio" is followed by the war of the personification allegory, whose ideal end in turn is followed by a return to the real, sin-tainted world of poet and audience outside the allegory. The pattern seems cyclical: the struggle implies its end, which implies the necessity to struggle, and so on. Against this, however, both major units of the *Psychomachia*, "Praefatio" and personification allegory, are histories of progress complete in themselves, with beginnings, middles, ends. Each of these two patterns is consistent with an aspect of Christian morality. Although a truly cyclical recurrence of events is alien to Christian morality and historiography (being accepted by neo-Platonists et al.), nevertheless the persistence of man's sinful nature and the consequent need for persistent moral engagement can be expressed formally by something like a cycle. On the other hand, human life and history are for a Christian (but not for a neo-Platonist) finite, and consequently encourage formal expression by means of progressive stages toward a goal. There is a certain tension between these formal tendencies in most Christian art and literature, and the *Psychomachia* is no exception. But this formal tension need not express any ethical contradiction. Christianity involves persistent moral engagement in a finite situation, which means not simply repetition of the moral act, but progressive moral action toward the goal of eternal life.

Experienced as a linear action, one following the illusion of space-time continuum created by epic narrative conventions, the allegory displays a stylized disorder followed by an alternately stylized order. The psychological truism so

119

arranged is that peace of mind comes after struggle against the confusion of sin. The *Psychomachia*'s aesthetic progress thus traces the history of conversion. Viewed statically, from outside the forward thrust of narrative, the allegory has an overall structural sophistication unequaled by any other hexameter poem excepting the *Dittochaeon* and the "Hymnus de Trinitate." The two main parts of the narrative, the sections of warfare and worship, balance each other thematically and symbolically (for example, the seven battles being complemented by the seven pillars of Wisdom's temple), and this balance is just one manifestation of structural order. More important is the vertical conformity of events in the "Praefatio" with events in the personification allegory. Such architectonics are surely meant to grant not just intelligibility but aesthetic perfection to the total moral action. Viewed statically, the process of conversion, moving and confusing to one engaged in it, becomes utterly rational (like its ideal end), utterly perfect (like the divine grace that orignates it) and, as it were, predestined. Viewed actively, however, the conversionary process is continually unfolding as its end remains desired rather than attained, as divine grace is continually renewed, as the free will continues to struggle toward its desired end.

The static form of the *Psychomachia* approaches symmetry on several levels. It is not, however, Prudentius' most perfectly symmetrical poem, for its symmetry is flawed or compromised in several respects. Of the two major sections of the plot, that on warfare is longer than that on peace, so that the midpoint of the action, the triumph of the virtuous army from the plain to the city, is off center. Then too, the seventh and final battle takes place after this transition, spilling over into the section of peaceful construction. Despite these imperfections, designed, I believe, to emphasize the tension between divine ideal and worldly actuality, the pattern of symmetry is quite visible.[8]

[8] Only after analysis of the scriptural emblems and of the "Prae-

PRAYER [. . . . . Allegorical Narrative . . . . .] PRAYER
   [BATTLES . . BATTLES] [CITY . . TEMPLE]
     [. . Warfare . . . . .] [. . . Peace . . . . .]

Sinful	Triumph	Charitable
Soul	of	Soul
	Conversion	

Symmetry is a principle of order which according to
Scripture follows the model of divine perfection.[9] The
Psychomachia emulates this principle. The *Dittochaeon*
embodies it. This series of hexameter quatrains deals exclusively with events and characters of scriptural history and,
moreover, with the typological concordances between the
Old and New Testaments. Each quatrain refers to a discrete
event or character or arrangement of symbolic things.
There is no narrative linking of one quatrain to the next—
indeed, enjambement and hypotaxis are rare even within the
quatrains. End-stopped lines are common, as is the struc-
turing of each quatrain into two groups of two lines. Because of these features, which are not characteristic of Prudentian hexameters and which therefore must be planned
for effect, the hexameters of the *Dittochaeon* do not move;
they are static. This condition draws attention to their
spatial arrangement. Of the forty-nine scriptural scenes, the
central twenty-fifth one concerns the Annunciation, the
cardinal moment of sacred history, that of Christ's Incarnation. This central quatrain is flanked by twenty-four representing Old Testament history and by twenty-four representing New Testament history. The total span of time
extends from the first to the last moment, from Creation
to Last Judgment. The *Dittochaeon*, then, is a schematic

---

fatio" in Chapter III will the structural sophistication of the *Psychomachia* be adequately appreciated.

  [9] Symmetry is holy form as manifested in the Cross, the Heavenly
Jerusalem of the Apocalypse, the Alpha and Omega; and as an aspect
of perfection in the order of creation. Thus Wisdom 11:21: *Sed
omnia in mensura, et numero, et pondere disposuisti* ("But thou hast
ordered all things in measure, and number, and weight").

121

outline of Scripture, and it strives for structural perfection.[10]
Its quatrains probably were meant to accompany and interpret the visual program on the side walls (for Old and New
Testaments, respectively) and apse (for the Annunciation)
of a basilica.

The *Psychomachia* belongs to a different order of beauty.
The form of the problematic psychological allegory can be
fitly compromised, that of sacred scriptural scenes cannot.
And the *Psychomachia* must exist as a narrative—which the
Dittochaeon is not—so that verbal movement continually
disturbs whatever ideal calm might be perceived in its
symmetry.[11] The tension between the ideal and the actual
in the *Psychomachia* more closely compares with a formal
dualism in the *Apotheosis*. This anti-heretical hexameter
oration is introduced by two shorter pieces, the first now
known as the "Hymnus de Trinitate," the second as the
"Praefatio." The two introductions differ greatly in form,
but each form can be said to influence the form of the main
hexameter section. The "Praefatio" of the *Apotheosis* resembles other prefaces in that it contains scriptural material
typologically relevant to the subject at hand: the parable
of the tares from Matthew's Gospel is applied to the poet's
need to uproot heretical ideas. Compared to the other prefaces, however, this one's movement is especially tortuous,
its structure uncertain. Beseechings of Christ's aid give way
to periodic reflections on the difficulty of the struggle versus
heresy, on the poet's inadequacy, and so forth. The meter

[10] The similar symmetry of Proba's *Cento* will be treated in Chapter IV. See p. 57, above, for the symmetrical frame of Ambrosian
meter in the *Liber Cathemerinon*. Roman art and early Christian art
confirm that this aesthetic principle of order was paramount in the
poet's day. The symmetry of the visual arts influences literature
directly in such works as shaped poems, mirror-image acrostics, and
inscribed epigrams.

[11] Symmetry may be considered a theme, as well as a formal principle, of the *Psychomachia*. As the narrative moves forward through
the city gates, symmetry is incrementally more visible until, with the
building of the temple, it is built.

(acatalectic iambic dimeter) creates a choppy, halting effect. In total contrast is the "Hymnus de Trinitate," the most balanced and symmetrical of all Prudentius' compositions:

> Est tria summa Deus, trinum specimen, vigor unus.
> corde Patris genita est Sapientia, Filius ipse est;
> Sanctus ab aeterno subsistit Spiritus ore.
> tempore nec senior Pater est, nec numine maior,
> nam sapiens retro semper Deus edidit ex se,
> per quod semper erat, gignenda ad saecula Verbum.
> edere sed Verbum Patris est, at cetera Verbi,
> adsumptum gestare hominem, reparare peremptum,
> conciliare Patri, dextraque in sede locare.
> Spiritus ista Dei conplet, Deus ipse: fideles
> in populos charisma suum diffundere promptus,
> et patris et Christi virtutem in corpora transfert.

[God is three supremes, threefold in person, one living power. Of the Father's love was begotten Wisdom, and the same is the Son; the Holy Spirit is from the everlasting lips. The Father is neither older in time nor greater in divinity; for God was wise through infinite time past, and gave forth from Himself, to bring the world into being, the Word whereby He ever was. But while to give forth the Word belongs to the Father, all else is of the Word, to take on and wear the nature of man and restore him from destruction, to reconcile him to the Father and set him at His right hand. This the Spirit of God accomplishes, who himself is God: ever ready to diffuse His gracious gift upon the faithful peoples, He transmits into their persons the power both of the Father and of the Christ.]

This poem forms a perfect square. The twelve verses are separated into four groups of three, the first group characterizing the Trinity by naming its three persons, and the three subsequent groups each treating a person of the Trinity. The three/nine structure is itself trinitarian (as

123

readers of Dante will recognize), but the four-square structure is surely intended to carry most of the symbolic weight. The shape of the Heavenly Jerusalem in the Apocalypse, its four walls each having three gates, is the shape of the "Hymnus de Trinitate." And the numerology may be extended. There are twelve verses, and each verse has twelve quantitative units (that is, half-feet). 12 × 12 might well be meant to remind us of the 144,000 Innocents who occupy the Heavenly Jerusalem.

Both of these introductions influence the hexameters of the *Apotheosis*. The "Praefatio" provides the dominant form. The main compositional technique in most sections of Prudentius' polemics, including the *Apotheosis*, is additive. Whether the poet is orating against heresy or against paganism, as he turns from one adversary to the next, from one theological point to the next, from the ridicule of one pagan divinity to the next, he piles up his arguments one atop another. The force of these arguments is cumulative, and there is little overriding principle of organization to be detected—at least at first glance. For example, it matters little in the *Apotheosis* whether the Sabellian (monarchian) or Jewish form of Christological error is defeated first. The very debates are themselves occasioned by the existence of evil—by the activity of Satan in the world, by Original Sin within man. Thus the Church in the service of God cuts down heresies as they crop up; but the order of the harvest is worldly rather than divine. In this way the form of the hexameter section of the *Apotheosis* mirrors imperfection. Yet there is also a higher order at work. How are the heresies cut down? By means of the Trinity. As if using the "Hymnus de Trinitate" as an outline, Prudentius asserts the distinct yet unchanging person of the Father against the modalists (1-320), the fully human yet fully divine person of the Son against the Arians (321-781), and the person of the Holy Spirit against the Manicheans (782-1084).[12]

---

[12] That the "Hymnus de Trinitate" thus functions as an outline for the *Apotheosis* is argued by Ronald G. Rank, "The *Apotheosis* of

Compared to the perfect symmetry of the "Hymnus de Trinitate," of course, the divine order is only darkly perceived amidst the anti-heretical contention, yet its presence is undeniable.

The *Psychomachia*'s first section of warfare also mirrors imperfection. From the standpoint of the virtues, there may be some formal rationality: Fides spans the action of the whole war, her participation in the first and last battles lending it a certain symmetry; and the virtues pair off against particular vices with some sense of fit order. But the order of battle is chaotic. No attempt to relate the particular sequence of battles to a larger psychological process is convincing; rather, the vices intrude themselves so as to suggest random attacks. Whether or not the vices actually initiate particular battles, their presence in the soul determines that these battles must be fought. If the soul had not fallen into sin, its temple would already have been perfectly formed. That the virtues need to struggle against the vices means that the soul is in a state of sin, and until the last vice is defeated, the soul remains in this state. Hence the appropriateness of the additive narrative technique, mirroring psychological imperfection. Prudentius puts this technique aside after the defeat of Discordia permits the building of the holy city. Once Fides and Concordia can take charge of the virtuous army without the intrusions of sin, their reasoned speech precedes action. (Beforehand on the battlefield, the speeches of the virtues had been in response to the exigencies of action.) Thus the city is first planned, then

---

Prudentius: A Structural Analysis," *Classical Folia*, 20 (1966), 18-31. Rank also offers a description of the "Hymnus de Trinitate" supporting my characterization of it as four-square: ". . . in each stanza, there is a four-fold characterization of the Person. For the Father, it is *nec senior, nec maior, sapiens, edidit Verbum*. Four infinitives are used for the Son: *gestare, reparare, conciliare, locare*. And for the Holy Spirit we have *conplet, promptus, diffundere, transfert*" (20). But in his treatment of the hexameter narrative, Rank errs in overemphasizing the principle of order (at the expense of the principle of disorder). He misses the moral complexity of the *Apotheosis*.

built. The randomness of events is no longer felt. The building of the city is accomplished in an orderly fashion, calmly, rationally, until perfection is reached.

Between warfare and worship is conversion, the transitional moment when the dialectic of sin and charity is resolved, if only provisionally.[13] The moment itself has no moral meaning apart from what precedes and follows it, and therefore it is truer to characterize the total before-and-after movement as essential conversionary experience. Expressed formally, the movement is from relative chaos to relative symmetry. (Because of God's grace, the chaos is relative; because of man's inherent sinfulness, the symmetry is relative.) Insofar as the conversionary experience is continually renewed in the soul of the Christian, it must remain provisional, relative, imperfect. At the same time, however, the pattern of this experience strives to conform with the divine image.

WARFARE AND WORSHIP IN CHRISTIAN TRADITION

The theme of warfare is so basic to salvation history that it should be unnecessary to discuss it here. But so many modern commentators on the *Psychomachia* have confused this theme with the epic mode in which it is presented that the poem's scriptural antecedents have been misestimated. Not that the "Praefatio" or the typological emblems within the allegory have been ignored. Recent critics have to some extent analyzed the relevance of Abraham's heroism against the kings of Sodom and Gomorrah and the relevance, for example, of Judith's heroism to Pudicitia. But these Old Testament characters have not seemed quite integrated into the action of the *Psychomachia*. Perhaps the confusion between the theme of scriptural warfare and the Vergilian mode has stemmed from a failure to appreciate the meaning of the scriptural theme itself, a meaning not inherent

[13] In the allegory, this is the triumphal procession of the virtues prefigured by the Red Sea Crossing. To be discussed in Chapter III.

in the literal deeds of the Old Testament characters. The battles of Deborah, David, of the Maccabees, were well known to Prudentius' contemporaries, but they were interpreted by way of St. Paul's exegesis. They were interpreted additionally, and sometimes in greater detail, in later patristic allegorization.

Let us examine first the New Testament theme of moral warfare.[14] In the sixth chapter of his epistle to the Ephesians, St. Paul communicates the idea that Christian morality has two aspects, fleshly and spiritual. "Children, obey your parents in the Lord, . . ." he admonishes, and from this he develops the theme that Christians should learn both fleshly and spiritual obedience. The lesser obedience is service to man, as in the Old Law Commandment to honor father and mother; the greater obedience is service to God. In this context, and with typical metaphoric flexibility, Paul urges the Ephesians to be strong in the Lord, and he develops the theme of Christian fortitude by means of military metaphors: "Put you on the armour of God, that you may be able to stand against the deceits of the devil. For our wrestling is not against flesh and blood, but against principalities and powers, against the rulers of the world of this darkness, against the spirits of wickedness in the high places. Therefore, take unto you the armour of God, that you may be able to resist in the evil day and to stand in all things perfect. Stand, therefore, having your loins girt about with truth and having on the breastplate of justice; and your feet shod with the preparation of the gospel of peace; in all things taking the shield of faith, wherewith you may be able to extinguish all the fiery darts of the most wicked one. And take unto you the helmet of salvation and the sword of the Spirit (which is the Word of God)" (Eph. 6:11-17).

[14] Many scriptural passages relevant to spiritual combat are given by Pier Franco Beatrice, "L'allegoria nella *Psychomachia* di Prudenzio" (cited Critical Introd., n. 26), 40-48. Beatrice acknowledges fully the influence of Paul (especially Ephesians 6:11) upon the Latin Fathers, but argues that this influence is rather indirect and of lesser importance than that of Origen.

127

Prudentius is certainly familiar with this. Whether the passage should properly be termed a scriptural source of the *Psychomachia* is an open question. Our poem details the armor of the several individualized virtues rather than presenting the entire soul as if it were a warrior whose members are protected by the virtues. But the distance between Paul and Prudentius is not so far: in both an extended metaphor of martial activity is joined with personified virtues, in both the spirituality of the soul's struggle against evil is tied to the goal of salvation, and in both Scripture (*verbum Dei*) serves as an important weapon in the struggle.

A second Pauline illustration uses the metaphorical concepts of spirit and flesh somewhat differently: not as complementary fields for the action of Christian charity toward God and neighbor, but as denotations of the opposing human motions of the soul toward God and the world. (No one except the Manicheans interpreted the following passage as supporting any inherent antagonism between the body and the soul.) "For the flesh lusteth against the spirit; and the spirit against the flesh. For these are contrary one to another; so that you do not the things that you would. But if you are led by the spirit, you are not under the law. Now the works of the flesh are manifest, which are: fornication, uncleanness, immodesty, luxury, idolatry, witchcrafts, enmities, contentions, emulations, wraths, quarrels, dissension, sects, envies, murders, drunkenness, revellings, and such like. Of the which I foretell you, as I have foretold to you, that they who do such things shall not obtain the kingdom of God. But the fruit of the Spirit is: charity, joy, peace, patience, benignity, goodness, longanimity, mildness, faith, modesty, continency, chastity. Against such there is no law." (Gal. 5:17-23). This passage also could qualify as a specific source. Some of its Latin nouns reappear as the virtues and vices of the *Psychomachia*: *fides, patientia,* and the opposite of *impudicitia* fight actively and are joined by *pax* in the city; on the negative side are *luxuria, ira,* and something very like *idolorum servitus*. The *sectae* are subsumed in the figure of Discordia, or Heresy. A more general influence could be in the struggle's outcome: the defeated vices are no more heard of, but the victorious virtues construct a symbolic kingdom of God.

Many other examples of the warfare theme could be cited from the New Testament, and key among these would be Paul's use of the *miles Christi* metaphor. Nor is the warfare of the Old Testament only historical—think of Job's pronouncement that life is a warfare. Prudentius is surely aware of this scriptural tradition and probably draws from it directly.

Turning to patristic literature, the following passage from Tertullian's treatise *De Spectaculis* has been suggested by several modern scholars as a source (or the source) of the *Psychomachia*.[15] The late second-century Father issues a sharp indictment of all forms of pagan mass culture, including the theater and gladiatorial contests. By means of metaphorical wordplay on the very features of this pagan culture, he offers Christianity as an attractive alternative. "[What greater pleasure] than to find yourself trampling underfoot the gods of the Gentiles, expelling demons, effecting cures, seeking revelations, living to God? These are the pleasures, the spectacles of Christians, holy, eternal, and free. Here find your games of the circus,—watch the race of time, the seasons slipping by, count the circuits, look for the goal of the great consummation, battle for the companies of the churches, rouse up at the signal of God, stand erect at the angel's trump, triumph in the palms of martyrdom. If the literature of the stage delight you, we have suffi-

---

[15] Puech (cited Critical Introd., n. 18), p. 248; A. L. Hench, "Sources of Prudentius' *Psychomachia*," *Classical Philology*, 19 (1924), 78-80; C. S. Lewis, *The Allegory of Love*, p. 68. More recent writers are less apt to take the Tertullian passage as the main source of the *Psychomachia*. For the general influence of Tertullian on Prudentius, see Maurice Lavarenne, *Étude sur la langue du poète Prudence* (Paris, 1933), p. 564. The relation of the *Hamartigenia* to Tertullian's *Adversus Marcionem* is discussed by J. Stam, ed., *Prudentius: Hamartigenia* (Amsterdam, 1940), pp. 8-11.

ciency of books, of poems, of aphorisms, sufficiency of songs and voices, not fable, those of ours, but truth; not artifice but simplicity. Would you have fightings and wrestlings? Here they are—things of no small account and plenty of them. See impurity overthrown by chastity, perfidy slain by faith, cruelty crushed by pity, impudence thrown into the shade by modesty; and such are the contests among us, and in them we are crowned. Have you a mind for blood? You have the blood of Christ."[16] Here the personified virtues and vices are imagined engaging each other in single combat. Personification allegory has been conceived, but not created! Despite this strikingly close literary similarity, Tertullian's thought is far from Prudentius'. There is no indication here, as in the Pauline epistles, that the moral contest is fought by or for the soul. Rather, this contest is an abstract and general characteristic of the Church at large.

Nearer to Prudentius' psychologizing of Christian warfare is a passage from the *De Mortalitate* by Cyprian of Carthage.[17] This treatise refers more immediately than did that of Tertullian to the issue of the Roman persecution and Christian martyrdom, and yet Cyprian focuses on the mental aspect of the moral struggle. "For the rest, what else is waged daily in the world but a battle against the devil, but a struggle with continual onsets against his darts and weapons? With avarice, with lewdness, with anger, with ambition, we have a conflict; with the vices of the flesh, with

[16] *De Spectaculis*, 29. Trans. from *Tertullian: Apology, De Spectaculis, and Minucius Felix* (Loeb Classical Library), ed. T. R. Glover and G. H. Rendall (London, 1931), pp. 295-297.

[17] I infer Prudentius' reading of Cyprian from *Peristephanon Liber* XIII, "Passio Cypriani": *incubat in Libya sanguis, sed ubique lingua pollet* (4); *dum liber ullus erit, dum scrinia sacra litterarum, / te leget omnis amans Christum, tua, Cypriane, discet* (7-8); and the concluding passage (96-106) in which Cyprian is described as having attained the kingdom of heaven even as he still instructs all the peoples of the Empire.

the allurements of the world, we have a continual and stub-
born fight. The mind of man [*mens hominis*] besieged and
surrounded on all sides by the assault of the devil with difficulty opposes these foes one by one, with difficulty resists
them. If avarice is cast to the ground, lust springs up; if
lust is put down, ambition takes its place; if ambition is dis-
dained, anger provokes, pride puffs up, drunkenness invites,
envy destroys harmony, jealousy severs friendships."[18]
Notice here the resemblance to the *Psychomachia* in the
pattern of successive combats, where one vice threatens the
mind after another has fallen, also in the individuation of
the characters of the vices. As with the other passages
quoted so far, however, there remains a significant difference. The mind (*mens hominis*) carries on its defensive
struggle as an integral power or faculty; it has no army of
virtues inside it. Moreover, Cyprian's *mens* faces the attacks
of the vices as these attacks are directed from outside, from
the world. This is not an inner struggle; the soul itself does
not contain the vices and is not divided against itself.

The point is not that Cyprian and Tertullian before him
were unable to conceptualize a *psychomachia*, for the general idea, basically Pauline, was before them; it is that these
Fathers could not express this idea in descriptive psychological language. Prudentius is known to have read Paul,
Tertullian, and Cyprian, and we assume that he drew upon
their treatments of Christian moral struggle.[19] Granting such
literary influences as I have been suggesting are possible,
however, the *Psychomachia* makes an entirely new departure: it turns a sometimes extended metaphor into epic allegorical narrative, and it gives the transformed metaphor
explicitly psychological content. That this departure can be
taken with such success, however, is largely due to the con-

[18] *De Mortalitate*, 4. Trans. from *Saint Cyprian: Treatises*, ed. Roy
Deferrari, The Fathers of the Church, Vol. 36 (New York, 1958),
p. 202.
[19] See above nn. 15 and 17.

ventionality of the metaphor. Its conventional meanings are gathered into the *Psychomachia*, making the allegory immediately lucid.

Let us retrace our steps through Scripture and patristic literature to follow the *Psychomachia*'s other major (and ultimate) metaphor, that of temple worship. In this case also the influences from the Christian tradition are thematically important but partial, and the *Psychomachia* marks an entirely new departure.

Prudentius very likely conceived of the poem's two-part sequence through reflection on the fifth chapter of I Kings. Solomon sends messengers to Hiram, saying: "Thou knowest the will of David my father, and that he could not build a house to the name of the Lord his God, because of the wars that were round about him, until the Lord put them under the soles of his feet. But now the Lord my God hath given me rest round about: and there is no adversary nor evil occurrence. Wherefore I purpose to build a temple to the name of the Lord my God, as the Lord spoke to David my father, saying: Thy son, whom I will set upon the throne in thy place, he shall build a house to my name" (III Kings 5:3-5). As the history continues, the materials and ground plan for Solomon's temple are detailed. Many of these materials and building techniques reappear in the temple of the *Psychomachia*. As the city of the virtues rises on its foundations, Fides clearly alludes to the episode in III Kings:

> unum opus egregio restat post bella labori,
> o proceres, regni quod tandem pacifer heres
> belligeri, armatae successor inermus et aulae,
> instituit Solomon, quoniam genitoris anheli
> fumarat calido regum de sanguine dextra. (804-808)

[One task alone, ye captains, now that war is over, remains for a noble effort to perform; the task that Solomon, the peaceful heir of a warlike throne, the unarmed successor to an armed court, set on foot, since his father

PSYCHIC WARFARE AND WORSHIP

panted from the slaughter and his hand reeked of the warm blood of kings.][20]

Fides combines in her person David and Solomon, warrior and peaceful heir. Having earlier led the virtues to battle, she here directs them in the construction of Sapientia's temple.

The temple of Solomon is one of the major religious symbols in the Old Testament. It epitomizes the strength of Israel in the Lord. Its destruction at the hands of the Assyrians and the subsequent Babylonian captivity are cardinal events of Hebrew history, events that in part determine the spirituality of the prophetic books. Christians interpreted the building of the temple by Solomon as a prefiguration of Christ's building of the new temple, the Church.[21] They saw the destruction of this temple—and of the rebuilt temple (authorized by Herod the Great) sacked by the Romans in A.D. 70—as a signal of God's intention to cast off the Jews, who would not acknowledge Christ.[22]

In John's Gospel, when Jesus alludes to the great temple of Jerusalem then standing, his use of metaphor signals a shift to new Christian significations: the idea of the temple has superseded the physical temple. "Jesus answered and

[20] Note that Abraham's slaughter of the kings is evoked in the person of David.

[21] Another prefiguration of the temple was the vision in Isaiah 6:1-3. The Lord sitting on a high throne, and the cries of "Holy, Holy, Holy," probably influence Prudentius' vision of Sapientia. For Sapientia, see Chapter III.

[22]   destructone iacent Solomonia saxa metallo
         aedificata manu? iacet illud nobile templum.   (*Apo.* 512-513)

—and the continuation until line 540. See also *Per.* X, 346ff., as background for the temple in the *Psychomachia*; and the quatrain of *Dittochaeon* 81-84:

   Aedificat templum Sapientia per Solomonis
   obsequium; regina austri grave congerit aurum.
   tempus adest quo templum hominis sub pectore Christus
   aedificet, quod Graia colant, quod barbara ditent.

133

said to them: Destroy this temple [*templum*]; and in three days I will raise it up. The Jews then said: Six and forty years was this temple in building; and wilt thou raise it up in three days? But he spoke of the temple of his body. When therefore he was risen again from the dead, his disciples remembered that he had said this; and they believed the scripture and the word that Jesus had said" (John 2:19-22). Whereas temple metaphors had heretofore been applied to Israel, to the chosen people as a nation, this usage is individualistic; for Christ speaks of his own body and refers to the mystery of his Resurrection. But of course no psychological sense is involved. In the Epistles to the Corinthians, Paul uses the metaphor with an expanded range of meanings: for the body itself (I Cor. 6:18-20), the entire human being (I Cor. 3:16-17), and the collective body of Christians who form the Church at Corinth: "And what concord hath Christ with Belial? Or what part hath the faithful with the unbeliever? And what agreement hath the temple of God with idols? For you are the temple of the living God; as God saith: I will dwell in them and walk among them; and I will be their God; and they shall be my people" (II Cor. 6:15-16).

Such figurative use of *templum* continues to flourish in the writings of the early Church Fathers. Two basic meanings coexist: each Christian is a temple of God; and the Church is the temple (the body of Christ), prefigured by the temple of Solomon and now formed of the unity of all who worship and are sanctified by God. Cyprian, for example, alludes often to the above Pauline passages, and he uses the word *templum* for a range of social and individual meanings; the baptized Christian is a *templum Dei* and the church is a *templum*.[23] Lactantius apparently puts more emphasis on the inwardness of the temple when he describes

[23] These references are listed in Michael Andrew Fahey, *Cyprian and the Bible: A Study in Third-Century Exegesis*, Beträge zur Geschichte der Biblischen Hermeneutik, 9 (Tübingen, 1971), pp. 444-445.

the Church as "the true temple of God, since it does not consist of walls but in the hearts and faithfulness of the men [*in corde ac fide hominum*] who believe in Him and are called the faithful. . . ."[24] But this is simply a case of synecdoche—the heart represents the faithful Christian—and Lactantius shows no interest in the psychological ramifications of such imagery.

These ante-Nicene passages quoted on the subjects of warfare and worship are representative of the tradition of Christian metaphor affecting the *Psychomachia*. Essentials of this tradition are, first, its historical foundation and, second, its dominant moral concern; thus, Christian metaphors, even when detached from their inevitable scriptural origins, function as shorthand tropological exegesis of Scripture. Paul's use of the warfare *topos* is unthinkable without his and his audience's received knowledge of Israel's military history; whether he cites a specific scriptural text and then allegorizes it (as he is wont) or not, the ethical sense is clear. Jesus' particular allusion to his own Resurrection as the rebuilding of the temple is not introduced with the phrase, "it is written," but his allusion depends for its effect upon the Jews' profound religious sentiments about Solomon's temple, about which sacred truths *are* written. Such Christian metaphor is not symbolic in any Platonic sense: it does not move from a less real to a more real sense. Rather, Christian metaphor embodies reality: verbally dependent upon history, it fulfills but does not transcend history by denoting its progress toward moral perfection.

Ante-Nicene metaphor, however, expresses tropology without fully delineating it. Christians should fight against the armies of Satan, Christians should be holy temples of Christ—the meaning can be (and was) explicated in detail in the course of a sermon, but is in itself vague. As the doctrine of the Trinity was only tentatively described at

[24] *Divinae Institutiones* 4. 13, from *Lactantius: Divine Institutes*, trans. Mary Francis McDonald, The Fathers of the Church, Vol. 49 (Washington, D.C., 1964), p. 276.

Nicaea but fully described at Constantinople, so the metaphors for Christian psychological states were much more sharply delineated toward the end of the fourth century. In the past chapter I argued that new heretical efforts by Apollinarians and by defenders of Origen's *On First Principles* probably sparked Church efforts to create a Christian psychology. Thus Ambrose writes a commentary, *De Isaac et Anima*, in which he relates the sacrifice of Isaac to the moral developments within the mind of a Christian. Although Philo had centuries earlier performed psychological exegesis of Scripture, and although Tertullian's *De Anima* and other patristic commentaries had treated the nature of the soul, the proliferation of interest at the close of the fourth century is unprecedented. Reading Ambrose, for example, gives the impression that psychology has become an almost popular subject, certainly a subject to linger over rather than an abstruse and minor difficulty. The quotation (in the next paragraph) from his *De Bono Mortis* is unthinkable at the beginning of his century. Its ideas are obviously of relevance to the theme of the *Psychomachia*; its careful, leisurely handling of these ideas gives a more important clue to Prudentius' cultural context.

Ambrose's opening question might be directed to Tertullian or to Cyprian: "But why speak of snares that are from outside? We must beware of our own internal snares. In this body of ours we are surrounded by snares, and we ought to avoid them. Let us not trust ourselves to this body, let us not join our soul with it. . . . For if there is a joining, the flesh, which is the lesser element, becomes better than the soul, which is the greater, because the soul [*anima*] gives life to the body, but the flesh pours death into the soul. And so the working of each element is brought into disorder. . . . But do not think that disorder occurs merely because the soul is infused into the body. Take for example the gift of light, for the light is poured out upon the earth and yet is not confounded with it. And so let the working of elements whose nature is unlike not be confounded, but

136

let the soul be in the body to give it life, to rule and enlighten it. Yet we cannot deny that it should have compassion on its body. For it also is afflicted, since Jesus says: 'My soul is sad, even unto death,' thus expressing the human emotion in Himself, and elsewhere He says: 'My soul is troubled,' since He shows compassion by His attitude and disposition. Just so the singer shows compassion with his melodies and with the sound of his pipe or cithera or organ, when he is sad at the sad sounds, joyful at the joyful ones, more excited at those that are sharper, more calm and gentle at those that are calmer. Thus in his own person he gains favor for the sounds of his songs and in some way controls their moods. The soul too, playing in moderation on the body as if on a musical stringed instrument, strikes the passions of the flesh as if they were notes on the strings, but with its fingertips, so to speak. Thus it produces music in euphonious accord with a virtuous way of life, and in all its thoughts and works sees to it that its counsels harmonize with its deeds. The soul, then, is the user, the body that which is being used, and thus the one is in command, the other in service; the one is what we are, the other what belongs to us."[25] This treatment is stylistically new in the unhurried geniality of the presentation, the absence of any abruptness or awkwardness. And it is conceptually new in the internalization of the moral consciousness: the vices of the world replaced by "internal snares," the moral struggle seen as taking place *within* the Christian rather than *between* the Christian and the world, the harmony to be achieved being, once again, an internal harmony.

But even St. Ambrose does not quite describe a psychological battle: his "internal snares" are, at least in origin, corporeal; and his moral solution is proper interaction of body and soul. The moral life he describes is therefore internal but not purely psychological. St. Augustine achieves a

[25] *De Bono Mortis*, 7 [26-27], from *Saint Ambrose: Seven Exegetical Works*, trans. Michael P. McHugh, The Fathers of the Church, Vol. 65 (Washington, D.C., 1972), pp. 90-91.

more sophisticated and more purely psychological analysis. His "soul-struggle" is not so much *on behalf of* the soul or *by* the soul—although it is these also—as *within the soul itself*. This is a key distinction, one upon which the *Confessions* depends, and one which Augustine expressly makes in the course of the *City of God*. "As things now stand, the soul [*animus*] is ashamed of the body's opposition to it, for the body is subject to it because of its lower nature. When the soul opposes itself in the case of other emotions, it feels less ashamed because when it is vanquished by itself, the soul is its own vanquisher. Although this victory of soul over soul is disorderly and morbid because it is a victory of constituents that should be subject to reason, yet it is a victory of its own constituents and therefore, as was said, a self-conquest. For when the soul vanquishes itself in an orderly fashion and thus subordinates its irrational emotions to the rule of a rational purpose, such a victory is laudable and virtuous, provided that its purpose in turn is subordinate to God."[26]

In the same work Augustine employs the metaphor of temple worship with emphasis on inner spirituality. Admittedly this passage, in contrast to the preceding one (and in greater contrast to *De Trinitate*), is not analytic. The soul is not partitioned. The metaphor is almost Pauline in its extended range and in its quality, in its evocation of sacred forms of worship to denote moral states. But notice that once Augustine internalizes the *templum*, his language—

[26] *De Civ. Dei* XIV, 23, from *Augustine: City of God* (Loeb Classical Library), 7 vols. (London, 1964-72), Vol. 4, pp. 381-383. The reader should note that Augustine uses *animus* rather than (as in the Ambrose passage) *anima*. The usual Augustinian term for soul is *anima*, but also used are *mens* (referring to *cogitatio*, the highest principle of *anima*), *spiritus* (designating *anima* generically), and *animus* (which suggests especially the faculty of will in *anima*). With Augustine these words are approaching precision; earlier they may be used interchangeably, although *anima* is standard for soul. Earlier authors could understand the distinctions in root senses well enough. See below, n. 29, for Prudentius' terminology.

amor, oblivio, humilitas, caritas—is clearly intended to define psychological reality. The Christian devotion to God is located squarely within the soul, *in ara cordis*. Perhaps the lack of analysis, then, reflects the charitable soul's unitary, mystical condition. "To [God] we owe the service which is called in Greek *latreia*, whether this service is embodied in certain sacraments or is within our very selves. For all of us together are his temple and all of us individually his temples, since he deigns to dwell both in the united heart of all and in each one separately. . . . When we lift our hearts to him, our hearts are his altar; with his only begotten Son as our priest we seek his favour. We sacrifice bleeding victims to him when we fight in defence of his truth even unto blood; we offer him the sweetest incense when in his sight we burn with pious and holy love, when we vow, and pay the vow, to devote to him his gifts bestowed on us and to devote ourselves with them; when we dedicate and consecrate to him a memorial of his benefits in solemn feasts on appointed days, lest, as time unrolls its scroll, a thankless forgetfulness should creep in; when we offer him on the altar of our hearts a sacrifice of humility and praise kindled by the fire of our love."[27]

In these early fifth-century passages, Augustine completes a tendency only sporadically felt from St. Paul to the post-Nicene period: the relocation of the moral life in the psyche. Paul had said that the spirit lusts against the flesh, but it was not always easy to tell the whereabouts of the spiritual-corporeal contest. Whereas the early Church had located the arena of moral struggle somewhere in the space between each individual Christian and the evils of the world (and between the Church and external Satanic forces), there had always been some interest in the inward effects of this moral struggle. Indeed, the whole Gospel message revolts against conventional righteousness and puts primary value on inward morality: on the intentions preceding the

[27] *De Civ. Dei* X, 3. Loeb, Vol. 3, p. 261.

139

act, even on the intentions without the act—for example, whoever looks on a woman to lust after her has committed adultery already in his heart (Matt. 5:28). And Paul, writing earlier than the evangelists, expounds the inward orientation of ethics. But not until the post-Nicene period do the complex conflicts or peaceful states within the soul, such as Augustine describes, become formulated and described in detail.

Before the *Psychomachia* was written, Augustine had investigated his own mind and produced perhaps the first intentional record of a personality in literary history. Charles N. Cochrane has commented on the *Confessions*, ". . . with Augustine each individual human being is envisaged as a centre of radiant energy. Born into a world of contacts, he presently develops a whole tissue of external relationships, but the 'subject' is not on that account to be resolved into any or all of the relationships thus established. On the contrary, it accepts the raw material of sense-perception streaming in through the various channels; recording, sorting, and assessing it in the light of standards which mature with maturing experience, only to make it the basis of further demands upon what appear to be the available sources of satisfaction. From this standpoint, the different so-called faculties may all be considered as functions of will. . . . It thus becomes apparent that, so far as concerns the human animal, the problem of life is a problem of consciousness."[28] These remarks are also useful in interpreting the two quotations (above) from the *City of God*, for what else does Augustine describe in them but two states of consciousness? The soul, affected by the reactions of its own faculties to the experience of the world, wills itself to respond to these faculties (its lower self) in the manner of a moral struggle. Again, the soul experiences willful love of God and manifests this love according to forms of worship-

[28] *Christianity and Classical Culture: A Study of Thought and Action from Augustus to Augustine* (rev. ed. 1944; rpt. New York, 1972), p. 389.

ful service. In both cases, the motions of the soul itself, rather than the interrelationship between this soul's faculties and body or world, are traced in language.

THE MENTAL SETTING OF WARFARE AND WORSHIP

These metaphorical passages in the *City of God* share literary affinities with the *Psychomachia* in their treatment of a hypothetical, general, or universal psyche. But it is one thing to delineate a psychology in a treatise, where the author is free to advance speculation and to qualify or retreat from it, to amass evidence from other authorities and from the world at large—in short, to argue; it is quite another to do this in a tightly controlled allegory. Nothing prevents the poet from arguing in his own person in the course of his allegory, but he must beware not to tread too heavily lest his allegorical fiction dissolve into something very like a treatise. The poet must let the nouns and verbs of the allegory carry the bulk of his meaning. Granted that Augustine culminates the development of a Christian psychology, can such a psychology admit of expression in allegory? In order to guarantee its allegorical meaning *as a psychology*, will the personifications themselves be explicitly mental? Will their actions describe explicitly mental processes, or will the setting of their actions be explicitly mental? It is obvious that the tradition of Christian metaphor allows the *Psychomachia*'s sequence of warfare and worship to refer somehow to psychological conversion. In the context of late fourth-century thought, the probability of such reference is very large. The poem's title would seem to contain conclusive evidence of mental locus, but perhaps the burden of proof should fall on the poem's characters and setting.

Our first somewhat unpromising discovery is that the names of the characters may be derived from non-psychological phenomena. In this respect they are the true subjects of the metaphorical verb systems activating them. If war-

141

fare and worship reflect scriptural history, its agents are from New Testament moral theology, from ecclesiastical history, and, in the case of certain vices, from pagan Roman history. The vice's names do not necessarily signify emotions or thoughts conceived as psychological phenomena, but universal moral ideas visible as social behavior. The soul may simply be the nexus of the vice's activity, the vice herself not psychological but a cause or effect of psychological events. Avaritia, for example, is surely a pattern of social behavior as well as an internal desire for wealth. The allegory's first vice, Cultura Deorum Veterum, is primarily a social fact even though she can also describe the "pagan" or idolatrous sentiments in the soul. Note the similarity to earlier Christian writings; the "dissension, sects, envies, murders, drunkenness" of Galatians 5 have no ethical reality except as they at least potentially leave the area of mental intention and are actualized in society.

That the virtues are more likely than the vices to denote essentially psychological states may relate to (if not explain) the fact that personified virtues appear later in the tradition of metaphorical battle than do the vices. When the ante-Nicene vices attack from the outside (being still essentially abstractions of social behavior), they are opposed by the virtuous singular soul, not by the plural virtues. Even when the single combats between vices and virtues are described, as in the Tertullian passage, there is no explicit characterization of these battles as psychological rather than social. Of Prudentius' virtues, some are by nature psychological faculties or states: most obviously Mens Humilis, Spes, Ratio. Others, however, could easily be used in another context as patterns of social behavior: Pudicitia, Sobrietas, Fides. The local ambiguity and its attendant literary problem remain. Can metaphors derived from moral universals or from patterns of socially visible behavior, military campaigns, and temple worship adequately express an invisible psychological reality?

The framing hexameter passages in which the poet argues

142

in his own person resolve this ambiguity by showing that Prudentius intends the allegory of soul-struggle to take place *in* the soul. In his invocation, he prays that Christ will say with what fighting force the soul (*mens*) is armed to cast out (*pellere*) sins from within our breast (*nostri de pectoris antro*). Christ is not being asked to say how sins may be cast out from the *body*. Disregarding the figurative vocabulary (*antro*), we note that the pectoral region was in Prudentius' day considered the seat or region of the soul. Christ is being asked, further, to describe the means of help when there is internal disorder (*turbatis sensibus intus / seditio*) and when the strife of evil passions vexes the spirit (*animam morborum rixa fatigat*). It will be noticed that in the course of the *Psychomachia* Prudentius employs a variety of words for the soul: *mens, anima, spiritus,* and others less descriptive and more metaphorical. These are not equivalent terms; they are used frequently with subtle poetic distinctions.[29] Yet they all refer in a general sense to the non-corporeal or spiritual nature of man. It must be granted that Prudentius the layman is no theologian and no metaphysician, so his psychological vocabulary is occasionally vague. One cannot always determine whether he describes divisions within the soul or between the soul and the surrounding body or bodily nature.[30] In his concluding prayer to Christ, for example, Prudentius describes the human condition:

> fervent bella horrida, fervent
> ossibus inclusa, fremit et discordibus armis
> non simplex natura hominis; nam viscera limo
> effigiata premunt animam. . . .　　　　(902-905)

[29] *Spiritus* is connected with *spirare*, therefore with the spiration of the Holy Spirit. See the quotation on p. 147 for this word play: *spiritus* (768) following *Spiritui* (766). Similarly *anima* is connected with *animare*. The play on *animat* (909), in this case not picked up by Thomson, is crucial in the interpretation of Prudentian psychology in this concluding prayer; see p. 144.

[30] See the discussion of setting below.

[Savage war rages hotly, rages within our bones, and man's two-sided nature is in an uproar of rebellion; for the flesh that was formed of clay bears down upon the spirit. . . .]

The context of the phrase *non simplex natura hominis* is without doubt the body-soul antagonism, but how literally is this antagonism to be taken? In what sense is the *bella* within our bones (*ossibus inclusa*)? This basic warfare inherent in mankind is hardly taking place within the bones themselves; the war is more likely raging throughout the body or, it seems to me even more likely, within the soul enclosed by the body. A few verses beyond is this: *distantesque animat duplex substantia vires* ("and our two-fold being inspires powers at variance with each other" [909]). The *duplex substantia* could well be the Pauline spirit-flesh duality, but the resultant *distantes . . . vires* cannot be equivalent and must logically be psychological forces of some sort. The very suggestive verb, *animat*, so confirms. Taking all of these indications together, it is difficult not to believe that the allegory of the *Psychomachia* takes place, in some sense, within the soul.

Perhaps this internal disorder, this *turbatis sensibus intus / seditio*, is twofold in a strikingly Augustinian sense. St. Augustine in the *City of God* has described simultaneous struggles between soul and body and within the soul. Both struggles are occasioned by sin, and both bring on shame as a result of the consciousness of sin; the will wills that both struggles be waged; the effects of both struggles are interrelated, a concord within the soul accompanying a concord between body and soul and the total human being therefore united in love of God. So it is in the *Psychomachia*. In one sense its subject is the successful defeat by the soul of the assaults of the body. Thus after all the single combats have been won, the camp of the virtues is united and whole in its lack of contamination by the body (or the bodily nature).[31]

[31] Paul often employs words for "body" and "flesh" in a meta-

concurrunt alacres castris ex omnibus omnes,
nulla latet pars Mentis iners, quae corporis ullo
intercepta sinu per conceptacula sese
degeneri languore tegat, tentoria apertis
cuncta patent velis, reserantur carbasa, ne quis
marceat obscuro stertens habitator operto.   (740-745)

[All assemble briskly from the whole camp. No member
of Soul lurks in idleness, shut off in a pocket of the body
and lying close in some retreat in ignoble sloth. All tents
stand exposed, their curtains drawn back, the canvas open,
so that no dweller therein shall lie lazily asleep in undis-
covered secrecy.]

Those assembling are the *Sensus*, the thoughts and sentiments dwelling in the soul and forming, under optimal religious conditions, a unified and peaceful society. Because
the soul retains its freedom of will, there exists the dangerous possibility of these *Sensus* again wandering off sinfully
to the hidden reaches of the body (or the bodily nature).
Sin recurs if the tent flaps are closed, if not all the thoughts
of the soul are present and accounted for by the will.

But the soul is not cut off from the body, nor does it
wish to be—unless it be a heretical, Manichean soul. What
the will of the converted Christian wants to avoid is not
contact with the body per se, but cupidinous contact with
the body.[32] Therefore the will guards against two manifestations of the bodily nature, the excesses of the body itself
and the "fleshly" or cupidinous motions of the soul. This
twofold Augustinian struggle may be visualized in the
Psychomachia's setting. The city of the soul is constructed
on the plain of the body. The city walls afford some protection against plain-dwelling enemies who might wish to
encircle the city with their assaults, but these walls do not

---

phorical sense, and later Christian writers follow this usage. Interpretation requires caution.

[32] Ambrose makes this distinction in the quotation above, pp.
136-137.

145

exclude the plain itself because the city rests on the plain. The tents within the city rest on this plain. What does all this signify? According to the model of the Roman Empire, especially in its Theodosian stage, the whole plain should be under the rule of the *urbs*, both city and country should form one unified and productive society. Translated into Christian psychology, the soul should rule both itself and the body in spiritual harmony.[33] That the army of virtues sallies forth from the city against invading vices on the plain signifies neither that the struggle occurs only in the body nor that the struggle is between soul and body. Instead, an all-inclusive struggle occurs within the human empire ruled by the soul. This human empire has been invaded by evil barbarians (in league with Satan), who have claimed and occupied the bodily nature, and who also can enter the soul (as Discordia demonstrates). The internal weakness of the soul has permitted this invasion to occur in the first place— hence the necessity for the will's continued psychomachic vigilance within the soul-city, even after the alien invaders have been repulsed. The moral action of the *Psychomachia* involves simultaneous struggles, the one between the will and the bodily impulses, the other between the will and the *Sensus*, who have let these bodily impulses pervert the ideal order of the psyche. This order has been provisionally restored when the thoughts and sentiments assemble to hear Concordia's victory speech.[34]

[33] Gnilka, *Studien zur Psychomachie des Prudentius*, pp. 9-18, discusses the "allegorical scenery" of *campus, castra, urbs*. Jerusalem, in lines 811-819, he interprets as the body purified, the seat of the temple of soul; the movement from country to city he takes as the body's change of state from sinfulness to purity.

[34] A recent critic has missed the point of Concordia's speech: "If the mind of man is conceived as a battlefield of warring *homunculi*, it is not surprising—just tedious—to discover that the *homunculi* themselves are composed of even tinier *homunculi*; and so on. . . . In other words: we have driven off our enemies the Vices, so don't let any discord rise up among yourselves, you Virtues! The Loeb editor gives no capital letters to *sententia discors* (though he does to

Concordia's speech provides a convenient gloss. Not only does it explain the topography of the allegory, it also confirms the mental locus of the battles or, to be more exact, the primacy of the battle within the soul in maintaining the continued health of the body-soul relationship. Concordia begins as follows:

> cumulata quidem iam gloria vobis,
> O Patris, o Domini fidissima pignera Christi,
> contigit: extincta est multo certamine saeva
> barbaries, sanctae quae circumsaepserat urbis
> indigenas, ferroque viros flammaque premebat.
> publica sed requies privatis rure foroque
> constat amicitiis: scissura domestica turbat
> rem populi, titubatque foris quod dissidet intus.
> ergo cavete, viri, ne sit sententia discors
> Sensibus in nostris, ne secta exotica tectis
> nascatur conflata odiis, quia fissa voluntas
> confundit variis arcana biformia fibris.
> quod sapimus coniungat amor; quod vivimus uno
> conspiret studio: nil dissociabile firmum est.
> utque homini atque Deo medius intervenit Iesus,
> qui sociat mortale Patri, ne carnea distent
> Spiritui aeterno sitque ut Deus unus utrumque,
> sic, quidquid gerimus mentisque et corporis actu,
> spiritus unimodis texat conpagibus unus.   (750-768)

[Abundant glory has come to you, ye faithful children of the Father and of Christ our Lord. With a great struggle have you wiped out the cruel savages that had beset the dwellers in the holy city round about with hard pressure of fire and sword. But the nation's peace depends on good will between its citizens in field and town. Division

---

Sensibus), but there is a Chinese Box here for all that."—A. D. Nuttall, *Two Concepts of Allegory: A Study of Shakespeare's The Tempest and the Logic of Allegorical Expression* (London, 1967), p. 39.

at home upsets the common weal and difference within means faltering abroad. Therefore be on the watch, my soldiers, that there be no discordant thought among our Sentiments, that no foreign faction arise in us from the occasion of hidden quarrels; *for a divided will creates disorder in our inmost nature, making two parties in a heart at variance.* Let our understanding be united by love, our life be in accord in a single aim; where there is separation there is no strength. And just as Jesus mediates between man and God, uniting mortality with the Father so that the fleshly shall not be separated from the eternal Spirit and that one God shall be both, *so let one spirit shape in single structure all that we do by action of soul and body.*][35] (Italics mine)

In his concluding prayer, Prudentius adds his own gloss, some of which we have read already. With Concordia, he stresses the psychological locus of the personification allegory. The key verses are those beginning the thanksgiving:

reddimus aeternas, indulgentissime doctor,
grates, Christe, tibi, meritosque sacramus honores
ore pio; nam cor vitiorum stercore sordet.
tu nos corporei latebrosa pericula operti
luctantisque animae voluisti agnoscere casus. (888-892)

[We give to Thee, O Christ, Thou tenderest of teachers, unending thanks and offer to Thee the honour that is thy due with loyal lips—for our heart is foul with the filth of sin. Thou didst wish us to learn the dangers that lurk unseen within the body, and the vicissitudes of our soul's struggle.]

And, at the end, the statement that the soul's *distantes . . . vires* will struggle:

[35] Prudentius' apostrophe to Pax, following this passage, may be compared to that of Augustine in *De Civ. Dei* XIX, 13.

donec praesidio Christus Deus adsit et omnes
virtutum gemmas conponat sede piata,
atque, ubi peccatum regnaverat, aurea templi
atria constituens texat spectamine morum
ornamenta animae, quibus oblectata decoro
aeternum solio dives Sapientia regnet.   (910-915)

[until Christ our God comes to our aid, orders all the
jewels of the virtues in a pure setting, and where sin
formerly reigned builds the golden courts of his temple,
creating for the soul, out of the trial of its conduct, ornaments for rich Wisdom to find delight in as she reigns
for ever on her beauteous throne.]

Two points are now clear. First, the narrative has shown us
according to the will of Christ the sinfulness within the
body (891) *and* within the soul (892).[36] Second, the narrative has shown us the means to overcome this state of sinfulness: the struggle within the soul. As an allegory of
Christian psychology, therefore, the *Psychomachia* is both
descriptive and prescriptive. We have needed to be shown
these things because we are ourselves in a state of sinfulness;
and only through the grace of Christ have they been shown.
Given this divine inspiration, its descriptive psychological
truthfulness cannot be doubted.

PERSONIFICATION

The *Psychomachia* could not exist without personifications. As embodied and animated moral ideas, they create
through their interactions the illusion of psychological space

[36] Likewise, in the *Hamartigenia*, a description of the soul's defense
against the onslaughts of Satan from the outside is thus qualified:

sed quid ego omne malum mundique hominumque maligni
hostis ad invidiam detorqueo, cum mala nostra
ex nostris concreta animis genus et caput et vim,
quid sint, quid valeant, sumant de corde parente?   (553-556)

149

and time without which the history of conversion is impossible. But these personifications do not represent psychological components as such; although they are real moral ideas, the soul is not composed of them. What then is the nature of their poetic truth?

Prior to the composition of the *Psychomachia*, no force of literary tradition compelled a poet to join the naming or abstraction of the virtues and vices with personification. The virtues and vices were one thing (ethical categories), personification another (a rhetorical trope); between the two was no necessary connection. In connecting the two, the *Psychomachia* was a watershed of literary history. Together with John Cassian's systematization of the seven capital sins, Prudentius' allegory spawned conventional medieval personification allegory. But there was nothing inevitable about Prudentius' use of the trope; neither Scripture nor classical tradition demanded it.

Personified virtues or moral ideas do occur in Scripture, as in Psalm 84: "Mercy and truth have met each other: justice and peace have kissed." But the great majority of personifications in both Old and New Testaments do not apply to such ethical categories—wine is more apt to be personified than drunkenness. Where a moral abstraction is personified, there is rarely any elaboration; a single noun-verb combination is usual, as when righteousness walks with a man. An important exception is Sapientia, personified extensively in the apocryphal Book of Wisdom and in Proverbs. She is of course the supreme personification of the *Psychomachia*, and Prudentius dramatizes Proverbs 9:1 toward the end of the allegory: "Wisdom [*Sapientia*] hath built herself a house: she hath hewn her out seven pillars." Many such verses follow one another in the Book of Wisdom and Proverbs, but the elaboration of the personification is additive: a series of discrete figurative impressions, each with intensive metaphorical depth, accompanies Sapientia. There is no roundness or solidity of personification—no character, that is—such as could be obtained by presenting inter-

150

connected and consistent features together. There are no instances in Scripture of personifications elaborated by means of the tableau description that typifies the characters of the *Psychomachia*. Nor do scriptural personifications ever form groups which might interact or exchange discourse within an illusion of space and time.

Tertullian's personification seems to represent a literary advance. The virtues and vices in *De Spectaculis* are said to be fighting one another all in the same arena. Here is perhaps the germ of the *Psychomachia*'s personification allegory—but only the germ. Prior to Prudentius, there is no elaborate and internally consistent personification of the Christian virtues and vices.

Perhaps Prudentius derived his personifications from classical literature?[37] Ever since Hesiod's *Theogony* there were writers willing to employ personifications, and with Vergil the trope takes on a certain mimetic roundness. Fama in the *Aeneid* (IV, 173-188) really acts like her name: she travels from place to place spreading rumors and instilling in men's heads the effects of rumors, such as fear and foolishness. The decorum of such personification is emulated not only by other pagans but by the Christian writers. It is probably responsible for the inner consistency of Tertullian's figurative gladiatorial contest, and it influences the personifications of the *Psychomachia* directly as well as by way of Tertullian. Prudentius' contemporary Claudian employs personification very much in the tradition of Vergil when he paints the tableau figures of Roma and Africa in the *De Bello Gildonico*. Claudian (like later panegyricists) expands the Vergilian trope considerably. Claudian's Roma is weak with hunger from grain withheld, she bears a rusty spear and an ill-fitting helmet showing her gray hairs and an un-

---

[37] The most complete treatment of classical personification and the *Psychomachia* is in Beatrice (cited Critical Introd., n. 27), 25-40. Beatrice accounts for epic personification but identifies the trope most closely with the tradition of the diatribe and with satire, whence the Christian apologists take it.

151

polished shield—the iconography forms a unified political picture even as it is elaborated in great detail; Roma's lengthy speech retraces this picture and adds emotional coloring to it. Similarly detailed elaboration is accorded the figure of Africa. Prudentius' technique is not unlike Claudian's: his virtues and vices also display a realistic combination of iconographic detail forming the illusion of personification as character, an illusion given credibility by human-like speech and action. Given our Christian *rhetor*'s proficiency in classical literature, his adaptation of this particular trope is easy to imagine. In his application of personification to virtues and vices, though, Prudentius departs sharply from his pagan countrymen.

Roman personification of virtues and vices rarely goes beyond mere naming, mere abstraction. Especially in the period of the late Empire there is a great proclivity toward abstraction, and this is evidenced by the proliferation of new divinities such as Fever and Victory, whom the Christian apologists are so fond of ridiculing. Their ridicule is directed at one of the weak spots of pagan ideology, its failure to achieve what the Christians were achieving in their general councils and anti-heresy campaigns: a coherent and all-inclusive ethical system. Among the crowded divinities in the pantheon stood a number of personified (or deified) virtues whose relationship to the other gods and goddesses never seems to have been defined. Nor was the relation between the ethical abstraction and its social manifestations particularly clear; by naming the divinity one acknowledged its reality and its power, but one did not thereby know how, when, or whether to worship it. In other words, there is a certain arbitrariness and accidental quality to the Roman personifications of virtues. Thus during the very period when some social and political conceptions such as Fama and, most important, Roma are being personified with great sophistication, other ethical categories that were to become the Christian psychological virtues and vices are merely named, merely abstracted.

Accompanying the throng of Egyptian divinities in Book VIII of the *Aeneid* is Discordia, exultant in her rent robe (*scissa gaudens vadit Discordia palla*, 702)—no further elaboration given. In the *Thebaid*, Statius' depictions of Virtus (X, 632-682) and Pietas (XI, 457-481) are detailed, and might be taken as the exception to this tendency toward mere abstraction. But Pietas is a public political virtue, and the sidereal Virtus must undergo a metamorphosis (to Manto) before she can be embodied in speech and action. More typical of Statius' personification is perhaps this:

non solitas acies nec Martia bella paramus,
sed fratrum—licet alma Fides Pietasque repugnent,
vincentur—fratrum stringendi comminus enses.
grande opus! ipsae odiis, ipsae discordibus armis
aptemur.   (*Thebaid* XI, 97-101)

['Tis no common fray or Martian battle that we prepare, but brothers—though kindly Faith and Duty resist, they will be overcome—ay, brothers shall draw the sword in combat hand-to-hand. A noble work! Gird we ourselves with deadly hate, with armed discord.][38]

[38] Text and trans. from *Statius* (Loeb Classical Library), ed. J. H. Mozley, 2 vols. (London, 1928), Vol. 2, pp. 396-397. C. S. Lewis has argued for the *Thebaid* as a major influence on Prudentius' decision to personify the virtues (p. 68)—an exaggerated view, corrected by Beatrice. But see also Alan Cameron, *Claudian* (cited Critical Introd., n. 4), pp. 254-255, where Claudian's use of personification in his panegyrics is felt to be mainly influenced by "Latin epic, above all Statius," and the *addendum* (pp. 490-491) to this statement, where the absence of personifications in the distinct Greek rhetorical tradition supports the idea that "they are an infusion from Latin epic, idiosyncratic among Easterners to Claudian and taken over from him and exaggerated by his Western successors." The relative influence of Vergil, Statius, and Claudian upon Prudentius in this regard is difficult to determine—especially in light of Beatrice's counterargument, n. 37 above. An important new study by David Vessey, *Statius and the Thebaid* (Cambridge, 1973), analyzes this epic in detail, including the entrance of the personifications Virtus and Pietas. Vessey does not isolate personification as a separate literary problem; but he does treat Statius' personification well in passing.

It is not that Latin literature shuns personification, but that its personification of most ethical qualities tends to be superficial. In Claudian we observe the following crowd of evils, vices, and misfortunes:

> glomerantur in unum
> innumerae pestes Erebi, quascumque sinistro
> Nox genuit fetu: nutrix Discordia belli,
> imperiosa Fames, leto vicina Senectus
> impatiensque sui Morbus Livorque secundis
> anxius et scisso maerens velamine Luctus
> et Timor et caeco praeceps Audacia vultu
> et Luxus populator opum, quem semper adhaerens
> infelix humili gressu comitatur Egestas,
> foedaque Avaritiae complexae pectora matris
> insomnes longo veniunt examine Curae.
>
> > (*In Rufinum* I, 28-38)

[Hell's numberless monsters are gathered together, Night's children of ill-omened birth. Discord, mother of war, imperious Hunger, Age, near neighbour to Death; Disease, whose life is a burden to himself; Envy that brooks not another's prosperity, woeful Sorrow with rent garments; Fear and foolhardy Rashness with sightless eyes; Luxury, destroyer of wealth, to whose side ever clings unhappy Want with humble tread, and the long company of sleepless Cares, hanging round the foul neck of their mother Avarice.][39]

Against the charge of pagan ethical confusion it can be argued that this picture of confusion is intended, is itself an ethical statement. The very form of cumulative parataxis by which the vices, social ills, political enemies, and their ilk are presented in classical literature is meant to be conspicuous by its disorder, its lack of symmetry. Prudentius himself is attuned to the significance of this mode of pre-

---

[39] *Claudian* (cited Chapter I, n. 45), Vol. I, pp. 28-29.

sentation, and in the *Psychomachia* he employs a rhetoric of confusion to depict the vices. Thus when Avaritia appears,

> Cura, Famis, Metus, Anxietas, Periuria, Pallor,
> Corruptela, Dolus, Commenta, Insomnia, Sordes,
> Eumenides variae monstri comitatus aguntur. (464-466)

> [Care, Hunger, Fear, Anguish, Perjuries, Pallor, Corruption, Treachery, Falsehood, Sleeplessness, Meanness, diverse fiends, go in attendance on the monster.]

Such randomness echoes in miniature the form of the sequence of battles. It is not unlike the technique used by the Christian apologist to point the finger of ridicule at one pagan god after another. The list of names creates a mob scene. Despite this similarity of technique, however, Prudentius differs from Claudian in his use of personification.

What distinguishes the Christian writers, at least in the post-Nicene period, from their pagan counterparts is that even though both employ the same rhetoric to attack the evils at hand, the Christians alone can present a cogent explanation for the existence of these evils. Whereas Claudian employs the by now worn-out machinery of Roman mythology to introduce the evils of his world (they play senator to Allecto's emperor in Hades), Prudentius rationalizes the existence of his vices by means of theological truth. To the Roman pagan, the very existence of goods and evils can be explained only by recourse to the concept of Fortune; correspondingly, virtues and vices which define typical characters are themselves of mysterious origin, the outcome of Fortune. To the Christian of Prudentius' day, however, all of these things are knowable through Christ.

Let us consider how the poet rationalizes the virtues and vices in the *Psychomachia*. He claims that the struggles between the virtues and vices are being revealed by Christ as true psychological events. This need not mean that the personifications of the virtues and vices are structural ele-

155

ments in our souls. The virtues and vices are not permanent faculties of the soul like memory and will and intellect. The soul may be said to contain virtue but not the virtues, Original Sin but not the vices. The vices are particular, occasional, temporary manifestations of sin; the virtues are manifestations of a particular, occasioned counterattack against the vices.

Several considerations lead to this interpretation. The first is an argument from tradition. Discussion of ethics in Scripture and in the early patristic period is almost entirely practical. When Paul enumerates certain vices, as in Romans 1:29-31 or I Corinthians 5, these concern offenses against the flesh, as well as malice, pride, selfishness, indifference toward others, and so on. While all of these vices are perversions of Christian charity, their existence is not systematically explained as such. Rather, the vices are treated as practical problems of applied morality. Whatever hints of an ethical systematization do exist in Scripture—for example, the seven gifts of the Spirit in Isaiah 11:2, the grouping of Faith, Hope, and Charity in I Corinthians 13—these are not employed by Prudentius. Thus Faith and Hope are present in the *Psychomachia*, but in different capacities; and Charity is absent.[40] If the poet wished to convince us that the virtues made up an essential part of the soul's structure, he would have employed the available if sparse scriptural precedents of ethical systematization. Instead, like Paul, he wishes to display virtues and vices as concrete worldly manifestations of essential spiritual reality.

Second, some literary observations. The virtues and vices in the *Psychomachia* are first introduced and later disposed of unsystematically.[41] There is no necessity for Ira to enter

---

[40] The word *caritas* is not to be found in Prudentius; nor are the three theological virtues systematized.

[41] But see *Hamartigenia*, 409-428. The prince of evil is said to have seven tribes of warriors at his command: Canaanites, Amorites, Girgashites, Jebusites, Hittites, Peruzzites, Hivites. (This passage follows

ahead of Superbia, or for Superbia to enter ahead of Luxuria. The very arbitrariness of the order of battles reflects the fickleness of the fleshly instinct from a Christian point of view: that individuals have proclivities toward individual vices at different times. That the vices are killed means that they are non-permanent features of the soul's activity. Similarly, while all the virtues survive, each virtue is only temporarily active. With the exception of Faith, the necessary sponsor of all the other Christian virtues and therefore present throughout the action, the virtues step forth as their special skills are required and retreat into anonymity as their mission is completed. It is as if the virtues gradually become subsumed in Virtue as the action progresses against the vices. Lacking the vices as present threats, the virtues are in effect transferred from active duty to the ready reserves, where they become anonymous. Such developments would be inappropiate for permanent faculties.

Third, Prudentius tells us explicitly in another poem that the virtues and vices are accidental rather than substantial features of the soul's makeup. An illuminating passage in the *Hamartigenia* (389-408) describes the origin of the vices: Because of original sin men do not love God properly but love the world instead; their wills choose sinfully, and this leaves them open to attack from outside. Thus welcomed by the sinful will, Satan steals in and plants his ministers, an assorted crew of vices, inside the soul. These vices are personified, and there is once again a randomness or arbitrariness to their names—one suspects that the list could go on indefinitely. (Some of these vices are battalion commanders in the *Psychomachia*, others for no apparent reason remain unnamed footsoldiers.) After the rollcall, the poet exclaims:

---

another in which vices are personified.) Perhaps here is the germ of a typological system showing the influence of Origen, who in *Hom. in Jeremiam* has the seven tribes of Palestine as the seven vices.

heu quantis mortale genus premit inprobus hostis
armigeris, quanto ferrata satellite ductor
bella gerit, quanta victos dicione triumphat!

(Ham. 406-408)

[Alas, with what armed forces does the ruthless enemy
press upon the race of men, with what attendant trains
under his command does he wage his iron wars, with
what dominion triumph over the conquered!]

In such straits, the soul must counterattack,[42] but where
does it obtain its fighting force? From Christ, answers
Prudentius in no uncertain terms. But the poet's answer was
not automatically forthcoming. The heretical doctrine of
Pelagianism was at this very moment beginning to present
a threat to the Church's doctrine of grace. A Pelagian would
argue that the soul is perfectible and man does not require
God's grace for salvation; that the soul generates its own
virtues to counterattack against the vices. In this respect,
Prudentius is again quite Augustinian, for prior to Augustine's theoretical activity in the Pelagian controversy it was
often assumed that Virtue was an inborn human trait. The
four cardinal virtues had been more or less appropriated
from pagan philosophy, and thinkers of the stature of
Origen had drawn attention to them as ethical principles
but without attaching any specific Christian significance.
Augustine himself first formulated an essentially Ciceronian
definition of virtue—*virtus est animi habitus naturae modo
atque rationi consentaneus* (*De Inventione* 2. 53)—but he
came more and more to emphasize that virtue is the art of
living rightly in respect to eternal happiness; that it must be

---

[42] The soul must certainly reject C. S. Lewis's dictum that fighting
is an activity not proper for most of the virtues. The poet thus cau-
tions about weak souls (*invalidas mentes*)—

quae simplicitate

indociles bellique rudes sub foedere falso
tristis amicitiae primum socia agmina credunt,
Mammoneamque fidem pacis sub amore sequuntur. (*Ham.* 425-428)

supernatural in its finality; and that it comes only with God's grace. In light of current Church thinking on this matter, the nature of Prudentius' virtuous personifications is not just timely, it is advanced.

Prudentius in his invocation describes the counterattack against the vices mounted from within the soul but equipped and led by Christ. The virtues come only with God's grace, and their active fighting is in turn an act of human charity.

> nec enim, bone ductor,
> magnarum Virtutum inopes nervisque carentes
> Christicolas Vitiis populantibus exposuisti.
> ipse salutiferas obsesso in corpore turmas
> depugnare iubes, ipse excellentibus armas
> artibus ingenium, quibus ad ludibria cordis
> oppugnanda potens tibi dimicet et tibi vincat. (11-17)

[For, O kind leader, Thou hast not exposed the followers of Christ to the ravages of the Sins without the help of great Virtues or devoid of strength. Thou thyself dost command relieving squadrons to fight the battle in the body close beset, Thou thyself dost arm the spirit with pre-eminent kinds of skill whereby it can be strong to attack the wantonness in the heart and fight for Thee, conquer for Thee.]

The virtues of the *Psychomachia* are these *excellentes artes* with which the soul is armed by Christ to meet the threats of particular vices, and the vices are the soldiers of the Enemy welcomed into the soul by the sinful will. Accordingly, the soul is sinful at the outset because of its inherent depravity. It is through the grace of God and specifically the agency of Christ that the soul is enabled to combat sin.

The Heroic

From a religious if not a literary point of view, the turning point of the *Psychomachia* has already been passed at its beginning, with the gift of Grace for the embattled soul. Prudentius does not picture for us the prior state of the newly baptized soul, its irresistible motion toward sin impelled by cupidity of will and occasioned by the soul's contact with the body, the stealthy invasion of the Enemy's vicious agents. Nor does he narrate Christ's arming of the soul with its necessary skills: Fides the chief, Pudicitia, Patientia, Mens Humilis, Spes, Sobrietas, Ratio, Operatio, and doubtless other such captains as well as the unnamed common soldiers of the mind, the thoughts and sentiments. He begins the action *in medias res*, armies massed to fight. Here is the first battle:

> prima petit campum dubia sub sorte duelli
> pugnatura Fides, agresti turbida cultu,
> nuda umeros, intonsa comas, exerta lacertos;
> namque repentinus laudis calor ad nova fervens
> proelia nec telis meminit nec tegmine cingi,
> pectore sed fidens valido membrisque retectis
> provocat insani frangenda pericula belli.
> ecce lacessentem conlatis viribus audet
> prima ferire Fidem Veterum Cultura Deorum.
> illa hostile caput phalerataque tempora vittis
> altior insurgens labefactat, et ora cruore
> de pecudum satiata solo adplicat et pede calcat
> elisos in morte oculos animamque malignam
> fracta intercepti commercia gutturis artant,
> difficilemque obitum suspiria longa fatigant.
> exultat victrix legio, quam mille coactam
> martyribus regina Fides animarat in hostem.
> nunc fortes socios parta pro laude coronat
> floribus ardentique iubet vestirier ostro.   (21-39)

[Faith first takes the field to face the doubtful chances of battle, her rough dress disordered, her shoulders bare, her hair untrimmed, her arms exposed; for the sudden glow of ambition, burning to enter fresh contests, takes no thought to gird on arms or armour, but trusting in a stout heart and unprotected limbs challenges the hazards of furious warfare, meaning to break them down. Lo, first Worship-of-the-Old-Gods ventures to match her strength against Faith's challenge and strike at her. But she, rising higher, smites her foe's head down, with its fillet-decked brows, lays in the dust that mouth that was sated with the blood of beasts, and tramples the eyes under foot, squeezing them out in death. The throat is choked and the scant breath confined by the stopping of its passage, and long gasps make a hard and agonizing death. Leaps for joy the conquering host which Faith, their queen, had assembled from a thousand martyrs and emboldened to face the foe; and now she crowns her brave comrades with flowers proportioned to the glory they have won, and bids them clothe themselves in flaming purple.]

Analysis of this scene should begin with the single phrase, *dubia sub sorte duelli / pugnatura Fides.* Why is Faith said to face the doubtful chances of battle? Is it because at first glance she seems weak and unarmed? It is possible to read this phrase as Prudentius' feeble attempt to lend suspense to the scene and to the poem, but such a reading would miss a more profound significance. That the turning point of the allegory has already occurred, Christ having armed the soul with the requisite virtues, does not mean that the action is predetermined. The free will can choose the way of sin even though it is possessed of the means to fight sin. Insofar as the *Psychomachia* is a record of the conversion within one Christian soul, that conversion may be said to be predestined by God; but in the course of Christian soul-struggle, the outcome of each spiritual battle is indeed doubtful. So it is no accident that the poet has begun the narrative action with this phrase, the importance of which is emphasized twice again in two near-reversals for the soul. First, Luxuria all but defeats the army of the virtues with

161

her sweet attractions. Flowers are her weapons, and her strange warfare causes most of the army of virtues to drop their weapons in a state of utter enfeeblement.[43] Later on, after victory has seemed assured and the virtues are marching home singing a song of triumph, Discordia cognomento Heresis is discovered to have insinuated herself among the virtues. As Concordia warns the assembled army even later, there remains the continual danger of new sin: even with Christ present the soul must be vigilant.

What do Faith's doubtful chances convey about her heroism? Faith, we observe, is drawn with little outline but intense color. Her style is not classical. Her paradoxical combination of inner strength and weak external appearance disqualifies her from a place in classical epic, where the hero or heroine must display a dignity of mien to match worthiness of character. Perhaps the most striking feature of this passage is the clash between the warm and vibrant tawdriness of this figure and the brutality she is able to inflict. Also striking is the suddenness with which the action—the shortest single combat of the poem—is completed. Faith may have the fierce courage of the underdog, but this alone cannot account for the speed of her victory, which transpires as if a mysterious metamorphosis were occurring before our eyes. In spite of the illusion of epic reality created through the details of costuming and physical action, the action is clearly "otherworldly" in the sense that it is spiritualized.

If we remember that this heroism takes place within the Christian soul, which in turn exists in spiritual continuity with Church history, its strangeness will disappear. The iconographical details of Faith's appearance do make some psychological sense. Since this is the first battle the soul wages against sin, Faith quite properly has the glow and enthusiasm of a neophyte. Her bedraggled appearance (lost in later scenes) suggests the unsophisticated, unphilosophi-

[43] This action should be glossed by *Ham.* 425-428, quoted n. 42.

cal basis of belief. Tertullian had confessed, "The Son of God was born, I am not ashamed of it because it is shameful; the Son of God died, it is credible for the very reason that it is silly; and, having been buried, He rose again, it is certain because it is impossible."[44] Such paradoxes of "foolish" credence were ridiculed by pagans throughout the decline and fall of paganism. The dying yet victorious heroes of the *Peristephanon Liber* offer witness to such paradoxes. In the *Psychomachia* as well, carried into soul's first battle are the conditions of the great historical contest between the two systems of belief, as the presence of the thousand martyrs on the mental battleground proves. That Cultura Deorum Veterum is the first attacker reflects the fourth-century ecclesiastical history. Faith's disordered dress and untrimmed hair evoke the Church's damaged condition at the time of the persecutions; later episodes will evoke more recent ecclesiastical history. Perhaps by analogy, Faith's condition suggests also the more recent Arian controversy. One is tempted to let the historical relevance of the passage span the century. Fides' soldiers are assembled from a thousand martyrs—their martyrdoms have already occurred, perhaps in the Diocletian persecution. In the present action the final crowning of these martyrs may be meant to symbolize the final crushing of paganism under Theodosius, the political victory of the Church. If so, the present attack of Cultura Deorum Veterum may evoke the circle of Praetextatus and Symmachus and Flavianus; and if so, the correspondence between historical and psychological reality is timely indeed.

However one judges this last issue, it is clear enough that Prudentius is communicating a great deal in a few words about *Romanitas* and the classical tradition. Demonstrably

[44] *De Carne Christi*, 5. Trans. in Cochrane (cited above n. 28), p. 223. Cochrane comments: "This is the notorious *credo quia absurdum* which, by asserting the shameful, the silly, and the impossible as against the evidences of good taste, probability, and reason itself, hurls a defiant challenge in the face of the classical world."

false is the oft repeated charge that he presents a bare allegory decorated by thematically irrelevant epic rhetoric. The reader who is familiar with Vergil and reads the passage above will undoubtedly recognize certain phrases drawn from the *Aeneid*.[45] Its vocabulary is at least sporadically Vergilian, and there is a cluster of actual quotations from the *Aeneid* embedded in this passage. This epic language is not merely decoration; its resonance is heard most loudly as Cultura Deorum Veterum is being trampled under foot. Certain gory details of her hard and agonizing death come right out of the *Aeneid*, and would be so recognized by Prudentius' highly literate audience. While a cluster of Vergilian quotations crowds the figure of Faith's antagonist, none is near Faith. The pattern is significant, for Faith is a Christian character and no fit heroine for the old epic world to accept. Prudentius has ordered epic language, costume, conventional action, and—in other single combats— discourse so as to evoke a heroic tradition associated with the vices. In terms of the larger two-part movement of conversion this association can be seen. It is the first part of the *Psychomachia*, the order of discord and confusion, which is by far the most "heroic" in its themes and which contains the great majority of epic reminiscences. The action of the second part does not break completely with what has preceded it, for here too exist epic tags and, most conspicuously, a number of heroic discourses. And even the building of Sapientia's temple is told in hexameter. Nonetheless, it is generally true that in the second part of the *Psychomachia* the conventions of the heroic are dissolved in the mystical symbolism of Scripture.

I intend to demonstrate in Chapter IV that the epic form of the *Psychomachia* is a vehicle for anti-pagan literary satire. This does not deny Christian heroism in the *Psychomachia*. The virtues may fight heroically as they should, yet this may be accompanied by Prudentius' insistence that the

[45] See Chapter IV.

tradition of Roman epic is now the irrevocable possession of the Church. In the *Psychomachia* the hard and agonizing death of the epic genre as it was known to the ancient world is accompanied by the birth of a new genre of spiritual allegory. Even with this metamorphosis, our poem remains a Roman document. The city of the soul is very much a copy of Rome herself: a strong ruler over the whole world, a stay against the barbarians, the commander of mighty legions. Roman imperial iconography can be located in the victory of the virtues over the vices. On late Roman coinage (possibly handled by Prudentius) the ruler, after victory, crushes underfoot his defeated enemy.[46] But if the heroism of the virtues is Roman, it is the Roman heroism that Prudentius saw in the victory of Theodosius at Frigidus, not in the victory of Augustus at Actium. The Roman legions have converted to Christ. Once again, the end of paganism:

> illa hostile caput phalerataque tempora vittis
> altior insurgens labefactat, et ora cruore
> de pecudum satiata solo adplicat et pede calcat
> elisos in morte oculos. . . .

> [But she (Fides), rising higher, smites her foe's head down, with its fillet-decked brows, lays in the dust that mouth that was sated with the blood of beasts, and tramples the eyes under foot, squeezing them out in death. . . .]

Even as Vergil is being mocked, we are reminded of the words of the Psalmist, a poet of God, prefiguring Christ's victory over the monsters of sin:

> Super aspidem et basiliscum ambulabis,
> Et conculcabis leonem et draconem. (Psalm 90:13)

> [Thou shalt walk upon the asp and the basilisk: and thou shalt trample under foot the lion and the dragon.]

[46] P. Verdier, "Virtues and Vices, Iconography of," *New Catholic Encyclopedia*, Vol. 14 (New York, 1967).

We shall come to appreciate that the *Psychomachia* is heroic narrative not because of its Vergilian presence but in spite of it. Its heroism is essentially scriptural, is in emulation of the patriarchs and other just warriors in the Old Testament, and follows the precepts of the Gospels and Pauline Epistles. As the process of Christian conversion moves forward within the poem, conventions of Roman epic become more and more exposed as vehicles of sin and error until the epic genre itself becomes converted to the scriptural genre of mystic vision. The next two chapters will take up the emulation of Scripture and the anti-Vergilian irony in detail. For the present, I may conclude that as an allegorical narrative the *Psychomachia* is essentially scriptural, for it imitates epic mainly in its first part—through which dangers Christians wish to pass—and for special effects in fragments; but not at all does it value epic's basic idea.

The *Psychomachia*, then, is a heroic poem about late fourth-century *milites Christi* within the soul of the Pauline *miles Christi*. Its mental locus of action responds to the new psychological interests of a post-Nicene audience; its allegorical mode, however, is very much the product of a single poetic intelligence. Prudentius has translated the authoritative scriptural metaphors of warfare and temple worship into one coherent personification allegory, thereby guaranteeing that the typical *historia* of the soul's conversion will be spiritually true and will be apprehended. Scripture, however, has not supplied him with all the literary techniques necessary to convey these truths to his aristocratic audience. His rounded personifications of the virtues and vices (but not his application of the trope to moral abstractions) reveal the influence of the literature learned in *rhetor*'s school, of Vergil and Statius especially, as well as the contemporary influence of Claudian. His employment of the classical illusion of space-time continuum reveals the general influence of Roman epic, only secondarily the influence of the historical narrative in Scripture. But these literary techniques are not of lasting importance. They create the rhetorical but not the substantial form of the allegory. Even the classical illusion of epic space and time soon becomes transformed into mystic vision; the tableau of personifications dissolves into purely spiritual, non-visual symbolism. The poet perhaps justly credits the totality of the allegory to Christ, for as the allegory proceeds toward its consummation, its scriptural themes leap out of their classical form and literally build new scriptural forms. The *Psychomachia*'s Christian themes create and dominate its form.

Salvation History and the Soul

THE *Psychomachia* begins with Genesis, ends with the Apocalypse, and has at its poetic center Christ's teaching. It thus resembles the *Dittochaeon* in its total scriptural design and movement. But whereas the *Dittochaeon* consists of a series of symmetrically arranged historical emblems (with Christ's Incarnation at the middle), the *Psychomachia*'s design is essentially moral rather than historical. Sacred history in the *Psychomachia* exists in order to generate a moral—specifically psychological—exegesis; the poet's selection of sacred historical referents is governed by the requirements of the Christ-inspired personification allegory. This tropological function of sacred history is evident in the periodic Old Testament emblems, which are arranged not chronologically but according to the allegorical situation at hand. Each of the seven combats (with the possible exception of that between Fides and Cultura Deorum Veterum)[1] has its prefiguration: the deeds of David, Judith, Job, and others are cited as relevant, and, indeed, operative upon the actions of the virtues and vices. On a larger scale, the career of the first believer, Abraham, is arranged in the "Praefatio" so as to parallel the allegorical career of the psyche. On the largest scale, the movement from Genesis to Apocalypse can be interpreted in terms of the soul's moral progress and final stasis with God.

This careful parallelism between soul-struggle and scriptural history is not gratuitous. It is not due solely to aesthetic considerations—although it produces much beauty. Prudentius' Christian moral outlook naturally perceives similarities

---

[1] Discussed below, p. 184.

between psychological and historical experience: both the soul and mankind collectively exist in a turmoil of imperfection; both desire God and struggle to progress toward God. Thus the temple symbolizing Pauline perfection in Christ is the goal of the soul-struggle, and the temple symbolizing New Jerusalem is the goal of salvation history. According to Christian eschatology, the two temples are in fact identical. The comparison between them, therefore, is not a simile or an anology and is not artificial. Rather, a vital and operative connection—usually termed figural or typological—joins the moral world of the allegory with the world of history at large.

A TYPOLOGICAL POET

Scripture is not for Prudentius a record of past history removed from the present. In the twin prefaces of the *Contra Orationem Symmachi*, he presents the figures of Peter and Paul as operative in his own tasks *contra paganos*. Similarly, the Cain and Abel of the *Hamartigenia* are not legendary figures of the dim past: they prefigure Marcion and Christ, who in turn manifest their presence among contemporary heretics and orthodox believers. Prudentius' prefaces put into practice a dictum of Cyprian on the relevance of Scripture. Commenting on Luke 21:31, where Jesus speaks of the signs of the world's dissolution, Cyprian asserts that the Gospel refers directly to the plague then (A.D. 252) raging in Carthage: "With the encouragement of His foreseeing Word (*providae vocis hortatu*), the Lord, instructing, teaching, preparing and strengthening the people of His Church for complete endurance of future events, predicted these coming events (*haec ventura praedixerit*)."[2]

In applying biblical texts to their own situations, Cyprian and Prudentius are merely extending a basic principle of interpretation held by Jesus, the four evangelists, and Paul.[3]

[2] *De Mortalitate*, 2. Trans. Fahey (cited Chapter II, n. 23), p. 50.
[3] For typological interpretation of the Old Testament—i.e., of what

169

Thus many events in the life of Christ are said to occur at least in part so that a particular prophecy might be fulfilled, and Christ's teachings are said not to have destroyed, but to have fulfilled, the Law of Moses. Erich Auerbach, who has done much good in bringing this Christian historical outlook to bear on criticism of Christian literature, explains: "Figural interpretation establishes a connection between two events or persons, the first of which signifies not only itself but also the second, while the second encompasses or fulfills the first. The two poles of the figure are separate in time, but both, being real events or figures, are within time, within the stream of historical life. Only the understanding of the two persons or events is a spiritual act, but this spiritual act deals with concrete events whether past, present, or future, and not with concepts or abstractions. . . ."[4] This definition is useful up to the last phrase. Auerbach correctly insists against the neo-Platonists, Manicheans, and modern symbolists, upon the essential historicity of Christianity. The Incarnation is meaningless if not a real event in the world, and in order to be morally operative it requires a context of past and future. The evolution of typological exegesis is closely tied to the Church's struggle against Marcion and other gnostics, who denied the validity of the Old Testament events in a salvational plan. In attempting to guarantee our appreciation of this, however, Auerbach has overstated the truth. He has failed to include in the figural scheme of Scripture great metaphorical structures of an ethical nature that were considered by Christ and Paul to

---

was then Scripture—by Jesus and Paul, see Matthew 12:39-40; Luke 11:29-30; John 5:46; Romans 5:14; Galatians 4:21-31; I Corinthians 10:6, 11; II Corinthians 3:14; Colossians 2:16-17. Also Luke 24:44: "And he said to them: These are the words which I spoke to you while I was yet with you, that all things must needs be fulfilled which are written in the law of Moses and in the prophets and in the psalms concerning me."

[4] "Figura," *Scenes from the Drama of European Literature* (cited Critical Introd., n. 32), p. 53.

have been prefigured by Old Testament events. Here the Prudentian themes of warfare and temple-building naturally come to mind, themes which do deal with concepts and, occasionally, with abstractions. Neither the New Testament figuralists, Jesus and Paul, nor patristic writers before Prudentius excluded concepts and abstractions from the category of reality.

Auerbach's definition may be supplemented with another: "Figural prophecy implies the interpretation of one worldly event through another; the first signifies the second, the second fulfills the first. Both remain historical events; yet both, looked at in this way, have something provisional and incomplete about them; they point to one another and both point to something in the future, something still to come, which will be the actual, real, and definitive event. This is true not only of Old Testament prefiguration, which points forward to the incarnation and the proclamation of the gospel, but also of these latter events, for they too are not the ultimate fulfillment, but themselves a promise of the end of time and the true kingdom of God."[5] Again a qualification is necessary. Auerbach correctly observes that the Christian historical viewpoint encompasses the entire length of time from Creation to Last Judgment. Events in the Old Testament prefigure the events of the Gospels, these in turn prefigure events in the Apocalypse. Perhaps erring in the direction of historical determinism, he leaves out the moral sense of Scripture in his time scheme; he fails to observe that the major reason why figural interpretation is a "spiritual act" (as he admits) is that it implies a present moral course of action for the interpreter to follow. How the interpreter of Scripture is able to approach ethical problems in the world and in his own soul will determine (God willing) his own status as sheep or goat at the Last Judgment. While God may be said to have foreknowledge of each person's condition at the end of time, it is the actions of each person which decide that condition.

[5] "Figura," *Scenes from the Drama of European Literature*, p. 58.

171

As a Christian conscious of his existence between Incarnation and Last Judgment and of his moral responsibility in light of the Incarnation, Prudentius considers the moral sense of Scripture to be the most important. Typology cannot be for him a matter of aesthetics; his point of view is not primarily from above the scheme of history, but from within it. Enveloped by the darkness of sin and ignorance, he finds that typological interpretation of Scripture provides some light, some hope, some knowledge of his place in the scheme of history, and consequently some aid for his will in choosing to love God rather than the world. As a poet, his use of scriptural types and imitation of typological structures is a moral act performed as a stay against sin's confusion. It stems from his own salvational desires and conforms with the practice of his Church, that is, with the interpretation of Scripture for the community of Christians.[6]

Prudentius' poems display a consistent desire to superimpose the pattern of sacred history upon the moral occasion. In the *Dittochaeon* most obviously, the pattern itself forms the subject, one suited to the poem's probable function in the design of a pictorial Church program. Amidst its overall pattern of concordance between the Old and New Testaments are many typological expressions, as when the twelve stones in the River Jordan (Joshua 3:4) are *in formam discipularum* ("prefiguring the disciples" [*Ditt.* 60]). The *Dittochaeon*'s quatrain on King David contains some important Christological figures used in the *Psychomachia*:

Regia mirifici fulgent insignia David,
sceptrum, oleum, cornu, diadema et purpura et ara.
omnia conveniunt Christo, chlamys atque corona,
virga potestatis, cornu crucis, altar, olivum. (*Ditt.*, 77-80)

[6] The interpretation of Scripture is the *sine qua non* of all early Christian sermons. It is not esoteric activity. For education of catechumens as the aim of Ambrose's exegesis, see below, p. 223.

[The marvellous David's royal emblems shine bright,—
sceptre, oil, horn, diadem, purple robe and altar. They
all befit Christ, the robe and crown, the rod of power, the
horn of the cross, the altar, the oil.]

In the *Liber Cathemerinon*, whose liturgical song would be
heard within the interior Church space ordered by the
Dittochaeon,[7] nearly every hymn evokes Old Testament
characters and events for their Christological sense. In the
"Hymn for Epiphany" (XII), for example, the antagonism
between Pharaoh and Moses prefigures that between Herod
and Christ; Christ is also the new Abraham and the new
David uniting all the warring nations in one Church. Unlike
that of the *Dittochaeon*, the typology of these hymns lacks
expression as structural symmetry, yet is more openly tropological. The Christological figure is taken forward into
the present and applied to the practical spirituality of worship at a particular time of day, season, or other occasion.
Thus the "Hymn for the Burial of the Dead" (X) displays
a fourfold exegetical movement, but does so without calling
attention to any system or structure. The subject naturally
calls up Lazarus, whose experience is prefigured by the
burial story of Tobit. Once this connection between Old
and New Testament events is visible, there follows a moral
discussion on the meaning of death and burial and on the
body-soul relationship, and this leads to the Christian duty
to care for the entombed bones of one's fellow men against
the resurrection of the body. As is typical of the *Cathemerinon*, the past and future events of Scripture are brought to
bear on the moral occasion.

The typology of the *Peristephanon Liber* also devolves
on the moral plane; but since this martyrological collection lacks the *Cathemerinon*'s diversity of seasonal and daily
occasions, its typology is quite limited. The martyrs' pas-

[7] See Chapter I, n. 2.

sions have been prefigured by the Passion of Christ.[8] All
Christians, in turn, are supposed to emulate the martyrs'
intermediary imitation of Christ by suffering willingly the
pains of this world. In *Peristephanon* X, St. Romanus argues
at length in the hope of converting his pagan torturers and
judges. After a sharp harangue against the gods of Rome,
he traces the sign of the cross through salvation history.

> crux ista Christi, quam novellam dicitis,
> nascente mundo factus ut primum est homo,
> *expressa signis*, expedita est litteris:
> adventus eius mille per miracula
> *praenuntiatus* ore vatum consono.
> reges, prophetae, iudicesque et principes
> virtute, bellis, cultibus, sacris, stilo
> non destiterunt pingere formam crucis.
> crux *praenotata*, crux *adumbrata* est prius,
> crucem vetusta conbiberunt saecula.
> tandem retectis vocibus propheticis
> aetate nostra conprobata antiquitas
> coram refulsit ore conspicabili,
> ne fluctuaret veritas dubia fide,
> si non pateret teste visu comminus.   (*Per.* X, 621-635)

[This cross of Christ which you call modern, when at
the world's birth man was first created, was clearly shown
by signs and set forth in writings, and his coming was
foretold through a thousand wonders by the mouth of
prophets all in harmony. Kings, prophets, judges and rulers by their prowess and wars, their rites and offerings
and their pen, did not cease to depict the form of the
cross; the cross was predicted, the cross was prefigured,
those olden times absorbed the idea of the cross. At last
the words of the prophets were made plain and in our

[8] An interesting exception is *Per.* V, 221-224, where the prefiguration is from II Maccabees 7 and from an apocryphal legend of the
martyrdom of Isaiah. Discussed in Thomson's *Prudentius* (Loeb),
Vol. 2, p. 201.

time antiquity was justified, shining before our eyes from
a visible countenance, so that truth should not be uncertain and its reliability in doubt through not being dis-
closed face to face, with the testimony of sight.][9]

This statement is of obvious relevance to the ordeals
Romanus is undergoing, and it amounts to his confession of
faith. A few lines later he says, "That cross is ours, *we*
mount the gibbet" (*crux illa nostra est, nos patibulum
ascendimus*, 641). But the meaning of *nostra* is not confined
to Romanus' own experience on the *patibulum*: it is quickly
expanded to include all Christians for whom Christ dies
and conquers death. The moralization, that is to say, is general and theological—beyond martyrology.

Prudentius varies his use of typology according to genre
and audience. The typological prefaces of the orations contain an elaborately specific, if not extravagant, application of
Scripture to the contemporary scene. When scriptural history is given expression as Church iconography, figuralism
is confined to prophetic Christological essentials, to the basic
Christian *mythos* already revealed in Scripture. The lyrics
contain many such figures but expand them outward to the
moral present in homiletic fashion. Granted this variation
in the application of typology, the same mental habit is evidenced in all of Prudentius' works. This should not surprise
us. Jerome and Augustine use figural arguments in their
letters to pagans as well as in their sermons, and Ambrose's
interpretation of Scripture is basically the same for other
Christians as against Symmachus' *Relatio*. Despite occasional brilliance and originality in its application, Prudentius' typology is without eccentricity in its method and conforms with late fourth-century practice.

Indeed, that Prudentius is self-consciously imitating his

[9] My italics emphasize the technical vocabulary of exegesis. Notice
the idea that not only events are prefiguring, but words and pictures.
Notice also the role of non-historical reality in typology: events are
said to have absorbed an idea.

175

fellow Church writers—not poets, but exegetes, homilists, theologians—is strongly suggested by his use of their technical vocabulary. Add to the italicized words in Romanus' speech, above, the following examples:

> sic stulta Pharaonis mali
> edicta quondam fugerat
> Christi *figuram praeferens*
> Moses, receptor civium.   (*Cath.* XII, 141-144)

[It was thus that Moses, the protector of his people, prefiguring Christ, once escaped the wicked Pharaoh's foolish proclamation.]

> ergo *ex futuris* prisca *coepit* fabula
> factoque primo *res notata est* ultima,
>
> . . . .
>
> agnosco nempe quem *figura haec denotet.* . . .
>   (*Ham.*, Prf., 25-32)

[So the tale of olden times took its beginning from things that were to be, and the last deed was indicated by the first. . . . It is plain to see whom this figure denotes. . . .]

> sed cadit in faciem plebs non visura *profundae*
> *legis in effigie* scriptum *per enigmata* Christum.
> infelix, quae luce oculos praestricta paventes
> texerit et presso faciem *velarit* amictu!
> at nos *reiecto* Christum *velamine* coram
> cernimus atque Deum vultu speculamur aperto,
> nec *sub lege* gravi depressa fronte iacemus,
> sed *legis radium* sublimi agnoscimus ore.   (*Apo.* 330-337)

[But the people fall on their faces and will not see Christ written symbolically in the figure of the law's mystery. Unhappy race, in that they covered their trembling eyes before the dazzling light and pressed close their garments to veil their faces! But we have thrown back the veil and see Christ in person, looking upon God with countenance uncovered, nor do we lie with head bowed down under the weight of the law, but with face lifted up we recognize the law's splendour.]

Prudentius' vocabulary includes these terms (with their variant inflections): *effigies*, *enigmata*, *exemplum*, *figura*, *historia*, *imago*, *mysterium*, *mysticus*, *sacramentum*, *signum*, *similis*, *species*, and *umbra*. In addition, a number of metaphors for seeing, veiling and unveiling, illuminating, and so on are associated with scriptural interpretation. Prefigurations of Christ are often denoted by means of verbs containing *prae*-suffixes. Finally, the *id est* so common to exegetical prose is carried silently into the poems, especially where the figural symbolism of things in the Old Testament is concerned—for example, in the phrase *cornu crucis* of the *Dittochaeon*. (Not part of this vocabulary are the words *allegoria* and *typus*, but this lack need not concern us.)[10] So nearly all the exegetical terms employed by authors known to Prudentius are in his poems. His exegetical conventionality does not negate literary creativity. The last quotation shows an especially imaginative use of typological vocabulary for ironic effect. An attack against the Jews, who of course will not subject their Scriptures to a Christian allegorization, is accomplished by means of negatives attached to exegetical jargon. The Jews will not see, they veil their faces against what should be unveiled as the true Christian mystery, they remain bowed *sub lege* and are therefore *infelix*. Prudentius, we may be assured, associates Christian felicity with the figural interpretation of Scripture then being promulgated by the Church.

The *Psychomachia*'s typological vocabulary and argument resemble that of other poems. They also offer the greatest proof of Prudentius' flexibility and creativity in this field. The *Psychomachia*'s typology is essential structure as in the *Dittochaeon*, and it is a recurring mode of interpreta-

---

[10] The absence of *allegoria* (used by Paul; not in Cyprian's works) and of *typus* is not startling: these terms have no specialized meaning at this time, and those used by Prudentius are interchangeable.

tion used when appropriate (in the manner of a sermon). Granted that the poem's goal of ideal stasis in Christian charity requires structural perfection, the linear movement of the action within the representative soul requires a concurrent stress on the occasional, practical tropology we have observed in the lyrical compositions. Even as the types together form a design signifying the soul's conformity with salvation history, these types singly answer the moral needs of the putative reader who is not saved, who himself experiences the attacks of the vices, who needs Christ to show him the excellent skills of the virtues.

Types of Moral Warfare

Scriptural characters have been marshalled forth to reinforce seven variations on the Pauline theme of moral warfare. Little purpose would be served by detailed discussion of every such character—the task would be too lengthy and too repetitive. Instead, I offer a schematic outline of the prefigurations (page 179) and supplement this with selective commentary. Within the several battle scenes, these characters' mode of existence varies: some prefigure the virtues, others the vices; while most are named by the personifications in their discourses, some are named by the poet's persona as relevant to the action at hand, and one (Job) is so named as a character present in the narrative. The number of types also varies from battle to battle, and so does the fullness of detail with which these types are drawn. My outline gives the types, their scriptural sources, and their mode of existence in the allegory. (Types contained in speeches of personifications are indicated by arrows from respective speakers; others occur as features of the poet's commentary or, in Job's case, in the action itself.)

The schematic outline reveals a pragmatism in the typology of the battle scenes. Inconsistencies of structure are obvious enough, and these derive from the moral themes themselves rather than simply from the need for aesthetic

I

	Fides	Veterum Cultura Deorum
Acts and Church History	1000 Martyrs	

II

	Pudicitia	Libido (the Sodomite)
Judith 13	Judith —————→	Holofernes
Matt. 1 and John 1	Mary	
Matt. 3:13	Jordan River: BAPTISM	

III

	Patientia	Ira
Job	Job	

IV

	Mens Humilis and Spes	Superbia
Genesis 2 and 3		Adam
I Kings 17	David ←	→ Goliath
Matt. 23:12	*sententia Christi*	

V

	Sobrietas	Luxuria
Exodus 17:3	Moses: water from rock	
Exodus 16:14	manna	
Matt. 26:26 etc.	*corpus Christi*: EUCHARIST	
I and II Kings	David	
I Kings 15:33	Samuel	
I Kings 14:43	Jonathan	

VI

	Ratio	Avaritia
Gospels and Acts 1:18		→ Iscariot
Joshua 7		→ Achar

TRANSITUS

	Triumphant Virtues	Defeated Vices
Job 38	God the thunderer	
Apoc. 3:21 and 4:1	Christ in majesty	
Exodus 14	Israel crossing Red Sea	Drowned Egyptians

VII

	Fides and Concordia	Discordia cognomento
		Heresis
Deut. 13:13 and II Cor. 6:15		Belial.

179

variety. For example, it is morally appropriate for Pride's way of introducing Adam to differ from the way Chastity introduces Judith and Mary. Variation of typological pattern in the battle scenes may be meant to mirror the order of confusion (caused by the state of sin) in the mind of the allegorical Christian. Within each battle scene, however, the moral message conveyed to the reader is quite clear. Particularities of the scriptural prefigurations befit the personified combatants; the rhetoric of the typological presentation sharpens the impact of the allegory's moral message.

Luxuria is the most dangerous of the vices because of her disarming effect, her weakening of the Christian will to struggle against the pleasures she brings. The grave danger posed by her is a fact according to the allegory: at Luxuria's entrance the foot soldiers of the virtuous army begin to swoon, and as she hurls scented flowers (strange warfare!) most of the army drops its weapons. This is amusing on one level, for even as the soldiers are disarmed we are shown that Luxuria is not very attractive—she is slobbering and retching after an all-night drinking bout. Vice is meant to be amusing, of course, but also to be taken seriously. The comedy is instructive: if the soul loses its battle against Luxuria, it will be damned. Such is the allegorical meaning as the virtuous soldiers forsake their moral potency. At this juncture enters Sobrietas, who is appropriately serious, sober, and full of awareness of the present danger to the soul.

In this most precarious of battles are no less than five scriptural references. All are directly intelligible, all can be discovered in early Christian sermons dealing with the subject of combatting "Luxuria." There is nothing abstruse or mystical in their typology, for these Old Testament persons can be emulated directly. Yet all are types of Christ. Rather than lessening the pragmatic worth of the typology, however, the Christological sense increases it in two ways. First and most importantly, it reminds the reader that the basic reason for fighting Luxuria is a Christian reason, that the

180

context of moral action is faith in the Incarnation and in the resultant possibilities of human salvation. Second, it reminds the reader that Christ the Savior fought Luxuria by fasting forty days in the desert, by living abstemiously and soberly, by embracing the opposite of Luxuria, pain and death, for our salvation. Now as imperfect human beings we cannot emulate the excellence of Christ's human nature, but the moral lessons of the Old Testament are accessible to us, and we can recognize in Samuel and Jonathan aids to a practical moral problem that we may face.

Prudentius' treatment of Job further reveals his awareness of the moral proximity of the Old Testament. There is no anachronism conveyed when this Old Testament character enters the very action of the personification allegory. Patientia at this juncture has witnessed the irate suicide of Ira, a frustrated response to Patientia's patient endurance of her weapons. As in the battle of Luxuria versus Sobrietas, the moral lesson is mainly revealed in the comic, mannered heroic action of the antagonists. Patientia drives home the point in a short speech: that the warfare of the new Christian virtues is often passive, yet is no less effective; that fury is its own enemy. Now Job is discovered, and his typology reinforces the moral lesson.

> haec effata secat medias inpune cohortes
> egregio comitata viro; nam proximus Iob
> haeserat invictae dura inter bella magistrae,
> fronte severus adhuc et multo funere anhelus,
> sed iam clausa truci subridens ulcera vultu,
> perque cicatricum numerum sudata recensens
> millia pugnarum, sua praemia, dedecus hostis.
> illum diva iubet tandem requiescere ab omni
> armorum strepitu, captis et perdita quaeque
> multiplicare opibus, nec iam peritura referre. (162-171)

[So saying, she makes her way unharmed through the midst of the battalions, escorted by a noble man; for Job had clung close to the side of his invincible mistress

181

throughout the hard battle, hitherto grave of look and panting from the slaughter of many a foe, but now with a smile on his stern face as he thought of his healed sores and, by the number of his scars, recounted his thousands of hard-won fights, his own glory and his foes' dishonour. Him the heavenly one bids rest at last from all the din of arms and with the riches of his spoils make manifold restitution for all his losses, carrying home things that shall no more be lost.]

Does this entry of a historical person into the allegorical battlefield violate decorum? I think not. For one thing, the placement of Job among the virtues and vices, the thoughts and sentiments, and other mental faculties may simply suggest that the representative Christian mind is filled with Scripture. In this sense, it makes no qualitative difference whether a scriptural character accompanies a virtue physically or occurs within a virtue's speech. For another thing, the same interchange between the moral and historical worlds occurs elsewhere with the movement reversed: when the psychological character Hope enters the Old Testament. After Spes has decapitated Superbia, she rehearses the apt story of David and Goliath, and she claims that she was physically present when David went forth against the Philistine champion: "That day the lad, in the ripening of his valour, followed me" (*me tunc ille puer virtutis pube secutus*, 300).

Job and Spes have in common that they exist throughout the time span of Scripture. David following Hope is not simply fighting a giant; as the ancestor (Matt. 1) and prefiguration of Christ, he is also, as psalmist, the hopeful prophet of Christ. Sharing this temporal field, Hope exists in Old Testament times and continues to exist after the Incarnation. Hope against Christ's Second Coming is present in the mind of each Christian. At the conclusion of her discourse, Hope leaves the battlefield and flies up to heaven, and the sense is anagogic.

> mirantur euntem
> Virtutes tolluntque animos in vota volentes
> ire simul, ni bella duces terrena retardent.
> configunt Vitiis seque ad sua praemia servant. (306-309)

[The Virtues marvel at her as she goes and lift up their
hearts in longing, desiring to go with her, did not earthly
warfare detain them in command. They join in conflict
with the Vices and reserve themselves for their own due
reward.]

Job also moves through history, through the representative
mind of the personification allegory, and upwards to
heaven; by the time he has received *sua praemia* and is
released from the struggle, he has increased in virtue incrementally. It may well be that Prudentius' Job owes his existence in part to the *De Interpellatione Job et David* of
Ambrose: ". . . no one receives the crown except him who
has contested lawfully. . . . Job suffered distress, but he
withstood and carried the burden of the words next to that
of the wounds. The president of the contest saw him; from
out of the cloud and the storm, He gave His hand to him
as he struggled, declared that Job's opponents had suffered
a grievous fall, proclaimed him the victor, and gave him the
crown."[11] The non-specificity of the commentary releases
Job from the Book of Job, makes him a soldier of God
under the New Law. Prudentius' Job is likewise a saved
Christian, deserving of eternal reward after his victory over
evil forces. His ulcers' scars have long since healed. Are
they not also the scars of the martyrs' thousand wounds?[12]

Job's and Spes's modernity accords with the other recent
ecclesiastical history in the *Psychomachia*. During the first

---

[11] *De Interpellatione Job et David*, 3 (7-8), from *Saint Ambrose:
Seven Exegetical Works* (cited Chapter II, n. 25), p. 357.

[12] For Job in the context of martyrdom see also Cyprian, *De Bono
Patientiae*, 18; Tertullian, *De Patientia*, 14. The Cyprian passage especially stands as a precedent for Prudentius' joining the type with the
virtue.

battle, Faith's emblematic thousand martyrs are of course drawn from post-New Testament times (although their numbers originate in the New Testament). Near the end of the poem (794), Concordia names the fourth-century heretics Photinus and Arius as exempla of the menaces to the soul's well-ordered society. There are other such allusions and evocations in between. References to recent Church history add to the basic effect gained by modeling the virtues' social organization on the Roman Empire; they offer poetic proof that the virtues work in the world, that they are more than psychological. Each time a virtue wins, the moral lesson also advertises the social well-being of the Church. The fact that many of these victorious Christian virtues are un-Roman and anti-heroic in terms of Roman traditions contributes much of the *Psychomachia*'s humor. Superbia, the most heroic and Roman vice of all, calls Mens Humilis a "newcomer" to the moral struggle: *nunc advena nudus / nititur antiquos, si fas est, pellere reges* (210-211). The repeated miracle of the battle scenes is that these passive newcomers, these underdogs and weaklings, get the victory. On this score, their heroism resembles that in the *Peristephanon Liber*. Because of inner faith in Christ, Theodosius wins at the Frigidus, the churches of Peter and Paul rise up as Rome's most conspicuous monuments, and the thousand martyrs wear the purple and the crowns of glory.

The sacred history depicted in the warfare section of the *Psychomachia*, then, includes scriptural and later events in an unbroken chain. This can be seen in the first battle where Faith, as we have already seen, is a radically modern virtue. She is followed by a thousand martyrs, and she would seem to be unique in being without an emblematic Old Testament prefiguration. Yet the personification allegory as it unfolds shows a series of allusions to Old Testament faith in Christ. And Faith is in fact prefigured by Abraham, the poem's most important Old Testament character. Abraham is a type of Faith because, as the first line of the "Praefatio" announces, he first showed the way of believing—*Senex fidelis prima credendi via / Abram.* A similar conflation of scriptural and ecclesiastical history is implied in Faith's antagonist. Paganism and the "old gods" are not the exclusive property of Rome. The bloody sacrifices so pleasing to Cultura Deorum Veterum occur not only in the *taurobolia* of the fourth-century mysteries, but in the Old Testament rites of Baal.[13]

This implied historical range is explicit in the second battle, between Pudicitia and Libido. Libido is once denoted "the Sodomite," which locates her ancestry in the moral history of the Old Testament.[14] At the same time Lust is an oft attacked vice in the early Christian period, one of concern to Prudentius and to many other writers. Both scriptural and recent history are united in the lengthy speech of the victorious Pudicitia (Chastity). She begins by offering an account of her own antecedents in Scripture. She cites the Old Testament heroine Judith, who saved her people by going to bed with Holofernes, the lecherous Assyrian tyrant, and by cutting off his head while yet preserving her chastity. Pudicitia explains the conventional Christological sense. Judith prefigured our times (*tempora nostra figurat*, 67) in that our times began with the Virgin Mary's bearing the divine child. The new flesh, created from a power on high, was pure, and made possible man's new purity. Lust lies conquered *post Mariam* (88) by authority of Chastity, who has now come to signify much more than bodily purity. In the course of her exposition of the Judith story, Chastity has offered a full treatment of the divine and

[13] Fides' last battle is set in figural relationship with the Old Testament, the prefiguration of Discordia-Hereses being Belial. Abraham is discussed later in this chapter.

[14] There is little reason to think that Prudentius wishes to elevate Sodomy (the monastic vice) to a major vice. "Sodomite" is a descriptive typological adjective, not part of the vice's name; she is elsewhere called simply Libido. For figurative, generalized use of Sodom, see *Ham.* 723-777. When Prudentius attacks effeminacy as a social vice (*Ham.* 279-299), he puts it among other manifestations of Luxuria, or Indulgence.

185

human natures of Christ, of the meaning of the Incarnation, and of man's possibilities of salvation. The virtue, it should be remembered, has been explaining her own evolving significance through history. Her significance within the Church, she now suggests metaphorically, is contained in the sacrament of Baptism. Her actions now demonstrate the typology she has expounded:

> dixerat haec et laeta Libidinis interfectae
> morte Pudicitia gladium Iordanis in undis
> abluit infectum, sanies cui rore rubenti
> haeserat et nitidum macularat vulnere ferrum.
> expiat ergo aciem fluviali docta lavacro
> victricem victrix, abolens baptismate labem
> hostilis iuguli; nec iam contenta piatum
> condere vaginae gladium, ne tecta rubigo
> occupet ablutum scabrosa sorde nitorem,
> catholico in templo divini fontis ad aram
> consecrat, aeterna splendens ubi luce coruscet.   (98-108)

[So spake Chastity, and rejoicing in the death of Lust, whom she had slain, washed her stained sword in the waters of Jordan; for a red dew of gore had clung to it and befouled the bright steel from the wound. So the conqueress deftly cleanses the conquering blade by bathing it in the stream, dipping it in to wash away the stain of blood that came from her foe's throat; and, no longer content to sheathe the purified sword, lest rust unseen engross the clean, bright surface with its dirty scruf, she dedicates it by the altar of the divine spring in a Catholic temple, there to shine and flash with unfading light.]

These actions occur within the era of the New Law. Although the Jordan River is mentioned throughout Scripture as a place of dramatic spiritual passages (for example, Elijah's), its main typological impact derives from the New Testament: Christ was baptized in its waters (Matt. 3:13).

The *fons* also is symbolically Christ.[15] The passage may more particularly represent the Church's present-day sacramental activity. While the constituent parts of Baptism, water and the blessing in the name of the Trinity, are attested in the New Testament (John 3:5; Matt. 28:19), the full force of the trinitarian blessing would not emerge until after the Council of Constantinople (381), when the nature of the Trinity is defined. While the word *catholicus* in our passage is not quite a neologism—first being used in a Christian sense by Ignatius of Antioch—its full force could not emerge till the fourth century.

As with the presence of Job in the allegory, such typology may seem to threaten decorum. In this case, how can the sacramental activity of the Church be located inside the representative soul? That sacraments affect the psyche is of course a matter of Christian doctrine, but this process involves a mystery perhaps inexpressible in language. The Pudicitia episode in its attempt to express this process creates a complex interaction between microcosm and macrocosm: allegory enfolds allegory. The episode raises theoretical questions as to whether narrative can convey multiplex senses that are logically dissociated.

In the passage (66-88) before the above quotation, a personified virtue within the mind, Pudicitia, has summoned up a pattern of history external to the mind in order to expand the meaning of the mental action. This pattern of history has consisted of the Judith-Mary-Christ-Baptism typology, and its complexity already requires high poetic intelligence to be rhetorically ordered. Presumably it is being so ordered, for though great typological and theological vistas are visible outside the world of the allegory, these are evoked from within the representative fictive mind. For this extra-mental reality is revealed by Pudicitia's indirect discourse. At this juncture, however, the mental personification performs an action (the washing of the sword) requir-

[15] See n. 22 below for the names of Christ.

187

ing a perspective from outside the mind; yet its agent is inside the mind. The bloody sword cleansed in the Jordan River is perhaps human nature, created in God's image; the blood the stain of sin; the water is Baptism in Christ; and the scabbard into which the sword will not be returned is the sinful flesh (metaphorically) of the fallen man. The cleansed sword will reside in the Catholic temple, where it will shine and flash with an unfading light; that is, salvation will be from within the Church. This is an allegory within the personification allegory, and one which complicates the inside-outside perspective of the narrative.

But this complication is only temporary, for the narrative movement of the basic personification allegory soon resumes. Prudentius' control over his allegory is evident in that such complications, inherent in the typological mode, are resolved so quickly. The allegory within allegory is surely intended to add meaning, and in this it succeeds. I doubt that Prudentius' audience experienced confusion over the inside-outside perspective in the *Psychomachia*; such confusion is a modern reaction to the strangeness of typological thinking. For the poet, all the spiritual reality of the *Psychomachia* exists on a continuum of faith, and this is a truer order than the fictive space-time continuum of classical literature. The personification allegory and the scriptural typology, then, merge as one mode, inseparable and mutually interdependent. When there is allegory within allegory, each means the other.

It follows from the idea of spiritual continuity (upon which typological thinking depends) that just as the battles between virtues and vices are all manifestations of the one Christian contest described by St. Paul, so their prefigurations are also interconnected.[16] Scripture being one Word of God revealing one plan of salvation, its major types tend

[16] The struggles' interconnectedness is asserted by Pudicitia (96-97), who has defeated Libido on behalf of all the worshippers of Christ (*Christicolas*); and by Sobrietas, who says that she will open a way for all the virtues: *pando viam cunctis virtutibus* (404).

to be interpreted similarly, that is, in relation to Christ. The advantage of a poet over an exegetical commentator is that the poet is free to select his types. This Prudentius does. He relies on the major types of the Old Testament, those which refer assuredly to Christ. Thus David prefigures Christ; Judith prefigures the Virgin Mother of Christ; the manna given by God prefigures the body of Christ in the Eucharist, and so on. A unity in the typology of the battle scenes obtains from the conventional magnitude of the types themselves.

There is also a basic uniformity of exegetical argument in the several battle scenes. A vice like Superbia we expect to misconstrue Scripture: she makes a hero of Adam by overemphasizing his aspect as the first fallen man—"If it weren't for me, he would still be running around naked!"—and by ignoring his function as a major type of Christ. Although Discordia correctly identifies her scriptural type and latter-day *praeceptor* as Belial, she lacks the moral proclivity to condemn him. But the virtues are virtuous, and they derive their typology conventionally. An Old Testament passage prefigures another in the Gospel, and their interrelation generates a tropological significance for the virtue's action. This exegetical movement may be explicit, as when Pudicitia derives the sequence JUDITH : MARY & CHRIST : CHRISTIAN PURITY (including both chastity and baptismal cleanness). Or it may be only implicit, as when Faith remains altogether silent about her postfiguration in Abraham; or, more characteristically, when Sobrietas derives the sequence DAVID : [CHRIST] : SOBERNESS. In this last case (386), the implied Christological meaning is so obvious that it makes little difference whether or not Christ is actually named. In fact, the name of Christ sounds throughout this passage, and only two lines earlier the Christian virtues have been called "the noble children of Judah" (*vos nobile Iudae / germen*). Even when such suggestive figural phrases are not proximate, the conventionality of a type precludes doubt as to the sequence from Old Testament history, to

189

New Testament history, to now. The eccentric typology of the vices reinforces our apprehension of the unity of Scripture because it is recognizably comic, unvirtuous, atypical. We are assured of a right way to relate Scripture to the moral battles in the mind by the regularity of Christological type and by the regularity of exegetical method.

Finally, the prefigurations themselves are often intersignifying. This creates long thematic chains of scriptural associations, the two most important of which follow the themes of warfare and temple building. We have seen that Concordia gives the prefiguration joining these two themes when she alludes to III Kings 5:3-5.[17] Sobrietas' citation of David supports this allusion:

> excitet egregias mentes celeberrima David
> gloria continuis bellorum exercita curis.   (386-387)

> [Let the renowned David, who never rested from the troubles of war, awake your noble spirits.]

This description is morally relevant to the situation at hand, the fight against Luxuria; it also prepares the expansive theme of David as the necessary warrior, David the warrior as the necessary parent of Solomon the temple-builder. In addition, Chastity's typology relates to the sacrament of Baptism, which in turn is associated with the temple. Such typological cross-references are regular in the *Psychomachia*.

Prudentius' handling of the Red Sea Crossing illustrates well the interconnectedness of types. Here in the only Vergilian simile of the *Psychomachia* are gathered many of the themes of the battles, and the following section of city life and temple building is previewed. The simile of the Red Sea Crossing is applied to the transitional scene of the narrative, the procession of the virtuous armies from the field of battle to the city. As a literal reader of the Old Testa-

---

[17] *Ps.* 804-808, quoted p. 132.

ment realizes, the destruction of the Egyptians does not mean that God's chosen people are home free; so in this scene we witness a false triumph, for the fight against Discordia cognomento Heresis must still be waged. But we also witness an exhilarating celebration of the potentiality of religious victory. When the personified virtues are likened to the Hebrew people fleeing Egypt, their homecoming procession takes on sacramental meaning. More than the deaths of certain vices, the scene celebrates the wonderful operation of God's saving Grace.

> non aliter cecinit respectans victor hiantem
> Istrahel rabiem ponti post terga minacis,
> cum iam progrediens calcaret litora sicco
> ulteriora pede, stridensque per extima calcis
> mons rueret pendentis aquae nigrosque relapso
> gurgite Nilicolas fundo deprenderet imo,
> ac refluente sinu iam redderet unda natatum
> piscibus et nudas praeceps operiret harenas.
> pulsavit resono modulantia tympana plectro
> turba Dei celebrans mirum ac memorabile saeclis
> omnipotentis opus, liquidas inter freta ripas
> fluctibus incisis et subsistente procella
> crescere suspensosque globos potuisse teneri.
> sic expugnata Vitiorum gente resultant
> mystica dulcimodis Virtutum carmina psalmis. (650-664)

[Just so sang victorious Israel, looking back on the yawning gulf of the sea that raged menacingly behind them, when now in their onward march they were treading the further shore dry-foot, as the hanging mountain of water crashed down hissing at their very heels and the flood falling back caught in the depths the dark-skinned people of the Nile, letting the fish swim again in the hollow as it filled, and with a rush covered the sand that had been bared. God's company beat loud the rhythmic timbrels to celebrate the marvellous work of the Almighty, a work to be told to all generations, how banks of water were

191

able to rise up with sea on either hand, cutting a path
through the waves while the wind stayed, and the masses
to be held poised on either side. So when the race of
Vices was subdued the Virtues' holy song rang out in
sweet, melodious psalms.][18]

These beautiful lines recall other references to the flight
from Egypt made during earlier battles. Sobrietas has already spoken of the Hebrews in the desert, the manna, the
water from the rock:

> excidit ergo animis eremi sitis, excidit ille
> fons patribus de rupe datus, quem mystica virga
> elicuit scissi salientem vertice saxi?
> angelicusne cibus prima in tentoria vestris
> fluxit avis, quem nunc sero felicior aevo
> vespertinus edit populus de corpore Christi?   (371-376)

[Have you forgotten, then, the thirst in the desert, the
spring that was given to your fathers from the rock, when
the mystic wand split the stone and brought water leap-
ing from its top? Did not food that angels brought flow
into your fathers' tents in early days, that food which
now with better fortune, in the lateness of time, near the
end of the world's day, the people eats from the body of
Christ?]

The spiritual food prefigured by the manna is of course the
Eucharist—this is explicit. Here it contrasts with the world-

---

[18] Note that in the explication of the simile the two hexameter
lines (663-664) turn pivotally from sins to virtues, from warfare to
hymnody. The total movement of the simile is from a picturing of
chaos to a picturing of divinely caused order. Reversing chronological
order, the drowning of the Egyptians is followed by the procession
of Israelites through the parted sea. Note also the expansion of time:
the horrible moment of destruction and (for the Jews) the exhilara-
tion of salvation realized becomes a later celebration of an earlier
event. Is this unique simile intended as a central miniature of the
action of the *Psychomachia*?

ly food of Luxuria, her all-night banquets of wasted foods and foaming wine. How then does Prudentius carry this sacramental association into the Red Sea Crossing? Not by poetic invention; nor just by drawing all this matter from the Exodus narrative, which has literal continuity. The spiritual continuity is also scriptural. Paul writes in his first Epistle to the Corinthians, "For I would not have you ignorant, brethren, that our fathers were all under the cloud; and all passed through the sea. And all in Moses were baptized, in the cloud and in the sea; and did all eat the same spiritual food; and all drank the same spiritual drink; (And they drank of the spiritual rock that followed them; and the rock was Christ). But with most of them God was not well pleased, for they were overthrown in the desert. Now, these things were done in a figure of us, that we should not covet evil things, as they also coveted" (I Cor. 10:1-6). Sobrietas speaks very much like Paul, mentioning the same details, allegorizing them, even referring to the Hebrews as "our fathers" as she addresses the virtues. There can be no doubt that Prudentius has the Pauline Epistle in mind during the battle between Sobrietas and Luxuria and during the later procession of the virtues. Such typological interconnections, existing already in Scripture and consciously fastened to the *Psychomachia*, let the personification allegory accommodate sacramental symbolism.

That combats between virtues and vices are mystically consummated in Baptism and Eucharist suits the basic conversionary shape of the *Psychomachia*. At this stage of the narrative, however, the sacramental sense is partly concealed by the condition of sinfulness. The virtues are virtuous but imperfect. A final battle, of which the virtues are ignorant, remains to be fought; and the temple of Christ remains to be built. Only when the psyche is ordered in the pure worship of Sapientia can it be well perceived.

Thus far, the virtues in the soul can trace their spiritual ancestry to Old Testament characters and can interpret their ancestry in the light of the New Law. They feel themselves chosen and beloved by God like the Old Testament types with whom they identify. All these scriptural characters are sons of Abraham who follow their patriarch in their belief in God and in willingness to act according to the moral law of God. But all the sons of Abraham are of Adam's lineage, are imbued with Original Sin, are in need of Christ's redemptive Grace. This dual spiritual ancestry generates paradoxical results. The virtues can and do gather a partial moral understanding from their Old Testament prefigurations, but full spiritual understanding can come only through Christ. Meanwhile a full spiritual understanding is impossible; only glimmers of sacramental light shine on the confusion of battle. That the virtues are Christian exegetes in effect guarantees their success in battle, yet this success remains incomplete. Even after six battles are won, the outcome of the war remains in doubt. Like the battles they fight for Christ, the virtues' interpretation of Scripture remains partial and tentative until the final mystic vision of the *Psychomachia*.

PERFECTION IN CHRIST

Sapientia is Christ. In the allegory of the *Psychomachia*, Sapientia cannot be wholly incorporated in the soul so long as the soul is engaged in its struggle against sin. Until the vices are defeated—including the most recent and most deceptive one, Discordia or Heresy—Sapientia's rule over the mind of the Christian remains only potential.

Nearly all of the early Church Fathers are agreed that Sapientia is the Word of God, or Christ. Prudentius asserts the equation in his meticulously doctrinal "Hymnus de Trinitate"—"Of the Father's love was begotten Wisdom, and the same is the Son" (*corde Patris genita est Sapientia, Filius ipse est* [2]). The conventionality of his treating Wisdom as a name of Christ is evidenced in another formulaic reference to the Trinity: *Deus et Sapientia vera / Spiritus*

et Sanctus. . . . (Ham. 164-165).[19] Augustine also uses the
word as a name of God—*Deus Sapientia*—in his early writings, and throughout his career especially as a name of the
second person of the Trinity.[20] According to Augustine,
this Christological meaning does not preclude that of man's
wisdom, but complements it: from the verbal identity
comes the spiritual analogy that man can participate with
the grace of God in the divine Wisdom.[21] While Augustine's treatment of the concept of Sapientia marks an intellectual advance over that of the earlier Fathers, the idea
that Sapientia is the Word of God, Christ, is already well
established. It is to be found conventionally expressed in the
exegetical writings of Ambrose, in the *De Abraham* and in
more accessible compositions. Nor is this Christological
sense confined to patristic writings and sophisticated
poetry. A fourth-century hexameter catalogue *De Cogno-
mentis Salvatoris* ("The Names of the Savior"), possibly
meant for popular memorization, includes *Sapientia* with
over a score of conventional Christological types.[22]

[19] For Sapientia, see also *Ham.* 197, 345, 402; *C. Symm.* I, Prf., 46;
II, 628; *Cath.* V, 161; X, 132; *Ditt.* 81.

[20] See the Appendix on Sapientia in the works of Augustine in
Henri-Irenée Marrou, *Saint Augustine et la fin de la culture antique*,
4th ed. (Paris, 1958), pp. 364-369.

[21] *De Trinitate* 14. 12 [15].

[22] Spes via vita salus ratio sapientia lumen
iudex porta gigas rex gemma propheta sacerdos
Messias Sabaoth Rabbi sponsus mediator
virga columba manus petra filius Emmanuelque
vinea pastor ovis pax radix vitis oliva
fons paries agnus vitulus leo propitiator
verbum homo rete lapis domus omnia Christus Iesus.

Anthologia Latinae Supplementa, Vol. 1 (cited Chapter I, n. 29), pp.
68-69. See also *De Epithetis Salvatoris Nostri, De Trinitate*, and
Explanatio Nominum Domini (in which the names of Christ are
moralized), all once attributed to Orientius, in *CSEL*, Vol. 16, ed.
Robinson Ellis (Vienna, 1888), pp. 243-249. This sort of poem almost
seems to have been a mini-genre. Prudentius reacts to it in the pas-

195

Sapientia, like other such names of Christ, depends for its meaning on scriptural authority. Paul's First Epistle to the Corinthians refers to "Christ, the power of God and the wisdom of God" (*Christum Dei virtutem, et Dei sapientiam*, 1:24). Luke on one occasion (11:49) calls Jesus the wisdom of God.

Such New Testament references prove that in the earliest period of the Church, perhaps with Jesus himself, there is an attempt to relate the Gospel message with Old Testament and apocryphal wisdom literature. This wisdom literature includes books attributed to Solomon, Proverbs and Wisdom, and to Jesus the son of Sirach, Ecclesiasticus. Without going into questions of the authenticity, history, and cultural role of these writings, I can briefly characterize the Hebrew concept of wisdom against which Luke, Paul, and the Church Fathers are bracing themselves. Wisdom is the epitome and source of all virtue in men, and as such it is located in the just, the prudent, the powerful: it is that quality by which kings rule well. More important to the Christian interest in it, wisdom is a transcendent quality of which man merely partakes. As the personified Wisdom explains, she was born of God before creation: "The Lord possessed me in the beginning of his ways, before he made anything from the beginning [*a principio*]. I was set up from eternity, and of old before the earth was made" (Prov. 8:22-23). Wisdom also takes part in creation: "When he compassed the sea with its bounds, and set a law to the waters that they should not pass their limits: when he balanced the foundations of the earth: I was with him

---

sage in *Apo.* 393-396, beginning *o nomen praedulce mihi*! It would be interesting to do a statistical analysis of these attested "names of Christ" in the works of Prudentius and other early Christian writers as a method of determining how symbolic their Latin vocabulary is. Notice that the syntax of the chain of names makes literal nonsense and spiritual sense: the thought process, from one Christological sense to the next, will be familiar to readers of (for example) Augustine's *Ennarationes in Psalmos*.

forming all things: and was delighted every day, playing before him at all times; playing in the world: and my delights were to be with the children of men" (Prov. 8:29-31). And Wisdom remains with God as a consort or as a refulgence of eternal light: "For wisdom is more active than all active things: and reacheth everywhere by reason of her purity. For she is a vapour of the power of God and a certain pure emanation of the glory of the almighty God: and therefore no defiled thing cometh into her. For she is the brightness of eternal light, and the unspotted mirror of God's majesty, and the image of his goodness" (Wis. 7:24-26). For a Christian after the Council of Nicaea, these descriptions of Wisdom must have recalled the "begotten not made" phrase of the creed. An inclination to read Old Testament Wisdom as Christ would be firmly supported by the opening verses of John's Gospel. The structure of John 1-18 closely follows that of Proverbs 8: both Wisdom and the Word are close to God, participate in creation, dwell among men, confer their benefits upon men.[23] Both are transcendental yet embodied in humanity. According to a fourth-century Christian reading of Old Testament wisdom literature, therefore, Sapientia and Christ are identical.

Strictly speaking, this identity is not typological.[24] Yet perceptions of Sapientia by men under the Old Law can prefigure later perceptions of Christ.[25] Matthew treats the supposed human author of the wisdom literature, Solomon, as the imperfect bearer of Christ's perfect wisdom: "The queen of the south shall rise in judgment with this genera-

[23] C. H. Dodd, *The Interpretation of the Fourth Gospel* (Cambridge, 1953), pp. 274-275; M. Boismard, *Saint John's Prologue* (Westminster, Md., 1957), pp. 74-76.

[24] A prefiguration of Christ must occur as a prior event or other sign qualitatively different from what is signified. Christ cannot be prior to or different from Christ, so that if Sapientia is Christ she is not a type of Christ.

[25] Prudentius believes that Abraham, for example, saw Christ: *Apo.* 9-80. Such perceptions are imperfect perceptions of perfect truth.

tion and shall condemn it; because she came from the ends of the earth to hear the wisdom of Solomon. And, behold, a greater than Solomon here" (Matt. 12:42; cf. Luke 11:49). If Christ is the fulfillment of Solomon, his teachings among men in a sense fulfill the wisdom literature authored by the Holy Spirit through Solomon. Insofar as Proverbs or Wisdom is the Word of God, it contains true doctrine concerning Christ; but insofar as it is clouded by the imperfect perceptions of the human author Solomon, its doctrine is incomplete. With Christ's own wisdom literature, the Gospel sayings, proverbs and parables, the authorship is perfectly divine.

Alongside of the relationship of identity between Sapientia and Christ, therefore, exists a relationship of difference: the two relationships together interact within history as a progressive perfection of man's perception of Christ. Sapientia is eternally Christ, yet in a limited and historical sense— which is that of scriptural typology as man perceives it— Sapientia prefigures Christ.

Nor does the exegetical movement halt at this point. Wisdom is also a mental quality, but on account of its Christological meaning it is a supernatural faculty. Sapientia reigning in the soul is the grace of Christ. The author of the Book of Wisdom writes: "But the things that are in heaven, who shall search out? And who shall know thy thought, except thou give wisdom, and send thy Holy Spirit from above" (Wis. 9:16-17).[26] Paul affirms this active sense of wisdom as inspiration when he prays that the Colossians "may be filled with the knowledge of his will, in all wisdom and spiritual understanding . . ." (Col. 1:9). This Pauline wisdom and spiritual understanding comes from Christ. Once in the mind, it operates to give spiritual peace and strength in spite of whatever suffering may be experienced in the world; passing beyond the internal ordering of the mind of the Christian, this wisdom governs the activity of good works

[26] See also Job 32:7-8.

198

in the world. Thus Paul characterizes the purpose of wisdom: "that you may walk worthy of God . . . being fruitful in every good work" (Col. 1:10). But such moral activity is not its own justification; it is performed out of love of Christ. Christ is both the original cause and the final cause of wisdom in man: ". . . Christ, in you the hope of glory. Whom we preach, admonishing every man and teaching every man in all wisdom, that we may present every man perfect in Christ Jesus" (Col. 1:27-28). The attainment of such spiritual perfection in Christ is what the personification allegory of the *Psychomachia* leads to: Sapientia enthroned in the mind, and the mind in a state of peaceful and ordered worship of Sapientia.

The allegory ends with a vision of perfection, which is then qualified by the poet's concluding prayer. The *donec* (910) and the subjunctive mood of this prayer emphasize that the allegory's final vision is not yet attained, that it may not be attained.[27] This perspective on the allegory is helped within its final vision by the contrasting present indicative tense, a tense utterly without narrative movement, a tense of the eternal present of the afterlife. What the framing prayer can only allude to hopefully (*aurea atria; decoro solio*) is richly elaborated in the allegory and then vivified in a passage of great spiritual beauty:[28]

at domus interior septem subnixa columnis
crystalli algentis vitrea de rupe recisis
construitur, quarum tegit edita calculus albens
in conum caesus capita et sinuamine subter
subductus conchae in speciem, quod mille talentis
margaritum ingens, opibusque et censibus hastae
addictis, animosa Fides mercata pararat.
hoc residet solio pollens Sapientia et omne
consilium regni celsa disponit ab aula,

[27] See quotation p. 149 and discussion below, p. 204.
[28] An excellent and detailed commentary of verses 823-887 is in Gnilka, *Studien zur Psychomachie des Prudentius*, pp. 93-124.

tutandique hominis leges sub corde retractat.
in manibus dominae sceptrum non arte politum
sed ligno vivum viridi est, quod stirpe recisum,
quamvis nullus alat terreni caespitis umor,
fronde tamen viret incolumi, tum sanguine tinctis
intertexta rosis candentia lilia miscet
nescia marcenti florem submittere collo.
huius forma fuit sceptri gestamen Aaron
floriferum, sicco quod germina cortice trudens
explicuit tenerum spe pubescente decorem
inque novos subito tumuit virga arida fetus.   (868-887)

[An inner chamber, too, is constructed, which rests on
seven pillars cut from a glassy rock of ice-like crystal and
topped with a white stone cut cone-wise and curved on
the lower part into the likeness of a shell, a great pearl
to buy which Faith had boldly sold at auction all her
substance and her property, and paid for it a thousand
talents. Here mighty Wisdom sits enthroned and from
her high court sets in order all the government of her
realm, meditating in her heart laws to safeguard mankind.
In the sovereign's hands is a sceptre, not finished with
craftsman's skill but a living rod of green wood; severed
from its stock, it draws no nurture from moist earthly
soil, yet puts forth perfect foliage and with blooms of
blood-red roses intermingles white lilies that never droop
on withering stem. This is the sceptre that was prefigured
by the flowering rod that Aaron carried, which, pushing
buds out of its dry bark, unfolded a tender grace with
burgeoning hope, and the parched twig suddenly swelled
into new fruits.]

Here is depicted the Pauline state of moral perfection in
Christ. Description of this moral state is extremely complex
in respect to both the symbolic associations of the picture
and the typology. Many names of Christ besides Sapientia
are sounded, often echoing earlier namings in the *Psychomachia*. These names form the decorative linguistic sym-

bolism of Sapientia's temple.[29] Regarding its structure, key typology is found in Proverbs 8 (the Christological chapter so pertinent to Nicene theology), where the personification Sapientia speaks of building herself a temple; and in the following chapter (9:1), where she speaks of its seven pillars. Prudentius draws upon a quarry of scriptural materials to construct other features of Sapientia's temple. The golden courts are mentioned in I Kings 6:22. The *margaritum ingens* is certainly the pearl of great price of Christ's parable in Matthew 13:45-46; Faith, like the merchant in the parable, sells all worldly goods for the one pearl, which is the kingdom of heaven.

Viewing such architectural features together, we see that the temple is modeled mainly on that in the kingdom of heaven. Here for the first time in the *Psychomachia* the great bulk of the typological material comes from the Apocalypse of John. Since Sapientia is eternal, she is located throughout Scripture, and her temple is fitly constructed from Old and New Testaments. But her presence is conspicuous at the aesthetically perfect stasis of the Last Judgment. *Hic sapientia est* (Apoc. 13:18). And Sapientia is one of the attributes of the enthroned Lamb (Apoc. 5:11-12). Not surprisingly, John's vision of the New Jerusalem in Apocalypse 21 is the source of much of this last section of the *Psychomachia*. The temple of Sapientia follows the ground plan of the New Jerusalem. After alluding to Solomon's temple in her victory speech, Fides encourages the virtues to erect a similar temple to receive Christ (just as Solomon's temple was built to receive the Ark). Then Fides and Concordia step down from their platform and measure out the four-square distances for the foundations of the temple. Faith's module is a golden reed. Each of the four walls has three gates, over each of the twelve gates is the name of one of the twelve disciples (prefigured by the twelve tribes of Israel), and each is set with a different precious stone, for example,

29 See n. 22 above.

ingens chrysolitus, nativo interlitus auro,
hinc sibi sapphirum sociaverat, inde beryllum,
distantesque nitor medius variabat honores. (854-856)

[A great chrysolite, speckled with natural gold, had part-
nered with it on one side a sapphire, on the other a beryl,
and the lustre between them gave varying tones to the
beauties it parted.]

After describing these gems and their symbolic beauty at
some length, Prudentius turns to the inner chamber and the
presentation of Sapientia as we have quoted it above. This
whole closing scene is selected paraphrase of Apocalypse
21:10-22: "And he took me up in spirit to a great and high
mountain; and he shewed me the holy city Jerusalem, coming down out of heaven from God, having the glory of
God. And the light thereof was like to a precious stone, as
to the jasper-stone, even as crystal. And it had a wall great
and high, having twelve gates, and in the gates twelve angels,
and names written thereon, which are the names of the
twelve tribes of the children of Israel. On the east, three
gates; and on the north, three gates; and on the south, three
gates; and on the west, three gates. And the wall of the city
had twelve foundations; and in them, the twelve names of
the twelve apostles of the Lamb. And he that spoke with
me had a measure of a reed of gold to measure the city and
the gates thereof and the wall. And the city lieth in a four-
square; and the length thereof is as great as the breadth. And
he measured the city with the golden reed for twelve thousand furlongs; and the length and the height and the breadth
thereof are equal. And he measured the wall thereof, a
hundred forty-four cubits, the measure of a man, which is
of an angel. And the building of the wall thereof was of
jasper-stone; but the city itself pure gold, like to clear glass.
And the foundations of the wall of the city were adorned
with all manner of precious stones. The first foundation was
jasper; the second, sapphire; the third, a chalcedony; the

fourth, an emerald; the fifth, sardonyx; the sixth, sardius; the seventh, chrysolite; the eighth, beryl; the ninth, a topaz; the tenth, a chrysoprasus; the eleventh, a jacinth; the twelfth, an amethyst. And the twelve gates are twelve pearls, one to each; and every several gate was of one several pearl. And the street of the city was pure gold, as it were, transparent glass. And I saw no temple therein; for the Lord God Almighty is the temple thereof, and the Lamb." Prudentius has transformed John's heavenly city of Jerusalem, which contains no separate temple, into a temple of Christ; within this temple, he has transformed John's vision of the Lamb enthroned into his own vision of Sapientia enthroned in the inner sanctum of this temple.[30] The spiritual meaning he has kept intact.

This typology is now prophetic rather than historical; or, to be more exact, it is derived from the scriptural history of the future. This temporal shift does not interrupt the continuity of the psychological history. Prudentius remarks that the four walls of the temple represent man's four ages (845-848). He pointedly presents a psychological allegorization of the twelve names of the apostles taken from the Apocalypse:

Spiritus his titulis arcana recondita Mentis
ambit et electos vocat in praecordia Sensus.   (840-841)

[With these inscriptions the Spirit encircles the unseen privacy of Soul, calling elect Sentiments into the heart.]

But the new scriptural source of the typology surrounding Sapientia lends a new and powerful anagogic pull to the moral-psychological allegory. It puts the future into the present. By bringing the heavenly Jerusalem of the Last Judgment into the final vision of the *Psychomachia*, the poet has stated once again the basic Christian moral doc-

---

[30] Solomon's temple was also symmetrical, it also had right angles, but was not four-square; it was adorned with gold, but not with the twelve precious stones, the pearls, the crystal.

trine: that the character of the soul's eternal life is decided by the activity of the will as it chooses folly or wisdom, Satan or Christ. But he has done more than this. He has turned narrative into mystical vision, transformed the moral soul-struggle in time into eternal aesthetic perfection.

In his concluding prayer, Prudentius reaffirms the importance of the moral choice as well as the dependency of the will on the grace of God. He reminds the reader that involved in the state of sin is the willingness to suffer damnation—

> nunc inclinatis virtutibus ad iuga vitae
> deteriora trahi seseque addicere noxis
> turpibus et propriae iacturam ferre salutis.   (896-898)

[when the virtues are worsted, are dragged away to live in bondage to the worse, making themselves the slaves of shameful sins, and content to suffer the loss of their salvation.]

And he concludes with the foreshortened vision, now subjunctive, of the heavenly city. After the glory and splendor of the vision of salvation, the terrors of Hell are understated, but they remain a real possibility. Only within the personification allegory is the psychological divine comedy consummated. Through the process of defeating the vices, of experiencing reversals in the moral struggle, of maintaining a watchful guard against the barbarian attackers of Satan, the virtues have gained a glimpse of Hell and have passed on to their reward. As framed by the poet's two prayers to Christ, the allegory is set apart and above. The putative reader below recognizes his moral choice and responsibility, sees that his own place in the idealized action just witnessed is foreknown only by God. The best he can do is to emulate the struggles of the virtues and, if victorious, to build a temple of Wisdom.

The *Psychomachia* ends with the Apocalypse, the end of salvation history. This does not create any moral hiatus with the present because the reader believes that he will then be judged. The Last Judgment may be said to freeze time, yet its two *status*, Paradise and Hell, are composed of the progressive sum of sacred history. Aaron's rod, the final typological emblem of the *Psychomachia*, therefore appropriately flowers in Old Testament times, with Christ, in the soul of the Christian, and eternally. As a symbol of its bearer's power, the scepter of Sapientia spans scriptural history. Appropriately for its placement in the *Psychomachia*, the scepter's scriptural source is found after the Red Sea Crossing, after the passage through the wilderness, in the promised land. "And Moses spoke to the children of Israel: and all the princes gave him rods one for every tribe. And there were twelve rods besides the rod of Aaron. And when Moses had laid them up before the Lord in the tabernacle of the testimony: he returned on the following day, and found that the rod of Aaron for the house of Levi was budded: and that the buds swelling, it had bloomed blossoms, which spreading the leaves were formed into almonds" (Numbers 17:6-8). As a type of Sapientia's scepter, Aaron's rod is grafted to the rod of Moses; and to Jesse's rod from which Christ—the *lignum vitae*—bloomed. Its significance is enlarged by Pauline commentary. In the Epistle to the Hebrews, Aaron's rod (*virga Aaron, quae fronduerat*, 9:4) is put with the most sacred objects of the Old Law—the golden censer, the ark, the tables of the covenant—in the second tabernacle; here the priest used to enter but once a year, and the place was called the Holy of Holies. "But Christ, being come a high priest of the good things to come, by a greater and more perfect tabernacle, not made with hands, that is, not of this creation; neither by the blood of goats or of calves, but by his own blood, entered once into the Holies, having obtained eternal redemption" (Heb. 9:11-12). Tracing the origin of Sapientia's scepter in Aaron's rod, Prudentius reviews the sacred history of temple worship, the priesthood, and the sacraments. The iconographic lesson of this history is clear: the way to future salvation is present worship in the temple of Wisdom, whose high priest is Christ. The scene is a memorable picture of redemptive grace flowering in the Christian soul. Amongst all the gold and crystal and precious stone of the heavenly city, the budding and blooming rod is a reminder of the priesthood of Christ present in the living souls of Christians here and now. The final vision of the *Psychomachia*, then, is more than prophetic or apocalyptic: it reverberates through scriptural history, remembering the past, hoping against the future, concentrating its moral energy on the present.

Abraham: Type of the Faithful Christian

Abraham's career in the "Praefatio" prefigures the plot of the personification allegory. As the first believer in Christ, Abraham is the forerunner of Fides, the chief virtue in the Christian soul. As an Old Testament character, the father of Israel is unable to see Sapientia face to face, but his successful warfare and fruitful homecoming show the way of the allegory to come. Christian readers able to comprehend the mystery of Abraham's 318 soldiers, of Melchisedech's blessing, and of Sarah's fertility will also comprehend the workings of Christ's grace in the psychological allegory.

The "Praefatio" divides into three parts: introduction (1-14), narrative (15-49), and conclusion (50-68). Its organization may best be characterized as narrative scriptural paraphrase plus exegetical frame. The exegesis guarantees figural interpretation of the scriptural paraphrase of Abraham's career, which in turn establishes the norm of figural interpretation for the main hexameter section. We have been studying how a representative Christian soul in spiritual crisis entertains a series of typological intrusions, and how this soul's reaction to Scripture is instrumental in its resolving the crisis of sin in Christian conversion. The "Praefatio" contains a similar interaction between psyche and salvation history, but with the interaction reversed: scriptural history is the stuff of the narrative, psychological moralization is appended. Unlike the personification allegory, the "Praefatio" is generically exactly like conventional scriptural exegesis.

As Prudentius assembles the three sections of his "Praefatio," he alters his literary technique for each section, His introduction presents the character of Abraham (or Abram) in the perfect tense: Abraham did this, this, and this, and he thereby taught us that, that, and that. Except that it runs on for fourteen lines, its piled up phrases forming a single period, this introduction is like one of the quatrains of the *Dittochaeon*. It is a static, hieratic emblem. The narrative section shifts to the present tense—historical present. Here Prudentius relates in swift succession three important events in the life of Abraham: the slaughter of the kings and Lot's rescue by Abraham and the 318 servants; Melchisedech's blessing of Abraham; and the entertainment of the three angels of God by Abraham and Sarah, with the subsequent fertility of Sarah. The conclusion offers commentary on this narrative as it restates some of the themes in the introduction. This commentary begins in the perfect tense, turns to the present tense as it offers psychological moralization, then turns to the future tense in order to utter prophetic statements about the relationship between the soul and God.

Features of each part of the "Praefatio" require detailed interpretation. Therefore I shall quote each part in full and then relate these to the personification allegory, offering relevant New Testament and patristic texts by way of commentary. Here is the introductory section:

Senex fidelis prima credendi via
Abram, beati seminis serus pater,
adiecta cuius nomen auxit syllaba
Abram parenti dictus, Abraham Deo,
senile pignus qui dicavit victimae,
docens ad aram cum litare quis velit,

207

quod dulce cordi, quod pium, quod unicum
Deo libenter offerendum credito,
pugnare nosmet cum profanis gentibus
suasit, suumque suasor exemplum dedit,
nec ante prolem coniugalem gignere
Deo placentem, matre Virtute editam,
quam strage multa bellicosus spiritus
portenta cordis servientis vicerit.   (Prf. 1-14)

[The faithful patriarch who first showed the way of
believing, Abram, late in life the father of a blessed
progeny, whose name was lengthened by a syllable (for
he was called Abram by his father, but Abraham by
God), he who offered in sacrifice the child of his old
age, teaching us thereby that when a man would make
an acceptable offering at the altar he must willingly and
with faith in God offer to Him that which is dear to his
heart and the object of his love, that of which he has
but one, has counselled us to war against the ungodly
tribes, himself giving us an example of his own counsel,
and shown that we beget no child of wedlock pleasing
to God, and whose mother is Virtue, till the spirit, bat-
tling valorously, has overcome with great slaughter the
monsters in the enslaved heart.]

Abraham teaches us lessons basic to the allegory of the
Psychomachia, that is, pertaining to the warfare against ungodly tribes and to the proper spirit of worship. But the
lessons seem cryptic. The addition of a syllable to the name
of Abram, for instance, requires some prior special knowledge to be interpreted or else promises further comment by
the poet. And the whole sentence is highly condensed with
figural meanings not immediately perceived. In fact, not
until we reach the hexameter narrative do certain striking
parallels show themselves. Abraham is the first to show the
way of believing. Who is the second? Certainly Christ.
"Abram" is the first name mentioned in the "Praefatio" and

"Christ" is the first word in the main hexameter section. So begins a detailed structural plan of typological fulfillment of the "Praefatio" by the hexameter section. The two names of Abraham are fulfilled in the hexameters: we worship "one God . . . under the two names" (*unum namque Deum colimus de nomine utroque*, 3). Furthermore, Abraham "has counselled us to war against the ungodly tribes" just as Christ himself commands the relieving squadrons in the mind and will reveal in the allegory the battle victorious. Abraham has the first *psychomachia* of sacred history to be resolved completely in favor of God; thus his obedient willingness to sacrifice his son Isaac. The allusion (5-8) is understated and non-dramatic, probably for the same reason that the sacrifice of Isaac is not treated in the later narrative paraphrase. (The "Praefatio" deals not with Abraham's moral-mental struggles, but with his external actions and good works which can be interpreted figuratively in a psychological sense. The events of Abraham's life are, with the exception of the Isaac story, figures of a *psychomachia* rather than themselves psychomachic.) Be that as it may, the moral lesson (not the typology) of the Isaac story is repeated in the opening of the hexameter section: the struggle in the soul can be resolved completely in favor of God, the virtues can win. In smaller details of theme and vocabulary too, the introduction of the "Praefatio" is answered by the invocatory prayer to Christ. In both the word *portenta* occurs in the last line. Both have phrases like *bellicosus spiritus*, *mens armata*, and verb forms of *pugno*, all of which present moral warfare in a psychological arena.

From the standpoint of literary theory, the most important parallel relates to the establishment of a typological relation between personification allegory and Scripture. It is striking how the *exemplum* of Abraham gives rise immediately to allegory. In the phrase *bellicosus spiritus*, *spiritus* is almost personified with the sounding of the adjective; the verb *vicerit* completes the personification. The *prolem coniugalem . . . Deo placentem* is in the scriptural source

209

Isaac, born from Sarah, and the son of Abraham's old age. With the phrase *matre Virtute*, we witness the birth of personification allegory out of Scripture. This process is fulfilled when in the introductory prayer of the hexameter section, Christ has been invoked with the imperative *dissere* and is about to reveal the allegory "if it is permitted" (*liceat*) to be viewed. In the initial passages of both the "Praefatio" and the hexameter section, allegory is claimed as closely allied if not identical to the Word of God, with revelation. We are counselled allegorically by Abraham, then by Christ; in both cases there is at least the illusion of direct discourse.

However revolutionary Prudentius' poetic use of it may be, the Abraham-Christ typology is wholly conventional. Augustine asks in Sermon 105: "What is Israel, but the seed of Abraham? What the seed of Abraham, but Christ?" With Augustine this typology is historiographically crucial. In the *City of God* he argues that the life of Abraham marks a turning point (*articulus temporis*) of salvation history, the beginning of the third age, after which "there are clearer indications of divine promises which we now see fulfilled in Christ" (XVI, 12). Abraham is historically the father of Israel, the only believer in the true God during a period of nearly universal wickedness, the founder of a line that alone maintained the worship of God prior to Christ's Incarnation. As disobedient as Adam was, Abraham was obedient (*City of God* XIV. 15). Thus with Abraham occurs a partial and imperfect restoration of mankind aptly prefiguring (at the sixth age) Christ's total and perfect redemption.

For earlier patristic writers, Abraham shows the first way of believing. Cyprian characterizes the patriarch as "trusting God and being the first to establish the root and foundation of faith."[31] Abraham institutes the foundation of faith in two ways. He is personally faithful to God and takes care to pass on his faith to his offspring, the seed of Israel;

31 *De Bono Patientiae*, 10. Trans. Roy Deferrari in *Saint Cyprian: Treatises* (cited Chapter II, n. 18), p. 272.

and he himself is a prophet of Christ as well as an unwitting prefiguration of Christ.

The origins of patristic Abraham typology possibly should be traced to the evangelists, to Jesus himself, or to John the Baptist.[32] Certainly Paul expands the Abraham-Christ typology into a form upon which the patristic writers draw with some authority. Quoting Genesis 15:6, Paul writes in the Epistle to the Galatians: "As it is written: Abraham believed God; and it was deputed to him unto justice. Know ye, therefore, that they who are of faith, the same are the children of Abraham. And the scripture, fore-seeing that God justifieth the Gentiles by faith, told unto Abraham before: In thee shall all nations be blessed. There-fore, they that are of faith shall be blessed with faithful Abraham" (Gal. 3:6-9). Paul argues that all who believe in Christ, whether Jew or Gentile, are the seed of Abraham, the spiritual heirs of Abraham. "For you are all one in Christ Jesus. And, if you be Christ's, then are you the seed of Abraham, heirs according to the promise" (Gal. 3:28-29). Given this Pauline and later patristic treatment of Abraham, it would be surprising if the Christians in Prudentius' audi-ence did not think of Christ upon hearing mention of Abra-ham. They would not consider the typological relation be-tween the introductions of the "Praefatio" and hexameter section either strange or artificial.

Prudentius' meticulous thematic and verbal parallels are of course extraordinary. Nothing quite like the typological density of these fourteen lines exists in other early Christian verse. Especially noteworthy is the facility with which a psychologically valid personification allegory is derived

[32] For Jesus' allusion to Abraham, see Luke 19:9-10. Jesus may have considered himself the new Abraham as well as the new Moses (Luke 24:44); John the Baptist is reported by Matthew (3:9) to say, "And think not to say within yourselves: we have Abraham for our father. For I tell you that God is able of these stones to raise up children to Abraham." Nor is Abraham typology confined to the New Testa-ment; see Judith 8:22 and I Maccabees 2:52. For Abraham see also *Apo.* 360-375; *Ditt.* 13-16.

211

from Scripture. Also noteworthy is thematic control: from
the patriarch's life are selected the two main figural emblems
of the allegory to follow. Abraham's warfare against the
ungodly tribes has taught us to fight the monstrous vices
within the enslaved heart. His sacrifice of Isaac has taught
us to offer that of which we have but one (that is, our soul)
to God—a prototypical Old Testament lesson in temple
worship. Both of these activities are as yet static, mystic,
cryptic emblems whose moral significance remains to be
interpreted clearly by Prudentius. These activities originate
in faith, and they somehow cooperate with divine Grace so
as to yield mysterious spiritual gifts: success in them will
confer a new name, divine rather than worldly, on the doer.

The narrative section of the "Praefatio" expands these
obscure matters and makes them somewhat more intelligible. Here the main scriptural sources are Genesis 14 and
Genesis 18:1-15. Representation of events from the life of
Abraham is even more selective than before, yet less condensed. Hence our impressions of greater clarity, of mysteries unclouded.

> victum feroces forte reges ceperant
> Loth immorantem criminosis urbibus
> Sodomae et Gomorrae, quas fovebat advena
> pollens honore patruelis gloriae.
> Abram sinistris excitatus nuntiis
> audit propinquum sorte captum bellica
> servire duris barbarorum vinculis:
> armat trecentos terque senos vernulas,
> pergant ut hostis terga euntis caedere,
> quem gaza dives ac triumphus nobilis
> captis tenebant inpeditum copiis.
> quin ipse ferrum stringit et plenus Deo
> reges superbos mole praedarum graves
> pellit fugatos, sauciatos proterit,
> frangit catenas et rapinam liberat:
> aurum, puellas, parvulos, monilia,

greges equarum, vasa, vestem, buculas.
Loth ipse ruptis expeditus nexibus
attrita bacis colla liber erigit.
Abram triumphi dissipator hostici
redit recepta prole fratris inclytus
ne quam fidelis sanguinis prosapiam
vis pessimorum possideret principum.
adhuc recentem caede de tanta virum
donat sacerdos ferculis caelestibus,
Dei sacerdos, rex et idem praepotens,
origo cuius fonte inenarrabili
secreta nullum prodit auctorem sui,
Melchisedech, qua stirpe, quis maioribus
ignotus, uni cognitus tantum Deo.
mox et triformis angelorum trinitas
senis revisit hospitis mapalia,
et iam vietam Sarra in alvum fertilis
munus iuventae mater exsanguis stupet,
herede gaudens, et cachinni paenitens.   (Prf. 15-49)

[It chanced that insolent kings overcame Lot and took
him captive when he was dwelling in the wicked cities
of Sodom and Gomorrah, to which he clung and where,
though but an immigrant, he was a great man because of
the honour paid to his uncle's fame. Called by a bearer of
the evil tidings, Abram learns that his kinsman, by the
fortune of war, has been taken and put into subjection to
hard bondage under the barbarians. He arms three hundred and eighteen servants born in his house, to pursue
the enemy and slay them on their march, encumbered as
they are and slowed down by the rich treasure of the
great spoils their glorious victory has won. He himself,
too, draws the sword and, being filled with the spirit of
God, drives off in flight those proud kings, weighed
down with their booty, or cuts them down and tramples
them under foot. He breaks the bonds and looses the
plunder—gold, maidens, little children, strings of jewels,

213

herds of mares, vessels, raiment, cattle. Lot himself, set at liberty by the bursting of his chains, straightens his neck in freedom, where the links had chafed. Abram, having scattered his enemies' triumph, returns in the glory of recovering his brother's son so that wicked kings should not keep a descendant of the faithful stock under their violent power. To the warrior fresh from this great slaughter the priest presents heavenly food, the priest of God, himself also a mighty king, whose mysterious birth from a source that cannot be named has no ostensible author—Melchisedech, whose line and forefathers no man knows, for they are known to God alone. Then also a triad of angels in the form of three persons visits the old man's cabin, and he entertains them; and Sara, conceiving, is amazed to find the function of youth come to her aged womb, becoming a mother when she has passed her time, and she rejoices in an heir, and repents of her laughter.]

The plot of this narrative is comic. So were the barely perceptible movements of the introductory section: from human to God-given name, from the pain to the reward of sacrificing what one holds dear, from the danger posed by the monstrous forces in the heart to complete victory over them. Through all this, Abraham remained the static *exemplum* of faith. Now the narrative movement carries some momentum and fluidity, and this permits its comic structure a measure of dramatic reversal. It is interesting that the first word of this narrative, *victum*, picks up the earlier verb *vicerit*. The active-to-passive linkage is surely intentional, and it jolts the reader by reverting from what Abraham has counselled (victory over the ungodly tribes) to the prior danger (the victory of the ungodly tribes) against which he must act. By means of his own heroic warfare as aided by the 318 servants, Abraham is able to reverse the triumph of the evil forces. Having gained the victory, he is blessed by Melchisedech and secures a fruitful homecoming.

This narrative section of the "Praefatio" parallels that of the personification allegory, for both feature Christian warfare followed by Christian peace—the comic structure of conversion. But the parallelism is more intricate and subtle than meets the eye at first reading. As earlier, it involves verbal as well as larger thematic and structural connections. For example, an expressly Christological vocabulary begins to reverberate in the "Praefatio" once Abraham's victory is assured, and especially so as he is blessed by Melchisedech: thus *origo, fons sacerdos, rex, praepotens,* etc. Theologically related is language denoting threeness: *triformis . . . trinitas.* Just such vocabulary begins to reverberate loudly toward the end of the personification allegory of the *Psychomachia.*

For another example, the negative terms attached to the hostile kings quite as obviously anticipate the personified vices. As Ira will be, the enemies of Abraham are *feroces;* as Superbia, *superbos;* as Avaritia, *gaza dives;* as Cultura Deorum Veterum and Discordia cognomento Heresis, hostile to the faithful one of God; as Libido, *Sodomae.* Such terms bridge the narrowing gap between Scripture and moral allegory as Scripture is paraphrased by the allegorical poet. Abraham remains the scriptural character, but he is also Faith. Abraham's army, aided by the 318 servants, slaughters the kings with killing techniques used by the virtues against the vices. So the kings cut down and trampled underfoot are historical persons, but they are also the monstrous forms of sins. Once again we see that personifications grow from salvation history, that even in the "Praefatio" Scripture and allegory are interrelating modes of Christian expression. Further demonstrating this, Abraham's moral justification in fighting the wicked kings is that of the virtues in the personification allegory. The two kinsmen, Abraham and Lot, signify allegorically the two directions of the will in the Christian soul, that is, toward God and toward sin. Lot has been captured by the wicked kings (of Sodom, Gomorrah, and elsewhere) through his own willfull error. He has

215

immigrated to Sodom, the city of sin. But his faithful kinsman Abraham wishes to rescue him and, filled with the spirit of God, is able to do so—

> ne quam fidelis sanguinis prosapiam
> vis pessimorum possideret principum.   (Prf. 36-37)

[so that wicked kings should not keep a descendant of the faithful stock under their violent power.]

Likewise with grace from Christ the faithful soul, armed with the virtues, is able to defeat the forces of sin.

For a final example of the interaction between "Praefatio" and personification allegory, we find the words *qua stirpe* associated with Melchisedech. It can hardly be a coincidence that Sapientia's scepter, prefigured by that of another *sacerdos* (Aaron), is *stirpe recisum* (879). The stock is cut off, unknown, mysterious, yet the branch flowers. Aaron and Melchisedech are both conventional types of Christ, and as priests both are naturally identified with Christ in an especially sacramental context. The verbal and thematic connection made by *sacerdos* and by *stirpe recisum* clarifies the typological justice by which both unite in the person of Sapientia.

Granting Prudentius' skill in paraphrastic arrangement of scriptural narrative, his moral-exegetical meanings are not at all eccentric. Augustine in the *City of God* devotes one chapter (XVI, 22) to the slaughter of the kings and the blessing of Melchisedech, and considerably more (XVI, 29-31) to the entertainment of the three men or angels and the birth of Isaac. Augustine does not allegorize the slaughter of the kings, but he does allegorize the blessing of Melchisedech and the later events, and he follows Paul's own interests in the Abraham story. In the Epistle to the Hebrews, Paul writes that Jesus is "made a high priest forever, according to the order of Melchisedech" (6:20). Paul continues: "For this Melchisedech was king of Salem, priest of the most high God, who met Abraham returning from the slaughter of the kings and blessed him; to whom also Abraham divided the tithes of all; who first indeed by interpretation is king of justice; and then also king of Salem, that is, king of peace; without father, without mother, without genealogy, having neither beginning of days nor end of life, but likened unto the Son of God, continueth a priest for ever" (Heb. 7:1-3). The order of Melchisedech is not the Levitical priesthood of Aaron, but is superior to it according to Paul. Aaron's order is of the Old Law, but Melchisedech's order participates in the mystery of Christ's priesthood. "For it was fitting that we should have such a high priest, holy, innocent, undefiled, separated from sinners, and made higher than the heavens" (Heb. 7:26). The distinction between these two orders of *sacerdotes* is made vigorously by some of the Church Fathers, including Augustine.[33] Others are less willing to degrade Aaron by the comparison; Cyprian, for instance, seems to consider Aaron as embodying equal greatness with Melchisedech, and treats both as important types of Christ.[34] Prudentius belongs with this latter group, as the *Psychomachia* proves.[35]

The conventional typology of Melchisedech highlights one aspect of his blessing of Abraham, the offering of bread and wine. In his homily on Psalm 109, Jerome names the

[33] *De Civ. Dei* XVI. 22; quoting Ps. 109.4: "*Tu es sacerdos in aeternum secundum ordinem Melchisedech*"; *non scilicet secundum ordinem Aaron, quo ordo fuerat auferendus inlucescentibus rebus quae illis umbris praenotabantur.* Augustine follows the Epistle to the Hebrews in opposing the two orders of *sacerdotes*, but he admits that some of his contemporaries deny its authenticity. The differing treatments of Aaron may reflect opinion on the placement of Hebrews in the canon, though in Prudentius' case this would be reflected indirectly only.

[34] See Fahey (cited Chapter II, n. 23), pp. 574-576, for a full account of *Aaron sacerdos* in Cyprian; Melchisedech is discussed pp. 564-565. Both priests are equally types of Christ, Melchisedech being distinguished only by his association with the sacrament of Eucharist.

[35] Based on the fulfillment of Melchisedech and Aaron together in Sapientia at the end of the *Psychomachia*. No other naming of Aaron or Melchisedech occurs in Prudentius.

Epistle to the Hebrews and praises Paul's exegesis. Jerome then treats the striking sacramental imagery of the Genesis story: "Just as Melchisedech, the king of Salem, offered bread and wine, even so shall You offer Your Body and Blood, true bread and true wine. This is our Melchisedech who gave us the divine sacrifice that we have. It is he who said: 'He who eats my flesh and drinks my blood,' according to the order of Melchisedech, He gave us His sacrament."[36] Prudentius' terminology of "heavenly food" (*ferculis caelestibus*) in the "Praefatio" conveys such sacramental associations. Melchisedech, in fact, introduces the rich typology of the Eucharist in the *Psychomachia*. Sobrietas recalls the manna fulfilled in present-day food eaten *de corpore Christi* (376); the lilies and roses blooming on Sapientia's scepter may symbolize the body and blood of Christ. Sacramental meanings aside, the resemblance in Scripture between Melchisedech and Sapientia is unmistakable—both are mysteriously eternal. In the *Psychomachia*, Sapientia fulfills the Levitical order of Aaron's priesthood even as, like Melchisedech, she is both ruler (*domina*; *Sapientia regnet*) and high priestess of her temple.

Also of major importance to the narrative section of the "Praefatio" is the figure of Sarah, the miracle of her fertility, and the subsequent birth of Isaac. Once again the patristic tradition is based in Paul, who derives an allegory based on Sarah and Agar. "For it is written that Abraham had two sons: the one by a bondwoman and the other by a free woman. But he who was of the bondwoman was born according to the flesh; but he of the free woman was by promise. Which things are said by an allegory [*per allegoriam dicta*]. For these are the two testaments. The one from mount Sinai, engendering unto bondage, which is Agar. For Sinai is a mountain in Arabia, which hath affinity to that Jerusalem which now is, and is in bondage

---

[36] *Tractatus de Psalmo 109*. From *The Homilies of Saint Jerome*, Vol. 1, trans. Marie L. Ewald, The Fathers of the Church, Vol. 48 (Washington, D.C., 1964), pp. 274-275.

with her children. But that Jerusalem which is above is free; which is our mother. For it is written: Rejoice thou barren, that bearest not; break forth and cry, thou that travailest not; for many are the children of the desolate, more than of her that hath a husband. Now we, brethren, as Isaac was, are the children of promise. But as then he that was born according to the flesh persecuted him that was after the spirit; so also it is now. But what saith the scripture? Cast out the bondwoman and her son; for the son of the bond-woman shall not be heir with the son of the free woman. So then, brethren, we are not the children of the bond-woman but of the free; by the freedom wherewith Christ has made us free" (Gal. 4:22-31). Prudentius emulates Paul generally by interpreting Abraham's career as *per allegoriam dicta*. He also has this particular—and most authoritative—allegorization in mind. Although of Abraham's children only Isaac, born of Sarah, is named in the "Praefatio," the child's full spiritual significance as Abraham's seed, as legitimate heir, as a cause of rejoicing, depends upon Galatians. Notice that there are no slaves in the city of the virtues; in this respect the city of the virtues is a most non-Roman, idealized, New Testament city. And already in the "Praefatio," Prudentius has dramatized the theme of liberation from slavery by Abraham's rescuing of Lot. In a moral sense, one is a slave to sin after one has been captured by sin—this is what has happened to Lot.[37] But Abraham releases Lot from his chains just as the various virtues will release the thoughts and sentiments of the mind from the danger of captivity by the vices. In his Epistle to the Galatians, Paul has conflated the themes of spiritual freedom, of conflict between the children of the free and the children of the enslaved, of contrast between the worldly and the heavenly Jerusalem, and of contrast between the Old and New Testaments. These are thematic tracks for Prudentius to follow. He has connected contingent events in Genesis with the conflict between flesh and spirit, or between the

[37] *Ham.* 723-777.

219

soul's corporeal and spiritual instincts. Following Paul in
the conflict's consummation also, Prudentius has chosen to
recreate the heavenly Jerusalem in the Christian soul. He has
done this not simply because the Heavenly Jerusalem is also
scriptural but because it is specifically linked to the Abraham story in Galatians. The typological narrative of the
"Praefatio" is more than Old Testament paraphrasis—it is
an imitation of Pauline Old Testament paraphrasis—and this
provides optimal authority for the personification allegory
to follow.

The "Praefatio" concludes with this exegesis:

> haec ad figuram praenotata est linea,
> quam nostra recto vita resculpat pede:
> vigilandum in armis pectorum fidelium,
> omnemque nostri portionem corporis,
> quae capta foedae serviat libidini,
> domi coactus liberandam viribus;
> nos esse large vernularum divites,
> si quid trecenti bis novenis additis
> possint figura noverimus mystica.
> mox ipse Christus, qui sacerdos verus est,
> parente inenarrabili atque uno satus,
> cibum beatis offerens victoribus
> parvam pudici cordis intrabit casam,
> monstrans honorem Trinitatis hospitae.
> animam deinde Spiritus conplexibus
> pie maritam, prolis expertem diu,
> faciet perenni fertilem de semine,
> tunc sera dotem possidens puerpera
> herede digno Patris inplebit domum.   (Prf. 50-68)

[This picture has been drawn beforehand to be a model
for our life to trace out again with true measure, showing that we must watch in the armour of faithful hearts,
and that every part of our body which is in captivity and
enslaved to foul desire must be set free by gathering our
forces at home; that we are abundantly rich in servants

born in the house if we know through the mystic symbol
what is the power of three hundred with eighteen more.
Then Christ himself, who is the true priest, born of a
Father unutterable and one, bringing food for the blessed
victors, will enter the humble abode of the pure heart
and give it the privilege of entertaining the Trinity; and
then the Spirit, embracing in holy marriage the soul that
has long been childless, will make her fertile by the seed
eternal, and the dowered bride will become a mother late
in life and give the Father's household a worthy heir.]

As with the first two sections of the "Praefatio," this last
one has its counterpart in the hexameter section of the
Psychomachia. Narrative movement has halted. Like the
poet's concluding prayer, these lines interpret preceding
allegory for the reader, who is urged to "trace out" the
allegory in his soul so that his soul may be at one with God.
Both conclusions give weight to the themes of bondage and
freedom, and the Pauline context of these themes is very
much felt: the soul of the Christian is strong in Christ, free
in Christ, a worthy heir in Christ. As later, the moral idea
in the "Praefatio" is that the Christian should out of love
of Christ and with the help of Christ engage in a *psychomachia* for his soul's future salvation.

There is an important difference between the two end-
ings, however, and this is suggested by the difference in
verb tenses. The last lines of the "Praefatio" are in the future
tense, the tense of prophecy; those of the hexameter prayer
are in the subjunctive, the tense of moral doubt against the
future. This contrast is not arbitrary. The entire treatment
of Abraham has been in light of the future New Law (as,
for a Christian, Old Testament events are supposed to be),
yet our intellectual perspective throughout the "Praefatio"
has been as if from within the Old Testament period. We
are surrounded by mysteries: events whose significance we
do not as yet comprehend, mystical number symbolism,
miraculous manifestations of divine power. Like Abraham

221

we interpret these events by faith, knowing that Christ is signified by them, but not as yet knowing why this is so. Our temporal point of view, reinforced by the poet's skillful manipulation of verb tenses, is that of the Hebrew prophets, looking back to father Abraham and forward to the new Abraham, Christ. Within Scripture, this is the historical equivalent of the psychological preconversion state. With the transition to the main part of the *Psychomachia* comes a new temporal perspective: Christ has come. He is addressed in the opening prayer directly in the present tense, and our temporal point of view is now that of the post-New Testament period. With the shift in time comes a new religious outlook. The very first hexameter line announces the two essentials of the Christian moral experience: Christ and the *graves hominum . . . labores*. Prophetic hope has given way to moral hope actualized in the allegorical soul-struggle for salvation. The previous clouds of mystery are blown away by spiritual understanding as the allegory progresses, and at its end, the prophetic voice is fulfilled by the Pauline voice of moral admonition. The assured hope for Christ's coming expressed at the end of the "Praefatio" is fulfilled by a fearful hope against Christ's second coming. Thus the *Psychomachia* progresses from Genesis to Apocalypse, from Old Testament to New Testament, and is in its totality an allegorical imitation of Scripture.

The Influence of Ambrose's *De Abraham*

Although Prudentian typology is for the most part conventional, and therefore not traceable to specific Christian authors (except Paul), certain features of the treatment of Abraham in the "Praefatio" suggest that the poet knew and used Ambrose's treatise.[38] Influence of the nearly contempo-

[38] Text in *S. Ambrosii Opera*, Part I, ed. C. Schenkl, *CSEL*, Vol. 32 (Vienna, 1897), pp. 500-638. This work has not been translated

rary *De Abraham* shows itself in two ways. First, the *De Abraham* contains all the relatively obscure or mysterious features, including numerology and etymology, to be found in Prudentius' adaptation of the Abraham story. The change of Abraham's name, the 318 servants, the entertainment of the holy threesome—these details in the *Psychomachia* may be interpreted by means of Ambrose's allegorization of them. Second, of the many patristic treatments of the Abraham story, the *De Abraham* contains the greatest interest in a sustained moral interpretation of a psychological nature.[39]

The treatise exists in two books, the first intended for the instruction of catechumens, the second for baptized Christians. Ambrose's literary strategy is similar for both books: he guides the reader line by line or scene by scene through those chapters of Genesis that deal with Abraham, roughly chapters 12 to 25. As he follows the chronological order of Scripture, he also gathers into his commentary pertinent passages from the Old Testament, especially Psalms, and from the Gospels, Epistles, and Apocalypse. Both books of the *De Abraham* constitute moralized sacred history based on the life of the patriarch. But their levels of moral understanding differ. The first reading of the life of Abraham is simple: *de quo nobis moralis primo erit tractatus et simplex*

---

before. The following translated passages were prepared jointly by Robert G. Moran and myself.

[39] Laura Cotogni (cited Critical Introd., n. 34), 441, asserted almost forty years ago that the *De Abraham* was the "principal source" of the *Psychomachia*'s "Praefatio," for "in both the exegesis of Abraham's overcoming Lot's enemies and being granted a son by God is that the soul, overcoming its enemies the passions, is worthy to receive the gift of grace." So the matter has stood until the recent discussion by P. F. Beatrice (cited Critical Introd., n. 27), 56-57 and 64. Beatrice describes the *De Abraham* in some detail and points to ingredients shared by the *Psychomachia*: the psychological interpretation of the Abraham story, the allegorization of the 318, Sarah, Isaac. He hesitates (64) to call the *De Abraham* "the only source," however, if only because it lacks the Eucharistic typology so important to the *Psychomachia*.

(I, 1). Here the patriarch is presented as a model for our moral activity in the world. His entertaiment of the three angels of God, for example, is said to teach the virtues of hospitality and almsgiving (I, 34-35). Such instruction pertains to social, external conduct. The second, more complex reading of the life of Abraham refers to the inner workings of the soul. Ambrose compares his purposes and introduces his new themes: "We have treated a moral topic with thoughts as simple as possible in order that our reader might be able to use the treatment as a moral guide. But just as a sword, sharp on both edges, can be wielded in battle from either side, so too the word of God, since it is sharper than the sharpest sword and penetrates to the very joints of the soul, will be found a ready weapon whichever way it is turned, able to pierce into the mind of the reader and reveal to him the mysteries of prophetic Scripture. And so I think it not incongruous to apply our understanding to loftier things and, through accounts of various persons to set forth the progress, as it were, of the nature of virtue, especially since we have already discerned in Adam the beginnings of a deeper intelligence. For Adam we have said to be mind [*mens*]; Eve we have designated as the senses [*sensus*]; and pleasure [*delectatio*] we have expressed by the form of the serpent. But in Eden, from a state of absolute bliss and natural enjoyment of virtue, man degenerated into vice through deception of the senses and the lure of pleasure; whereas here the progress of the mind [*processum mentis*] has been held up to view. And this the divine law-giver has provided with great foresight: namely, as much as he has pointed out the failing of the mind in order that we might beware of these paths of error, so much has he indicated the progress of the mind and even a return to greater heights, so that we might learn to just what extent a broken mind is able to be revitalized" (II, 1). The Flood (historically between Adam and Abraham), which represents the purgation of human weakness (*fragilitas*), does not permit mankind to progress in virtue. Therefore God intervenes in history to

224

provide more positive instruction. "Abraham was introduced in place of mind [*mentis loco*]. And at last he was called a mediary [*transitus*]. And so, in order that mind [*mens*] which, in the form of Adam, had given itself over completely to pleasure and the delights of the body might pass over into the form and appearance of virtue, a wise man [*vir sapiens*] was placed before us for emulation" (II, 1).

As a new Adam placed before mankind for moral instruction, Abraham quite obviously prefigures Christ. But Ambrose only hints at this allegorical dimension, preferring instead to extrude as much psychology as possible from the Abraham story. He begins: "This mind [*mens*], then, was in Charra, that is, was in a cave bound to the different passions [*in cavernis obnoxia variis passionibus*]" (II, 2). Despite the different vocabulary, I suspect that the *Psychomachia*'s *mens* endeavoring to expel sins *de pectoris antro* (6) is influenced by this beginning. Here is Ambrose's continuation: "And likewise it was said to him: 'Depart from your land,' that is, from your body. He has departed 'this land' whose abode is in heaven. 'And,' it was said, 'from your near relations.' By this is meant the senses of the body, for these are near relations of our soul. For our soul is divided into two parts: that having reason and that not having reason. The senses belong to the non-rational part. Therefore they are 'related' to the rational part, that is, the mind" (II, 2). By his ranking of the senses as footsoldiers in the virtuous army, Prudentius may be influenced by these conceptions. Yet Ambrose, as will be seen, is more oriented toward Platonism than is Prudentius; and Prudentius diverges from the Bishop of Milan frequently.

For the remainder of Book II, the exegesis deals with inner psychological experience. Abraham's journey to Egypt is the soul's descent to sinful contact with the body: *descendit in Aegyptum, hoc est in adflictionem carnis* (II, 14) . . . *hoc est ad feros et barbaros mores* (II, 15). But Abraham sets an example for us by not allowing himself

225

to become contaminated by Egyptian customs. He increases in spiritual wealth by ruling the passions: *merito dives erat Abraham, quia regebat sensus inrationabiles* (II, 20). The relationship between Abraham and Lot is of special interest to Ambrose, for this relationship represents the tenuous kinship between the rational and the non-rational mind. It is right for the rational mind to wish to allow the non-rational mind to depart if it cannot prevent its deviating into sin (II, 32). As Lot immigrates to Sodom, "we can clearly learn how much mind can attain when non-rational interests do not interfere, and how much evil an unbroken succession of vices can bring" (II, 37). Prudentius' treatment of Lot is compatible with this. But Abraham's subsequent battle against the five kings and his rescue and liberation of Lot, an episode so important to Prudentius, is given a fairly hurried treatment by Ambrose. The five kings are the five senses: *quinque reges quinque sensus corporis nostri sunt, visus odoratus gustatus tactus auditus* (II, 41); neither this Platonized interpretation nor its static form of presentation have much in common with the *Psychomachia*.

Yet Ambrose elsewhere shows himself very much concerned with the division of the soul, the battle between virtues and vices, and similar Prudentian interests. The following draws on II Corinthians for some of its phraseology: "And so various lords wish to hold us in slavery. The devil presses on, his servants work their wickedness, the passions and movements of the body stir restlessly like internal enemies within the house. 'Battle outside, fear within; battle outside, desire within.' The substance of the body itself is contrary to purity of heart and so struggles against it or at least is repelled by it. Thus, there is daily war [*bellum cotidianum*] and grim battle between these camps [*intra castra*], until [*donec*—see *Ps.* 91off.] God in His mercy should pass judgment on the devil and his ministers; and extinguish the passions and subdue them beneath a watchful mind; and put our souls on trial for all the offenses they have committed and dangers they have caused" (II, 62).

Possibly influencing the seventh battle of the *Psychomachia*, the word *discordia* is frequent in the *De Abraham*, where it is verbally countered by *concordia*. *Bellum* and *pax* are set against each other in much the same way. In his commentary on Ephesians 2:14-16, where Paul calls Christ "our peace" who unifies man, making "the two . . . into one new man, making peace," Ambrose states: "Rightly therefore did the Apostle speak of himself as a miserable man, for he suffered within himself such a war as he himself could not quell" (II, 28).

Like Prudentius, Ambrose seems to believe that the struggle in the mind is resolved by Christ and by wisdom, *Sapientia* and *sapientia* in tandem. The *De Abraham*'s references to *sapientia* are dense. Ambrose often quotes Solomon (or pseudo-Solomon) so as to let the concept of wisdom operate in its dual function, theological and psychological. In a passage not unlike the invocatory prayer of the *Psychomachia*, Ambrose tells how the mind should be directed to see the sins of the world by the grace of Christ, and how the *mens sapientis* should respond: "For his [Abraham's] mind was directed toward the grace of Christ and he saw that this world is full of sin and that sin flies, as it were, from the height of the heavens and weighs down upon the depths of the earth; that modesty, good faith, and honesty are the slaves of no passions, that avarice and care for material things, by which those who possess the delights of riches are stifled, are lashed about and rent asunder. On account of which, riches and concern for earthly things are called cares, because they distract the mind and split it in two and drag it along contrary paths and do not allow it to remain whole and uncorrupted. Therefore a man of peaceful mind sits down and reflects to what extent he can do battle against these evils and put a stop to them, evils that oppress mankind. For the mind of a wise and just man strives to find remedies for human misery and to check and stop the troubles of our souls [*prohibere ac resecare animarum nostrarum labores*]" (II, 60).

227

Where Ambrose puts great emphasis on the rational mind's detachment from sins, Prudentius is more apt to stress the mind's active struggle against these sins. Ambrose's Platonism is evidenced by his wholesale borrowing from the Genesis commentary of Philo Judaeus, especially from his treatise of the same title, the *De Abrahamo*.[40] Prudentius pares away the Platonic elements as he finds them. Prudentius is more moralistic than Ambrose, more acridly and militantly Christian, more outspoken against the pagan philosophy used by Ambrose in support of his intellectual methods. Despite their basic differences in outlook on Hellenism and humanism, and despite their resultant differences in literary technique, both the bishop and the lay poet show a similarity of interest in Christian psychology. In attempting to describe the conditions within the soul, both writers employ metaphors (and allegories) of warfare (civil and imperialist), division, subjection, alienation. Both rely heavily on wisdom literature and on the Pauline epistles for their psychological themes. And both relate the struggle of the soul against sin to the anagogic themes and imagery of the Apocalypse.[41] Given the psychological exegesis by Ambrose in the *De Abraham*, combined as it is with these themes so basic to the *Psychomachia*, it is unlikely that Prudentius' choice of the Abraham story as the major typological preface for his psychological allegory is fortuitous.

Other features of the *De Abraham* confirm direct influ-

[40] The borrowings are cited in footnotes in the *CSEL* edition (cited n. 38 above). Morton W. Bloomfield, "A Source of Prudentius' *Psychomachia*," *Speculum*, 28 (1943), 87-90, mentions that the Abraham story is allegorized by Philo "at least three times," but he appears not to know of Ambrose's treatise. Bloomfield offers a number of possible sources, helpfully countering C. S. Lewis's nomination of Statius as the major source and suggesting that we search for Christian sources. But many of the sources that Bloomfield nominates are Greek or quite early. I see no reason to believe that Prudentius knew Philo; if Prudentius did know Philo, he need not have gone to Philo with the far more accessible treatise of Ambrose before him.

[41] See especially *De Abraham* II, 22.

ence upon the *Psychomachia*. First, the 318 servants from Genesis 14:14. In Book I, Ambrose explicates this number by means of its Greek letters: thus 318 is τιη, τ or 300 is the cross of the Passion, ιη or 10 and 8 are the first two letters in the name ιεσυς.[42] When Scripture says that Abraham went out with his 318 servants, therefore, this means that Abraham conquered by his faith in Christ rather than by the host of soldiers: *fidei ergo merito Abraham vicit, non populoso exercitu* (I, 15).[43] Having presented this numerological theory in the first book, Ambrose builds upon it in the second. "It is the number of life. In it is life, if we believe in the name and passion of our Lord Jesus. The embattled mind knows the recruits it should take to itself to consummate the battle; with what weapons it should take the field; under what banners it should lead the charge. It carries forth no dragons nor images of eagles, but marches out to battle with the cross of Christ and in the name of Jesus, from this sign taking courage, from this banner learning loyalty. Justly, therefore, is the mind embattled which has taken to itself the true wisdom (Wisdom) of a just man (Man) [*vera sapientia iusti viri*]" (II, 42). Perhaps these passages are the source of the *figura mystica* (58) of Prudentius' "Praefatio." Not only does the phrase *Christi pro nomine* (775) occur in the speech of Concordia, and not only are the names of Christ, both literal and figurative, abundant in the *Psychomachia*, but in the "Praefatio" itself the idea of mystic knowledge of the power of the 318 generates the appearance or inspiration of Christ. Immediately after the 318 is mentioned come the words: *mox ipse Christus . . . intrabit*—and Christ is the first word of the hexameter section.[44]

[42] 318 is also the number of bishops at the Council of Nicaea!

[43] The Ambrosian numerological allegorization of the 318 is not original with him. It first occurs in the probably Alexandrian *Epistle of Barnabas* (late first century), and is known in the East thereafter. But Prudentius' most likely source for it is surely Ambrose.

[44] The first word (Word) and almost the last: *Sapientia regnet*. Is

229

The second relatively obscure feature Prudentius may have derived from the *De Abraham* is the trinitarian interpretation of the three angels entertained by Abraham under the oak at Mambre (Genesis 18). This is no doubt related to the stormy emergence of orthodox doctrine—the Nicene party zealously searching for prefigurations of its *credo* in the Old Testament. Such exegesis of the mysterious threesome may seem no more fanciful than other exegeses quoted above, but it was not so universally accepted. Augustine, in the *City of God*, condemns such a reading sharply, instead arguing for the angelic nature of Abraham's guests.[45] But Ambrose accepts the vision of the Trinity. "First see this mystery of faith: God appeared to Abraham, and he saw three beings. He whom God illuminates sees the Trinity: for no one can worship the Father without the Son, nor profess the Son without the Holy Spirit" (I, 33). This is explicit. While Prudentius calls the guests angels (*angelorum*), possibly meaning to qualify Ambrose, he accompanies this literal statement with suggestive words: *triformis angelorum trinitas* in the narrative section of the "Praefatio," a straightforward *Trinitas hospitae* in its conclusion. Therefore I doubt that Prudentius would take issue with Ambrose's reading, and he may well be following it.

A final obscurity is the name change of Abram to Abraham (Genesis 17:5). We recall that Prudentius alludes rather cryptically to this name change and later presents the name of Christ in a structurally parallel manner.[46] Ambrose writes that Abram means "father," Abraham "the venerable father" or "the father elect" (I, 27). Ambrose now follows the Pauline allegory of the two sons, the fleshly and the spiritual, in the Epistle to the Hebrews. When Abram had offspring from the bondswoman, he was merely Abram,

---

Prudentius thinking of the A and Ω of Apoc. 22:13? If so, is the structure of the words *pater . . . Pater* in the "Praefatio" intended to parallel the structure of *primus et novissimus, principium et finis*?

[45] *De Civ. Dei* XVI, 24. [46] See p. 209.

merely a father; when his offspring was spiritual, not fleshly, he became Abraham. Read through this Pauline interpretation, the addition of a syllable becomes an important
symbol of conversion from sin to God, from Old Law to
New Law.[47] The addition of a syllable makes Abraham the
elect father of nations; his seed is Israel, the children of
promise fulfilled by the grace of Christ as the faithful of
Christ's Church.

The influence of the *De Abraham* upon the *Psychomachia* should be studied in far greater detail; my treatment has only touched upon some of the more visible correspondences. Ambrose has a great deal more to say about
Lot in Sodom (I, 44-58; II, 25-41), about the laughter of
Sarra (II, 86), and about the sacrifice of Isaac (I, 62-76).[48]
From our limited examination we have seen that some of the
more obscure features of the "Praefatio" can be located—
with their probable interpretations at hand—in the *De
Abraham*. The interpretations offered by Ambrose often
illuminate the *Psychomachia*, and this is true for conventional subjects (the order of Melchisedech, etc.) as well as
for those examined here.

What is most interesting about the *De Abraham* is not
its treatment of specific themes and characters, but its overall method. The *De Abraham* is a serious attempt to bring
Scripture to bear on an analysis of the soul's structure, its
conflicting motions, and the religious solution to these motions. In using this work, Prudentius' great achievement was
to accept the typological connection between Scripture and
detailed psychology in a spirit of poetic restraint. In turning Ambrose's voluminous treatise into a compact poem,

[47] For the addition of a letter in Sarah's name (Sara-Sarra), see *De
Abraham* II, 85. (The source is Genesis 17:15.) Prudentius uses the
spelling "Sarra"—that is, the superior form in Ambrose's allegorization.

[48] For Isaac as the perfected and graced soul, see p. 220. Beatrice (cited Critical Introd., n. 27), 61, believes that Isaac signifies
Christ, that is, virtue; I would prefer an interpretation as perfection
in Christ (the Pauline concept).

Prudentius disposed of much repetitive verbiage and strained exegesis. He selected and simplified the scriptural events thereby increasing the intelligibility as well as the dramatic impact of the plot of the life of Abraham. He took an almost shapeless mass of material and formed it into a design of figural symmetry.

Although the *De Abraham* can treat of *anima*, "which merits being named a temple of God" (II, 11), Ambrose's influence upon the *Psychomachia* is not literary so much as ideological or spiritual. Perhaps the *Dittochaeon* provides the best clue to the *Psychomachia*'s formal genesis. Scenes from scriptural history are the appropriate pictures for the walls of the Christian temple, be that temple the Church or the Christian soul. Church architecture is built upon the structure of Scripture, its formal symmetry based on the symmetry of salvation history; the Church's sacraments offered to believers from the central place where Christ, the center of salvation history, is pictured. In that the *Psychomachia* is sacramental poetry, written to save souls at the Last Judgment by the conversion of its readers, it likewise conforms with the form of Scripture. The *Psychomachia*, Prudentius claims, is a temple built by Christ, and therefore it mirrors its ideal subject, the soul in a state of charity. The perfect soul is a temple itself, and contains a temple, Christ. The *Psychomachia* contains many typologically related temples: the temple of Solomon, the temple of the pure heart, the anagogic temple of the New Jerusalem, and the temple of Sapientia. In the *De Abraham*, Ambrose writes that the best mind will contemplate the beginning and end, that is, the good. "But the good is Wisdom, for 'no one is good but the one God.' From Him we have come forth and have been created; to Him we return because it is better by far to be with Christ. And in order that you might know (because it is good) to equate the beginning and the end, He Himself, the good Lord Jesus, said: 'I am alpha and omega, the beginning and the end'. Let our mind ever be with Him, let it never depart from

His temple, from His Word. Let it ever be in the reading of Scripture . . ." (II, 21-22). The *Psychomachia* is itself a *lectio scripturarum*, a selective gathering and a reading of Scripture. In the temple of Sapientia, the beginning and end whom our mind is meant to contemplate, the allegorical *mens* is never far from the richly ordered Word of God.

The Assault Upon Vergil

To PROVE the *Psychomachia*'s extraordinary affinities with Scripture is not to explain its peculiar interspersal of Vergilian themes and language. Statistically, one hexameter verse in ten contains direct borrowings; this is a high density of Vergil in a work whose basic metaphors and historical allusions are scriptural and whose allegorical vision evolves toward scriptural paraphrase.[1] But the conventions of the Latin epic are in fact as conspicuous as the typological design. The warfare section is enveloped in an archaic heroic atmosphere, its single combats bearing no resemblance to the efficient fighting style of the Roman legions under Theodosius, its combatants' diction of formal harangue evoking ancient days. Even Fides tends to act and speak more as Aeneas than as St. Paul—a tendency not wholly traceable to the dactylic hexameter. Such classical features of theme and style are no more accidental than their verbal relations: the quotations from and allusions to Vergil's *Aeneid*. Indeed, Prudentius advertises his use of Vergil by constructing his very first hexameter from a well-known verse in the *Aeneid*; by spacing quotations in a con-

---

[1] The 1:10 ratio applies not to actual vocabulary (in which case it would be higher), but to lines containing recognizable Vergil. In this category, I include those listed in the notes of Lavarenne's 1933 edition of the *Psychomachia* (cited Critical Introd., n. 1); and in Lavarenne, *Étude sur la langue du poète Prudence* (Paris, 1933), pp. 562-596 ["Emprunts, imitations, allusions littéraires"], where ascription of the Vergilian borrowings is overly cautious. I include also the "probable" and a few of the "possible" quotations listed by Albertus Mahoney, *Vergil in the Works of Prudentius* (cited Critical Introd., n. 13). See n. 59 below for additional remarks on principles of ascribing borrowings.

spicuous pattern of clusters; by alluding pointedly, requiring the reader to compare and contrast the original context with the new one. The Vergilian presence in the *Psychomachia* being far more than rhetorical color,[2] we must acknowledge that Prudentius, for whatever purpose, is working on more than one level of meaning with the one Latin language at his disposal.

Many critics have not so acknowledged. By underestimating both Prudentius' artistry and his audience's responsiveness to the Roman tradition, they have concurred with Comparetti's stern judgment of fourth-century literature: "... every work of art during this period is a mere unintelligent imitation. . . ."[3] The underlying assumption here is that because Vergil (and other Augustan poets) had been absorbed by rote learning and by *imitatio* in the schools of rhetoric and had in turn been employed in panegyrics and *centones*, received knowledge of Vergil was necessarily shallow, however broad. When Lubac describes the *Psychomachia* as "pétrie d'expressions virgiliennes" or when the editor Lavarenne refers disdainfully to "ce pastiche perpetuel du style virgilien," they mean that Prudentius' quotations and allusions are practically meaningless.[4] The notion that this major feature of the *Psychomachia* is "mere convention" has persisted stubbornly. Even Albertus Mahoney, who has studied the matter most thoroughly and has discovered many cases of local thematic relevance in the Vergilian quotations, is embarrassed by the "epic trappings—the well-known epithets, the familiar verse tags, and the tedious harangues."[5]

[2] But it is also that—see discussion below.

[3] Domenico Comparetti, *Vergil in the Middle Ages*, trans. E.F.M. Benecke, 2d. ed. (1908; rpt. Hamden, Conn., 1966), p. 50.

[4] Lavarenne, *Prudence: Psychomachie* (1933), p. 77, on the authority of P. de Labriolle, *Histoire de la littérature latine chrétienne*, p. 619: "Altogether, the poem leaves an impression of ugly pedantry, which values a nearly continual pastiche of Vergilian epic style." For Lubac citation, see Critical Introd., n. 33.

[5] Mahoney, p. 76. See "Conclusion," pp. 194-195, for the view that

I find that the content of the *Psychomachia*'s Vergilian language, far from being negligible or morally neutral, is mock-classical, mock-epic expression; and that its proper context, more than a culturally elite's nostalgic preservation of the classics, includes bitter Christian-pagan antagonism. Prudentius, it seems to me, is reacting against a real cult of Vergil at the close of the fourth century, and he conceives of this aristocratic movement as a form of pagan idolatry. He fights this movement on its own turf, using Vergil as a weapon against Vergil. In so doing, his stance towards the literary tradition is that of an extremist, his poetic techniques radically Christian.

Prudentius' contemporary St. Jerome, who is usually a moderate and a humanist on such matters, poses the basic theoretical questions in his letter to Eustochium. While attempting to convince this high-born Roman lady to give up the world for the sake of God, Jerome turns to the topic of *adulterium linguae*, the sinful and extra-religious preference for classical literature over the Word of God. " 'What communion hath light with darkness? What concord hath Christ with Belial?' What has Horace to do with the Psalter, Virgil with the Gospels and Cicero with Paul? Is not a brother made to stumble if he sees you sitting at table in an idol's temple? Although 'unto the pure all things are pure' and 'nothing is to be refused if it be received with thanksgiving,' still we ought not to drink the cup of Christ and

---

Prudentian Vergil is, first, rhetorical and, second, of local thematic importance. Mahoney's study, despite the limitations of its conclusions, is extraordinary in its thoroughness and its perception of Prudentius' craft. My present chapter would not be possible without his efforts. The unpublished dissertation of Stella Marie Hanley, "Classical Sources of Prudentius" (Cornell, 1959), contains additional discussion of the thematic importance of Vergil, but Hanley's argument suffers gravely from the humanistic fallacy: e.g., "Prudentius exemplifies the view, justified from his day to ours, that the pagan classics deserve to be honored and studied as part of the tradition of culture which is our inheritance from the ancient world" (p. 329).

the cup of devils at the same time."[6] If Jerome's dictum can serve as a criterion for poetic creation as well as literary criticism, the language of the *Psychomachia* is not beyond adultery, not so liberated from the Christian claim to exclusive truth that it can serve two traditions honorably.

It seems likely that Prudentius is knowingly guilty of *adulterium linguae*, which he commits in order to provide his audience with the moral exemplum. The mingling of the two literary systems is too obtrusive not to be spiritually shocking. The contradictions between Vergil and the Gospels are not smoothly resolved or synthesized—yet the display of these contradictions is morally instructive. It is interesting that the poet avoids an easy handling of tension: he does not fill his warfare section with Vergilian reminiscences only to allow these to become ever rarer until, in Sapientia's temple, only Scripture is heard in unison. True, Discordia (wounder of Concord, enemy of Faith, prefigured by Belial) is rent to pieces at the gates of the virtues' camp. True, within the city are unity, concord, symmetry—the aesthetic indices of moral purity. Yet within the New Jerusalem of the soul, Discordia continues to lurk as a literary presence, surely by the poet's design. Amidst the wealth of scriptural words forming Sapientia's temple are scattered recognizably non-scriptural, Vergilian words, and one of the *Psychomachia*'s most obtrusive clusters of phrases from the *Aeneid* is located at Sapientia's feet, even in her blooming scepter. This being so, the Christian reader cannot respond only to the anagogic vision; his critical faculties must be additionally engaged.

Others before me have argued the existence of this second substantive dimension of meaning in the *Psychomachia*, but they have not appreciated its negative force. According to W.T.H. Jackson, the *Psychomachia* "assumes, as does the Vergilian epic, a struggle between two opposed views of

[6] Letter 22. 29, from *Jerome: Selected Letters* (Loeb Classical Library), ed. F. A. Wright (London, 1954), p. 125.

existence—the new Trojan and the old Italian in the *Aeneid*, the combats between brothers in the *Thebaid* of Statius, and it assumes also the possibility of the resolution of the struggle between these forces by the outcome of one titanic conflict. . . . By using these epic techniques, Prudentius lends to the Christian's daily struggle with evil the grandeur and majesty as well as the authority of the epic. . . . The implication of an 'epic' struggle dignifies the effort to make virtue conquer vice and universalizes it."[7] The main idea here being developed by Jackson is that personified abstractions require behavior to be believable and that, being unable simply to move into everyday life, they therefore require another milieu within the reader's experience. The use of an established literary frame, the epic, creates this milieu for allegory. But Jackson's secondary idea is that these epic conventions elevate and dignify the *Psychomachia* by evoking the precedent of civilizing struggle, and here I must disagree. It is not unreasonable to find in the two-part plot of warfare and city construction a reflex of the *Aeneid*, but the analogy does not hold, at least not positively. In the *Aeneid*, a tragic gloom overshadows the new civilization, but in Prudentius' soul-city everything glitters. In the *Aeneid*, the city's limits are prematurely marked out (Book VII); the city is never seen rising on its foundations; even as Turnus expels his last breath, the building of New Troy remains a matter of prophecy. The *Psychomachia* corrects all this. If comparisons are to be made with the plot of *Aeneid*, these must show Vergil's tragic resolution unsatisfactory in contrast to the brilliance of the scriptural edifice. In this ironic sense, the points of contact with the world of epic or with Augustan historiography may be said to dignify the *Psychomachia*.

Writing several decades before Jackson, H. J. Thomson anticipates his conclusions in the course of a more detailed

[7] W.T.H. Jackson, "Allegory and Allegorization" (cited Chapter II, n. 1), 165.

analysis of the problem. Up to the point that Prudentius' reaction to Vergil is characterized, the anti-pagan irony overlooked, Thomson's argument is compelling. Thomson begins by countering the theory of unintelligent imitation: "It is a great exaggeration to speak of the *Psychomachia* as almost a *cento* of Virgil; and it is unjust to accuse Prudentius of transferring Virgilian phrases and ideas to his poem in a mechanical and unintelligent way. After full allowance is made for the extent to which his mind was soaked in Virgil, there is a considerable residuum which shows that he could use borrowed material in his own way, making it live anew in true adaptation to his own purpose, which is what Virgil himself often did with conspicuous success. A good example is in the incident of Avarice, who, finding that in her own character she cannot harm the Virtues, disguises herself as the Virtue Thrift, and in that array does much execution. The device is suggested by Coroebus in *Aeneid* II putting on the harness of the Greek Androgeos, but here it is used with particular appropriateness and with true observation."[8] It is regrettable that after his perceptive observation Thomson offers so few examples of this local thematic relevance, but thanks to Mahoney we now possess many. Thomson's opposition to the then standard deprecation of the *Psychomachia* as a *cento* is correct insofar as it demonstrates the meaningfulness and control of the Vergilian element. But in some respects the *Psychomachia is* like a *cento*. Thomson, who probably has no quarrel with Comparetti's assessment of the genre as mechanical and unintelligent, does not perceive that the Christian *cento* in the hands of a good poet can be a sophisticated anti-Vergilian satire. I contend that Prudentius' employment of phrases from Vergil is meant to create the impression of simultaneous relevance (such as Thomson notes) and irrelevance,

[8] H. J. Thomson, "The *Psychomachia* of Prudentius," *The Classical Review*, 44 (1930), 111. Thomson here also refers in a note to this passage's debt to *Aeneid*, VII, 415, where Allecto changes into the likeness of Calybe.

and that the combination of the two involves irony and *cento*-like ridicule.[9] This occurs locally, in the periodic clusters of Vergilian quotations.

My qualified appreciation of Thomson's *Classical Review* article extends to his summary of the significance of Vergil in the *Psychomachia*: "I suggest that Prudentius conceived the war of Aeneas as in a way 'prefiguring' the moral warfare in the soul, divine law and peace subduing selfish passions, just as incidents of the Old Testament were often interpreted as prefiguring events of Christian history or elements of Christian experience."[10] By way of support, at least half of the Vergilian borrowings are discovered to have been taken from Books IX to XII, a quarter of them from Book XII alone. "Nowhere else in Prudentius," Thomson explains, "do these books figure to anything like this extent, and it is clear that while composing this poem he had Aeneas' conflict with Turnus much in mind. It is not the mere imitation of Virgil that is significant, but the suggestions which come to Prudentius from the contest of the divinely commissioned Trojans with the present inhabitants of their promised land under 'proud Turnus.' "[11] This intriguing notion of Vergilian typology is wide of the mark. Prudentius hardly ascribes sacredness to Vergil and his failure to name Vergil does not bespeak a sense of the master's importance; he offers no positive evidence that the methods of scriptural exegesis are meant to apply to secular literature. While some of his Vergilian borrowings are, loosely speaking, "figural," that is, referring to events in the *Aeneid* analogous to events in the soul, others work according to "negative typology," *in malo* by means of ironic contrast; still others are purposefully irrelevant, having no connection whatsover with the mental action. Such lack of consistency is in sharp contrast to the overall consistency of scriptural typology in the *Psychomachia*.

9 Below, p. 259. 10 Thomson, 112.
11 Thomson, 111.

Furthermore, there is no Roman counterpart to Abraham in the *Psychomachia*, no Roman figure who functions to anchor the psychological action to a progressive or rationally conceived Roman history. Prudentius nowhere shows that he cares a whit about Aeneas. It is true that in the *Apotheosis* the Roman emperor is placed in the traditional line of succession from Aeneas, but this detail is meant to further emphasize the conversion of Rome:

> iam purpura supplex
> sternitur Aeneadae rectoris ad atria Christi,
> vexillumque crucis summus dominator adorat.
>
> (*Apo.* 446-448)

[Now the successor of Aeneas, in the imperial purple, prostrates himself in prayer at the house of Christ, and the supreme lord adores the banner of the cross.]

Prior to these lines is a lengthy catalogue of the barbarian tribes Christianized and of the pagan gods (worshipped by Aeneas) now impotent; following these lines is the story of the confoundment of Julian the Apostate. The context of this passage, then, is hardly the glorification of Roman tradition. Aeneas is not mentioned in the *Psychomachia*, but neither is Turnus, and there is no indication that Prudentius favors one hero over the other. Even if there were reason to believe that Prudentius approved Aeneas' conquest of Latium—perhaps his Roman patriotism so permitted, or perhaps his faith in God's providence—this would not suggest a prefiguration of the Christian virtues. The virtues fight for the soul's salvation and for the soul's perfection in Christ, in which respect they are justly prefigured by Abraham. Only the vices in the *Psychomachia* could be "prefigured" by the characters in the *Aeneid*. All fighting in the *Aeneid* is carried on by mortals who have no salvational desire—they are all doomed, Aeneas along with Turnus.

I do not wish to suggest that all early Christian writers,

241

in recognition of Vergil's damnable qualities, simply cast
him in Hell and turn to the Bible for inspiration. Prudentius'
manipulation of Vergil is a special response to special social
exigencies;[12] others, particularly at the beginning of the
fourth century, imitate Vergil almost enthusiastically.[13]
Jerome speaks for these other writers when he allegorizes
the purification of captives (Deut. 21:10-13) in reference
to the pagan classics: "Is it surprising that I too, admiring
the fairness of her form and the grace of her eloquence,
desire to make that secular wisdom which is my captive
and my handmaid, a matron of the true Israel? Or that
shaving off and cutting away all in her that is dead whether
this be idolatry, pleasure, error, or lust, I take her myself
clean and pure and beget by her servants for the Lord of
Sabaoth? My efforts promote the advantage of Christ's family, my so-called defilement with an alien increases the
number of my fellow servants."[14] Presumably all Christian
writers understand the difference between the beautiful
captive's prior condition of impurity and her shorn and
trimmed condition. Jerome's statement of Christian humanism, it should be noticed, does not deny the alien status of
the captive; nor does it suggest that his use of classical forms
and eloquence is based on more than a cynical appreciation
of their practical value in winning souls. I am aware of no
fourth-century writer who holds that Vergil is a Christian
poet or "says the same thing" as Scripture,[15] but some of

[12] See the end of Chapter I.

[13] See discussion of Juvencus *et al.* above, p. 104, and below, p. 248.

[14] Letter 70. 2. Trans. in D. W. Robertson, Jr., *A Preface to Chaucer* (Princeton, 1962), p. 340.

[15] Augustine, in Letter 137 and in *De Civ. Dei* X. 27, points to the Fourth Eclogue as containing a prophecy of Christ; but he does not claim that the poet Vergil prophesies Christ. Lines 13-14 of Vergil's poem are said to be *veraciter . . . si ad ipsum referas*—an important "if"—and line 4 is cited as evidence that the Cumaean Sibyl, not Vergil, prophesied Christ. For Augustine's more typical anti-Vergilian stance, see below, p. 245. Jerome, in Letter 53.7, ridicules any Christian interpretation of the Fourth Eclogue.

these writers show an implicit awareness of Vergil as a pagan whose works glorify Satan's.[16] Their attitudes toward the pagan classics range from caution and uneasiness (Jerome) to open hostility (the apologists). An author will quote Vergil in order to gain a pleasing effect, in order to remind a pagan reader that one can be civilized in spite of one's Christianity; or an author will lambast Vergil's inconsistencies, his advocacy of immorality, his elevation of outmoded myths and divinities. Both techniques are conversionary. That both are meant for an audience of pagans and lukewarm Christians is suggested by the fact that neither Jerome nor Augustine are wont to quote Vergil or attack Vergil in their letters and treatises directed to other ecclesiastics.[17] At the same time, their letters to pagan aristocrats and their apologetic writings respond to an obviously strong and widespread love of this greatest—yet (alas!) pagan—Roman poet. Augustine, Jerome, and other Christian authors, all of them having passed through the Roman educational system, occasionally confess frank admiration for the Augustan poets.[18] But in a sense they all know better: there is no real ambiguity in their religious estimation of Vergil.

Prudentius, the early Christian master of the hexameter, believes as strongly as any other poet that the *Aeneid* is what Jerome calls a cup of devils, an idol's temple. Prudentius is incapable of Jerome's rhetorical generosity and sin-

[16] See discussions of *Confessions* and Proba's *Cento* below. Meyer Reinhold, "The Unhero Aeneas," *Classica et Mediaevalia*, 27 (1966), 195-207, discusses statements by Tertullian, Lactantius, and Orosius *contra* Aeneas.

[17] For the quotation of Vergil by Jerome and Augustine, see Harald Hagendahl, *Latin Fathers and the Classics: A Study of the Apologists, Jerome, and Other Christian Writers* (Göteborg, 1958); and *Augustine and the Latin Classics*, 2 vols. (Göteborg, 1967).

[18] Thus Jerome in Letter 70, quoted above, and Augustine, retrospectively, in the *Confessions*, treated below, p. 245. All must admit that Vergil is the best of the *poets*—but the term may sometimes be loaded.

243

cere pathos, which allows the comparison of Alaric's sack of Rome (410) with not just the fall of Moab (Isaiah 15:1) and the fall of Jerusalem (Psalm 78), but the fall of Troy (*Aeneid* II, 361-365).[19] When such large comparisons occur in the *Psychomachia*, they are fundamentally ironic. They could be termed negative or parodic typology if such terms did not obscure the poet's own clear distinction between the Word of God and the impure ancillary, the beautiful captive violated. Prudentius' disrespect toward the captive Vergil is understandable because of the closeness of the pagan revival, the veneration still felt in Rome for Flavianus and Praetextatus. The occasional nastiness of his disrespect is perhaps mitigated by its high artistry. The Vergilian presence in the *Psychomachia* amounts to a sophisticated literary attack, rhetorically interesting, and having nothing in common with the typically crude Christian lambast except for its basic meaning—that the *Aeneid* is a monstrous form, a work of Satan. This meaning and its mode of presentation, I think, were meant for the aristocratic descendants of Flavianus and Praetextatus.

FOURTH-CENTURY VERGIL

Far from any typological fulfillment, the *Psychomachia* seems to reverse and ultimately disregard the structure of the *Aeneid*. Granted that the bulk of the borrowings are from *Aeneid* IX-XII, those books narrating the warfare between the Trojans and the confederated Italians, these should be thematically appropriate, as Thomson claims, to the battle section of the *Psychomachia*. Such is their arrangement: the end of the *Aeneid* informs the beginning of the *Psychomachia*. Since Prudentius shows favoritism toward neither antagonist of Vergil's poem, this structural reversal may suggest that the state of sin *in toto* corresponds with the founding of the Roman state, a morally neutral

---

[19] In Letter 127. 12. Text and trans. is in *Jerome: Selected Letters* (cited above, n. 6), pp. 462-463.

historical process. But Book XII of the *Aeneid* is additionally evoked at the end of the *Psychomachia*, Latinus' scepter
figuring in the scepter of Sapientia. The weight of tragedy
contained in this reminiscence is increased by other tragic
allusions—to Dido, to the fall of Troy—and the effect of all
these upon the *Psychomachia*'s comic resolution is, ironically, negligible. The heroic narrative of arms and the man
is not permitted to move forward through the *Psychomachia*. Having suggested the state of sin during the warfare section, *Aeneid* IX-XII continues to do so—by self-
reminiscence—during the scene of Christian worship.[20]

Probably the greatest example of structural manipulation
of the *Aeneid* in early Christian literature is Augustine's
Confessions. Unlike Prudentius, Augustine purposefully
establishes straight parallels between his plot, that of his
own career, and that of the *Aeneid*; yet very much like
Prudentius, Augustine plays off the Christian resolution
against the vain and false activity of Aeneas. Early in the
Confessions occurs the famous critique of the role of pagan
poetry in the Roman educational system, and this critique
sets up the later interplay between the careers of Augustine
and Aeneas. As a converted Christian scanning his previous
life of sin, Augustine recognizes that his schooling in grammar had been beneficial only insofar as it taught him how
to read and write. "For those first rudiments were better,
because more certain, (seeing that by them, that skill was
and is wrought in me, that I am able to read what I find
written, and of myself to write what I will) than these
latter; by which I was enforced to commit to memory the
wanderings [*errores*] of I know not what Aeneas, while I
forgat mine own [*errores*]: and to bewail dead [*mortuam*]
Dido, because she killed herself for love; when in the mean
time (wretch that I was) I with dry eyes endured myself
dying towards thee [*a te morientem*], O God my Life!"[21]

[20] Discussed at the end of this chapter.
[21] *Confessions* I. 13, from *St. Augustine's Confessions* (Loeb Classical Library), ed. W.H.D. Rouse, trans. [1631] William Watts (Lon-

Due to sinfulness as well as the circumstances of fortune, Augustine's *errores* follow the tracks of Aeneas' *errores*. "To Carthage I came, where a whole frying-pan full of abominable loves crackled round about me, and on every side" (III, 1). As Augustine departs for Rome, his separation from his mother Monica recalls that of Aeneas from Dido. "That night I privily stole aboard, but she did not: she tarried behind in weeping and prayer. . . . The wind blew fair, and swelled our sails, and the shore withdrew itself from our sight. There on the morrow she fell into an extreme passion of sorrow, and with complaints and lamentations she even filled thine ears, which for that little seem to regard them: when through the strength of mine own desires, thou didst hurry me away, that thou mightest at once put an end to those same desires: and that her carnal affection towards me might be justly punished by the scourge of sorrows."[22] As in the *Aeneid*, the hero of the *Confessions*, still ignorant of God's total plan for him, severs a "carnal" relationship in the interest of furthering his career. If much of the irony is self-directed, it is also against Augustan historiography. At every reminder of the *Aeneid*, new Christian meanings emerge from the parallel circumstances. The recollection of these parallel circumstances proclaims a hiatus of moral experience. Augustine's goal is not Rome at all, but (at this point unbeknownst to him) God, and after he arrives in Italy the correspondences with

---

don, 1931), Vol. I, p. 39. In this passage Augustine, despite his confessed past sympathy for Dido, shows no preference for Dido over Aeneas, or vice versa.

[22] *Confessions* V. 8. *sed ea nocte clanculo ego profectus sum, illa autem non; mansit orando et flendo. . . . flavit ventus et implevit vela nostra, et litus subtraxit aspectibus nostris, in quo mane illa insaniebat dolore et querellis et gemitu implebat aures tuas contemnentis ista, cum et me cupiditatibus raperes ad finiendas ipsas cupiditates, et illius carnale desiderium iusto dolorum flagello vapularet.* Text and trans. Loeb Vol. I, pp. 236-237. See also IX. 9, where Monica is described as is Lavinia in the *Aeneid*. See Robert Hollander, *Allegory in Dante's Commedia* (Princeton, 1969), p. 12 and n.

the *Aeneid* almost cease. Among the last such correspondences are the battles between Augustine the rhetorician and his antagonists (especially his pupils) at Rome; finally, the struggle between Aeneas and Turnus recurs within Augustine's soul and reaches its crisis just prior to his conversion in the garden of Milan. Thus the concluding books of the *Confessions*, those containing the exegesis of Genesis 1, are beyond the experience of the *Aeneid*. There is no Vergil in Augustine's post-conversionary confession of faith; rather, the commentary on Genesis continues the chain of Scripture whose links run through the *Confessions*. And the commentary is part and parcel of Augustine's formal subordination of narrative autobiography to prayerful devotion. What has Vergil to do with the Gospels? In the *Confessions*, Vergil reminds us of the *errores* and battles associated with the state of sin. That we are reminded of the career of Aeneas amidst a continual flow of quotations from Scripture suggests that the moral struggle is also a literary one. That is, it is wrong to weep for Dido when, with the Psalmist, we should be weeping for the state of our souls, and so long as we follow the career of Aeneas our wills are misdirected by sin and ignorance.

Augustine's use of Vergil in the *Confessions* amounts to an implicit literary attack against him. This attack is not unexpected. The *Aeneid* glorifies the city of man, the dynasty of Augustus Caesar; it is idolatrous not only in its direct praises of pagan gods and religious piety, but in its civil piety. In the *City of God*, Augustine often refers to "this Vergil of theirs" (*hunc Vergilium*) or, more contemptuously without the name, "their poet." A passage from the very beginning of the *City of God* characterizes the quintessence of Vergilian political theory (VI, 853—the destiny of Rome prophesied by Anchises) as sinful. "For the King and Founder of this City, which is the subject of my discourse, has revealed in the scripture of his people a statement of divine law, which I quote: 'God resists the proud but gives grace to the humble [James 4:6].' Indeed,

247

it is this distinction, which belongs to God, that the inflated fancy of a proud spirit assumes when it chooses to be praised in the following terms: 'To spare the fallen and subdue the proud' [*Parcere subiectis et debellare superbos*]. This is why I cannot, in so far as the plan of my undertaking demands and my own ability permits, pass over in silence that earthly city which, when it seeks for mastery, though the nations are its slaves, has as its own master that very lust for mastery."[23] Prudentius likewise cannot pass over in silence the history of the earthly city, Rome, as he relates the building of the heavenly city in the soul. Like Augustine also, Prudentius links the earthly city with Vergil, its greatest apologist.

Augustine's sustained quarrel with Vergil as the mouthpiece of *Romanitas* is linked to the historical situation around the fall of Rome: to the refusal of pagan ideology to yield to Christianity without a struggle, specifically to the pagan revival of the 390's and its continuing effect upon Roman thinking into the fifth century. Conditions at the beginning of the fourth century were much different, and these encouraged reconciliation of Christianity with the spirit as well as the forms of classical culture.[24] Both poets and prose writers of the Constantine period quote Vergil mainly for rhetorical effect; in so doing, they betray little awareness of literary or ideological incongruity. Juvencus' *Evangeliorum Libri* is, as Curtius has correctly said, an imitation of the *Aeneid*. When Juvencus paraphrases Matthew 14:22-23, the episode of Christ's walking on water during the storm at night, he arranges his storm in Vergilian manner and borrows heavily from the *Aeneid* to do so (III, 93-132). God the Father takes on several of the poetic features of Vergil's Jove: thus he is *repertor* (I, 35), as in Vergil's *hominum rerumque repertor* (XII, 829)—the translation is doctrinally sound, rhetorically pleasing. Only occa-

---

[23] *De Civ. Dei*, I, "Praefatio." Loeb Vol. I, pp. 11-13.
[24] See the discussion of paganism in Chapter I.

sionally will Juvencus gently and playfully bring in the context of the *Aeneid* in such a way as to remind us of its inadequacy. Thus when Satan tempts Christ with the rule over worldly kingdoms, Satan's speech contains a parody of that of Mercury to Aeneas in Book IV, 272, during which the hero is reminded of his mission to found Rome: *Ostendens illi fulgentia regna per orbem: / 'Cernis, ait, quae sit tantarum gloria rerum?'* (I, 399-400). This sort of ironic contextual relevance, located regularly in the *Psychomachia*, is only sporadic in Juvencus' *Evangeliorum Libri*.[25] The great majority of Juvencus' borrowings are morally

[25] Text in *Iuvenci Evangeliorum Libri Quattuor*, ed. Huemer, *CSEL*, Vol. 24 (Vienna, 1891). Juvencus' awareness, too, of a higher Christian purpose can be seen in his "Praefatio." Although he praises Vergil (and Homer)—

> Hos celsi cantus, Smyrnae de fonte fluentes,
> Illos Minciadae celebrat dulcedo Maronis.　　　　　(9-10)

—Juvencus also distances himself from this tradition. Long-lasting fame for honor and virtue is gained through poets' praises, but this is impermanent like all worldly things.

> Inmortale nihil mundi conpage tenetur,
> Non orbis, non regna hominum, non aurea Roma,
> Non mare, non tellus, non ignea sidera caeli.
> Nam statuit genitor rerum inrevocabile tempus,
> Quo cunctum torrens rapiat flamma ultima mundum.　　　　　(1-5)

This allusion to the Last Judgment puts the created universe, including man's socio-political institutions, under God's rule; the Vergilian subject matter is thus subordinate to the subject matter of Juvencus' Gospel poem. Vergil's glory is *aeternae similis, dum saecla volabunt* (12), but Juvencus will sing an eternal subject. Note how the word *inmortale* is picked up from line 1:

> Quod si tam longam meruerunt carmina famam,
> Quae veterum gestis hominum mendacia nectunt,
> Nobis certa fides aeternae in saecula laudis
> Inmortale decus tribuet meritumque rependet.
> Nam mihi carmen erit Christi vitalia gesta,
> Divinum populis falsi sine crimine donum.　　　　　(15-20)

And when flames ravish the world, this work (unlike Vergil's, surely) will be spared by Christ the Judge.

249

neutral and seem intended to create an elegant epic style for the Gospel narrative, a style perhaps befitting the imperial court.[26]

Lactantius' effort to unite Christianity with pagan culture is even greater. The myth of the phoenix, already the common property of pagan and Jewish poets and philosophers, he translates smoothly into a Christian allegory. The *De Ave Phoenice* concerns Christ, whose miraculous resurrection resembles that of the mythical bird; yet the story contains no overtly Christian referent. According to the allegory, God the Father is Apollo: "Phoebus she obeys, and to him she yields her homage, a remarkable satellite . . ." (*Paret et obsequitur Phoebo memoranda satelles*, 33). The Paradise where the phoenix makes her home is strongly reminiscent of Vergil's *Georgics*—a rhetorical feature of conventional fourth-century Christian Paradises. This Paradise is the negation of Vergil's hell—the personifications of *Aeneid* VI, 274-276 are expressly excluded from it:

> Non huc exsangues morbi, non aegra senectus,
>   Nec mors crudelis nec metus asper adest. . . .   (15-16)

[Not to this place come any enfeebling disease, no weak old age; neither cruel death nor poignant fear is present. . . .][27]

Yet such negation carries no irony against Vergil. Rather, the poem achieves an easy blending of scriptural idea and classical imagery. Phrases like *ter quater* abound; the dawn is rosy Aurora, obtrusively classical; as the phoenix bird prepares for her resurrection, Aeolus encloses the winds in his cave (73). Such patent willingness to embrace Roman mythology as Christian symbol is unthinkable in a Pruden-

---

[26] See the concluding praise of Constantine: VI, 806-812.

[27] Latin text from *L. Caeli Firmiani Lactantii Opera Omnia*, Pars 2, ed. Brandt and Laubmann, *CSEL*, Vol. 27 (Vienna, 1893), p. 136; trans. M. F. McDonald, *Lactantius: The Minor Works*, The Fathers of the Church, Vol. 54 (Washington, D.C., 1965), p. 213.

tius or an Augustine. Lactantius' Apollo is practically a manifestation of Christ—the diametrical opposite of Prudentius' Apollo. In his use of mythology, Lactantius is perhaps the extreme of a general tendency of Caesaropapal culture: the desire to reconcile Horace with the Psalmist, Vergil with the Evangelists.[28] In both Lactantius and Juvencus this cultural liberalism shows itself in the willingness to make rhetorical borrowings from the classical writers, and especially from Vergil, with little or no indication of ideological tension.

However, it would be misleading to imply that confident rhetorical use of Vergil is confined to the first part of the fourth century. I have already mentioned Jerome's likening of the fall of Rome to the fall of Troy—a rhetorical usage by a Christian humanist able to praise Juvencus. Among late fourth-century Christian authors, Ambrose is also noteworthy for his elegant manner of Vergilian borrowing, and in this he betrays his class origins in the Roman aristocracy. His *Hexaemeron* is an exposition of the six days of Creation as revealed in Genesis. The subject is conducive to praise and thanksgiving for all created things, and Ambrose shows a great interest in natural history. Commenting on the beauties and utilities of the small things of nature, he relies heavily on Vergil's *Georgics* and *Eclogues*. It is generally true that if Vergil has written verses on a creature Ambrose wishes to treat, these verses will turn up as slightly reworked phrases of Ambrose's prose. For example, accounts of waterfowl (V, 43) and bee colonies (V, 67) in the *Hexaemeron* are imitations of *Georgics* I, 360ff. and IV, 153ff. respec-

[28] The only credible pieces of evidence presented by Comparetti to support widespread fourth-century belief in Vergil's Messianic Eclogue come from the period of Constantine. Thus Eusebius relates in his *Vita Constantini* (IV. 32) that the Emperor heard a Greek translation of the Fourth Eclogue and an accompanying Christological interpretation of it. Thus Lactantius in the *Divinae Institutiones* (VII. 24) interprets the poem as referring to the second coming of Christ. Discussed in *Vergil in the Middle Ages*, pp. 100-101.

251

tively. Similar use of Vergil occurs in all of Ambrose's exegetical writings, especially when the subject at hand is creation, and as a rule the Ambrosian context closely parallels that of Vergil. There is no hint of ironic quotation; rather, the Vergil in Ambrose functions as stylistic embellishment.[29]

Another rhetorical appropriator of Vergil is the Spanish Pope Damasus (366-384), who generously pads his verses with Vergilian borrowings. Either the context in Vergil is completely irrelevant or else has a certain association with the matter Damasus treats, but in neither case is the usage anything but straightforward. Two verses from a tomb inscription for a sister Irene show borrowings from the *Aeneid* without regard for context. In the first, *voverat haec sese Christo cum vita maneret* (10, 3) the last three words are probably taken from *Aeneid* VI, 608, where the tag is attached to the fratricides and patricides in Hades. Because the meaning of the borrowing is rather inconspicuous, and because there is no reason to assume that Damasus wishes to denigrate this Irene through association with the Vergilian context, the instance is undoubtedly one of requiring the words only. Much the same applies to the second verse, *magnificos fructus dederat melioribus annis* (10, 8), where the last two words come from *Aeneid* VI, 649, and refer to the "happier years" of Teucer's line before the battle at Troy. I suspect that Damasus, as he composed this inscription, read over fifty or so lines of *Aeneid* VI in search of filler. One might conceivably argue that since this is a tomb inscription, the context of Book VI is appropriate, yet if the author wished to advertise this context he surely could have found more memorable quotations.

But another poem by Damasus shows more relevant borrowing. This is a song in praise of David, some of its lines treating David's victory over Goliath and given as reminiscence of several battles in the *Aeneid*. The phrase *trun-*

[29] So concludes the dissertation of Mary D. Diederich, *Vergil in the Works of St. Ambrose*, The Catholic University of America Patristic Studies, Vol. 29 (Washington, D.C., 1931), p. 126.

cumque reliquit recalls Nisus' beheading of Remus in *Aeneid* IX, 332, and Turnus' beheading of Phegeus in *Aeneid* XII, 382. Just about all the vocabulary is Vergilian:

> ingentem clipeoque gravi frustraque minantem
> impia, maledicum, faleras telaque gerentem,
> surdorum demens coleret qui templa deorum,
> mactavit saxo tereti truncumque reliquit,
> iudicioque dei ingenti mox caede peracta
> monstravit populis tulerat quae ex hoste tropaea.
>
> (I, 11-16)

[This giant with his heavy shield threatening wicked deeds in vain, foul-mouthed, bearing breast-plate and spears, a raving creature who would honor the temples of the deaf gods—him David killed with a smooth stone, left the trunk remaining. Having quickly performed a mighty slaughter by God's judgment, he showed the people what trophies he had won from the enemy.][30]

The heroic accoutrement of the *Aeneid* (worn, with a possibly intended irony, by Goliath) fits the context, and even certain actions (the beheading) are thematically appropriate.

There is of course a great disparity in quality between this poem by Damasus and Prudentius' battle scenes. Damasus' words, but not the movement of his lines, are Vergilian, while in the *Psychomachia* both words (often ironically) and movement are Vergilian.[31] Yet both poets try for some

[30] Text from *Anthologia Latinae Supplementa*, Vol. 1, ed. Ihm (cited Chapter I, n. 29), p. 1; trans. mine.

[31] E. K. Rand, *Founders of the Middle Ages* (Cambridge, Mass., 1941), p. 184: Prudentius "has mastered the art of the Virgilian hexameter with more delicacy than those martial and resonant singers, Juvenal, Lucan, and Claudian." On the basis of his analysis of metrical schemata (or patterns), George E. Duckworth, *Vergil and Classical Hexameter Poetry* (Ann Arbor, 1969), p. 133, finds Prudentius more Ovidian than Vergilian—that is, having less spondaic and more dactylic character. But in other respects Prudentius and Paulinus of

of the same effects. Quality aside, the crucial difference between them is that while Damasus' borrowing from Vergil remains almost entirely rhetorical, Prudentius' borrowing is rhetorical only as it mounts a full-scale literary attack.

Before leaving the subject of rhetorical Vergilian allusion in fourth-century Christian literature, I frankly admit a lack of sure criteria for determining these authors' compositional intentions. It is sometimes difficult to judge whether a particular Vergilian quotation is indeed a quotation. When Damasus uses the phrase *truncumque reliquit*, I suspect that he knows his allusion; but a phrase such as *cum vita maneret* could well result from unconscious recollection of Vergil. This ambiguity of intentionality exists in Prudentius' borrowings in the *Psychomachia*, where it poses interpretive problems.

A related critical problem stems from the likelihood that a number of borrowings in Christian poetry of the fourth century are indirect. Christian hexameter poets from Juvencus onwards gradually collected their own conventional formulae, many of which are ultimately Vergilian (as we recognize, perhaps as these writers also recognized) but may not have been meaningfully felt as such. An example is the formula *tunc [dum, cum,* etc.] *pater omnipotens. . .* , which introduces any sentence the subject of which is God the Father and carries the meter as far as the caesura: thus *sed Deus omnipotens (Apo.*, 726). Since this expression has become a Christian commonplace, it would seem a small matter whether a given poet is aware that Ovid used it in *Metamorphoses* I, 154. The neutrality of such formulae in respect to their pagan ancestry is shared by certain longer themes. In a number of early Christian poems dealing with

---

Nola are judged "the most Vergilian" of the Christian poets of the late Empire: e.g., in variety of patterns, in the avoidance of repeat clusters, and in the infrequency of repeats. Given the mannered quality of sections of Prudentius' verse, nevertheless our poet can imitate Vergil very well indeed when he wants to. Duckworth's analysis on the whole supports Rand's assessment.

the Creation is felt the strong influence of *Georgics* III,
242 ff.

Omne adeo genus in terris hominumque ferarumque,
et genus aequoreum, pecudes pictaeque volucres,
in furias ignemque ruunt: amor omnibus idem.

[Yea, every single race on earth, man and beast, the tribes
of the sea, cattle and birds brilliant of hue, rush into fires
of passion: all feel the same Love.]

—and of these lines from Anchises' speech to Aeneas in the
underworld:

Principio caelum ac terras camposque liquentis
lucentemque globum lunae Titaniaque astra
spiritus intus alit, totamque infusa per artus
mens agitat molem et magno se corpore miscet.
inde hominum pecudumque genus, vitaeque volantum,
et quae marmoreo fert monstra sub aequore pontus.

(VI, 724-729)

[First, the heaven and earth, and the watery plains, the
shining orb of the moon and Titan's stars, a spirit within
sustains, and mind, pervading its members, sways the
whole mass and mingles with its mighty frame. Thence
the race of man and beast, the life of winged things, and
the strange shapes ocean bears beneath his glassy floor.]

Christianization of these two passages involves no insuper-
able difficulty for a poet without intensive theological insight, for there are clear correspondences with the creation
story in Genesis.[32] When a Christian poet employs phrases
from these passages, he is much more likely than with the
formula naming God the Father to be conscious of their

[32] E.g., Proba's *Cento*, 40-41, etc., cited n. 49 below; "Hilary," *In
Genesin*, text in *Cypriani Galli Poetae* . . . , ed. R. Peiper, CSEL,
Vol. 23 (Vienna, 1881), pp. 231-239. For a cluster of quotations from
Georgics in Prudentius, see *Ham.* 199-223, where we see not Para-
dise, but the cruel realities of fallen Nature.

classical origin. He will have memorized these passages in the course of education in rhetoric. Yet once one or two poets have thus Christianized Vergil, a third poet with full knowledge of pagan literary source may rely on the authority of his Christian predecessors for the usage. In this manner a certain quantity of Vergilian language perhaps passes over into conventional Christian language. Encountering certain "Vergilian" phrases in Prudentius, therefore, we shall be wise to refrain from being totally convinced of their conscious or direct pagan origin.

Nevertheless, critical judgments about the meaning of allusions are possible. In our examination of fourth-century poets' rhetorical use of Vergil, we have observed variation in the effective appropriateness of the original context. Granting a certain range of ambiguity within this variation, the extremes are usually identifiable. Sometimes a poet will borrow—consciously or unconsciously—Vergil's words in such a way that their original context either is irrelevant or would confuse the sense of the new passage. At other times a poet will bring Vergil's context to bear on his own, and we judge this to have happened when the original and later contexts either are parallel or are obliquely or conversely related so as to create wit or irony. We have seen that a purely rhetorical use of Vergil occurs throughout the fourth century when authors appropriate only words (for padding) and when they rely on non-ironic contextual parallels; we have also seen that as early as Juvencus there is a slight tendency toward ironic quotation. How do these uses relate one to another? Our analysis of contextual relationships is hampered by the lack of detailed scholarly treatment of the conventions of early Christian poetry. Yet the literary history of Vergilian allusion could be written— its outlines may be already visible. If one compares Juvencus with a late fifth-century poet like Avitus, one easily detects a change away from decorative rhetorical quotation and toward contextually sophisticated quotation.

Avitus' hexameter poem on Genesis occasionally displays true wit in its borrowing technique. Thus when God speaks to the newly created Adam and Eve, he instructs them to go forth and multiply and fill the earth with their seed. He says that they will have eternal life (*non annis numerus vitae*), and then, "I have granted a race without end . . ." (*progeniem sine fide dedi*).[33] Thus God the Father is made to paraphrase the words of Jove to Venus prophesying the endless rule of the Roman Empire:

his ego nec metas rerum nec tempora pono;
imperium sine fine dedi.   (I, 278-279)

[For these I set neither bounds nor periods of empire; dominion without end have I bestowed.]

The irony is complex and far-reaching. Since by Avitus' time the fall or at least the political decline of Rome was quite evident to everyone, this quotation from the *Aeneid* exposes Vergil as a false prophet and *Romanitas* as an inadequate ideal. Furthermore, Augustine had already employed the same quotation with the same effect in the *City of God*, and had thereby established its analogical Christian spiritual significance without losing the ironic sense that Vergil had never intended this higher significance. "Lay hold without delay on the heavenly fatherland, which will cost you but the slightest toil and will enable you to reign in the true sense and forever. There thou shalt have no fire of Vesta, no Capitoline stone, but the one true God 'no times, no bounds will set to action / But grant an empire without end [*imperium sine fine dabit*].' Do not pursue false and fallacious gods. Abandon them rather, and despite them, break away into true liberty."[34] Now when with this authoritative precedent Avitus has God speak as Vergil's Jove, Avitus at

[33] *De Mundi Initio*, 174, 175. Text ed. Abraham Schippers (Kampen, 1945).
[34] *De Civ. Dei* II, 29. Loeb Vol. I, p. 261.

one and the same time propounds a divine truth and alludes to a human falsehood. The divine truth is that there is eternal life for mankind: it is available to the first humans in Paradise, and it will be restored later by the redemptive grace of Christ. The human falsehood is twofold: first, Vergil's own falsehood; second, the general falsehood inherent in man's free choice of sin which, in Avitus' specific context in the Genesis story, creates dramatic irony in relation to the imminent Fall. In comparison with Juvencus, then, Avitus shows a substantial development in the sophisticated use of Vergil.

In both Augustine and Avitus we find more than simple irony, which would occur if a linguistic statement were supposed to mean something else besides what it seems to mean. Here the irony is complex, for two or more true (real) meanings obtain simultaneously: Vergil *in bono* and *in malo*. Jerome's famous citation of the fall of Troy does not function in this manner; it is a positive vehicle of pathos, bearing no extra cargo of irony. Nor is the whole tradition of rhetorical quotation of Vergil ironic. Yet ironic usage emerges from within the rhetorical tradition; indeed, where else could it come from? As we have seen, the quotation of Vergil for color, for elegance of expression, involves a wide range of possible consciousness of the original Vergilian context. Where the original context is invisible or inconsequential, no irony is possible; but where the original context is visible, irony is possible—not merely possible, but probable. For there are very few passages in the *Aeneid* (besides VI, 724ff.) readily lending themselves—at least until the twelfth century, with the school of Chartres—to Christianization.[35] The pagan content of Vergil and the other Augustan poets is usually too blatant for the late fourth- and fifth-century reader to gloss over except by

[35] For twelfth-century allegorization of Vergil, see Bernardus Silvestrus' commentary of *Aeneid* I-VI; and John of Salisbury's *Polycraticus*.

means of total allegorization.[36] Once the Vergilian context is advertised by a literary artist, therefore, it will most likely expose, and be intended to expose, the falsehood of Vergil. But Augustine and Avitus carry this process one step further; they Christianize the ironic Vergilian passage as an addendum, allowing the sense *in bono* to accompany the sense *in malo*.

This evolution is behind the complexity of the heroic narrative in the *Psychomachia*. The heroic warfare of the *Aeneid* is between pagans who know not God, who have no salvational hopes—this is true for "good" pagans like Aeneas, Evander, Latinus, as well as for "bad" pagans like Turnus, Mazentius, Ulysses. Consequently, quotations advertising the context of their battles are essentially *in malo*, and thus fittingly the whole heroic atmosphere in the *Psychomachia* is associated with the state of the soul immersed in sin. But the virtues are from Christ, and their heroism must be qualitatively different from that of the vices. Therefore the *in bono* sense of heroism accompanies the other: the Vergilian epic machinery associated with the virtues recalls the alternate heroic mode of Abraham, David, and Judith. Thus Roman and scriptural heroism operate simultaneously in the *Psychomachia* and may, insofar as they surface in recognizable Vergilian borrowings, be apprehended by means of complex irony.

THE *Cento*

Our analysis of Vergil in Prudentius demands consideration of the *cento*, a genre whose structural principal is related to complex irony. The *cento* is held in such ill repute today that it may seem futile to attempt a serious critical assessment of it, but this assessment is needed because the *Psychomachia*'s Vergilian clusters are *cento*-like. I may

[36] See the *De Continentia Vergiliana* by the Christian Fulgentius (no later than the sixth century).

259

admit that most *centones* are bad poems without defining the genre itself prejudicially. Ausonius' *Cento Nuptialis*, in point of fact, is a good poem even though it is neither "serious" nor "profound," and Proba's Christian *cento* is more successful, given its poetic assumptions, than is generally understood. But perhaps there is something inherent in the *cento* that inspires distrust in modern critics.[37] Without having read through the Vergilian *centones*, Comparetti offers this judgment: "[Vergil's] chief office now was to teach children in the schools and so give them the means of emphasizing their childishness when they grew up. In fact, he was so thoroughly studied at school that to know his works by heart from one end to the other was no uncommon feat. This great familiarity with his writings, coupled with the general poverty of ideas of the period, led to the production of the 'Centos,' in which, by the adroit combination of isolated lines and hemistichs, Vergil was made to say the most unexpected things. The idea of such 'Centos' could only have arisen among people who had learnt Vergil mechanically and did not know of any better use to which to put all these verses with which they had loaded their brains."[38]

In his epistolary introduction to his *Cento Nuptialis*, Ausonius freely admits the essential playfulness of the form: "They who first trifled with this form of compilation call it a 'cento.'" (*Centonem vocant, qui primi hac concinnatione luserunt.*)[39] Ausonius (d.c. 395) is not so serious-minded as Comparetti; but, being a contemporary of Prudentius and engaging in a still living genre, his views are probably more valuable to us. By what he says and by his

[37] Its capacity for playful profanation of poetry?

[38] *Vergil in the Middle Ages*, p. 53. Comparetti could not have read more than the first half of Proba's *Cento*, for he says that she "told the story of the Old Testament in Vergilian verses" (p. 54).

[39] This and subsequent quotations from the *Cento Nuptialis* from *Ausonius* (Loeb Classical Library), 2 vols., ed. and trans. Hugh G. Evelyn White (London, 1951), Vol. 1, pp. 370-393.

tone, Ausonius makes it clear that the *cento* is one of the lower or minor genres: " 'Tis a task for the memory only, which has to gather up scattered tags and fit these mangled scraps together into a whole, and so is more likely to provoke your laughter than your praise" (*solae memoriae negotium sparsa colligere et integrare lacerata, quod ridere magis quam laudare possis*). He defines it as "a poem compactly built out of a variety of passages and different meanings, in such a way that either two half-lines are joined together to form one, or one line and the following half with another half." Now follows a technical metrical justification of this definition in terms of the structure of the dactylic hexameter and its alternative caesurae. Part of the delight of the *cento* is in the technical skill with which it is put together, a skill likened to that required for excellence with the Greek bone-puzzle known as the *ostomachia*. One struggles with the bone shapes which resist combination; and if one is skillful one can produce a delightful picture, perhaps of a brutal boar or of a goose in flight, but an unskillful hand will produce only a grotesque jumble. Thus a good *cento* is one which is able to conceal the natural tensions among the disparate pieces of the puzzle. "And so this little work, the *Cento*, is handled in the same way as the game [*ludus*] described, so as to harmonize different meanings, to make pieces arbitrarily connected seem naturally related, to let foreign elements show no chink of light between, to prevent the far-fetched from proclaiming the force which united them, the closely packed from bulging unduly, the loosely knit from gaping."

Now any artist can form a picture of a brutal boar without using a bone-puzzle; a poet can describe a wedding night without using half-lines from Vergil. It is the very artificiality of the *cento* composition which appeals; rather than disguising this artificiality, a good *cento* will solicit our amazement at it. Comparetti has correctly observed that the *cento* is unthinkable without poets and an audience so fluent in Vergil that every hemistich could be identified, or almost

261

identified, at first hearing. We can only imagine the amusement of this audience (since we ourselves know no poet so well as this audience knew Vergil) at hearing a description of sexual intercourse made up of such disparate parts as the golden bough, the god Pan "crimsoned with vermillion and blood-red elderberries," Polypheme (*monstrum horrendum, informe, ingens*), and countless thrusts and parries of the *Aeneid*'s heroic warriors. Allusions are recognized with simultaneous dual associations: the original context mingles with the new context, giving in this *cento* a ridiculous but lighthearted effect. "For it is vexing," explains the poet, "to have Virgil's majestic verse degraded with such a comic theme" (*piget enim Vergiliani carminis dignitatem tam ioculari dehonestasse materia*).[40] For this *cento*, composed as an *opusculum*, and an amusing (*festiva*) one, it would be inaccurate to employ the term "irony" as we have been using it for the Christian borrowings of Vergil. But its basic technique is related, the basic difference being that here the same technique is continually repeated so as to become a structural principal of composition. Ausonius calls his *Cento Nuptialis* "absurd, though of grave materials" (*de seriis ludicrum*); a Christian poet would reverse the formulation, composing a *cento* "grave, though of absurd materials," but he would appreciate the same juxtaposition of contexts for its ridiculous, or ironic, effect.

We turn to the most famous Christian *cento*.[41] Faltonia

[40] Quintilian seems to understand the possibilities both for degradation and for humor in *cento*-like quotations. As rhetorical fault: . . . *vitium est apud nos, si quis sublimia humilibus, vetera novis, poetica vulgaribus misceat. Id enim tale monstrum, quale Horatius in prima parte libri de arte poetica fingit: "Humano capiti cervicem pictor equinam / Iungere si velit," et cetera ex diversis naturis subiiciat* (VIII. 3. 60). And as witty effect: *Adiuvant urbanitatem et versus commode positi, seu toti ut sunt (quod adeo facile est, ut Ovidius ex tetrastichon Macri carmine librum in malos poetas composuerit), quod fit gratius, si qua etiam ambiguitate conditur* (VI. 3. 96).

[41] Text in *Poetae Christiani Minores*, Pars I, ed. C. Schenkl, *CSEL*,

Proba, who composed it around the middle of the fourth century, was an important woman of Roman aristocracy, the wife of one consul and the mother of another.[42] She certainly knew Vergil well in order to write a *cento*, and being a well-educated Roman and a Christian, she probably associated with high ecclesiastical authorities. Her literary output, that is to say, in all probability conforms with the needs of the Roman Church and should not be characterized as closet eccentricity. How and why then does she assemble pieces of Vergilian hexameter in order to harmonize them in a new Christian order? Her poem begins with a prayer asking God for his acceptance of the *cento* and explaining its purpose, technique, and relation to the heroic tradition. During the course of this prayer, which is not itself a *cento*, the form gradually evolves: lines from Vergil are inserted into the prayer at an increasing rate until, at its conclusion, it is made up of Vergil. The remainder of the composition is all Vergil, and it is precisely when Vergil "takes over" as the poetic voice that Proba ceases to speak in her own poetic voice and foregoes all *inventio*. The *cento* proper is a paraphrase of Scripture. Like the *Dittochaeon*, it divides into two perfectly symmetrical sections, an Old Testament part and a New Testament part.[43] The first paraphrases the be-

---

Vol. 16 (Vienna, 1888), p. 513ff. The other Christian *centones* are in this volume also. For all of the pagan *centones* except that by Ausonius, see *Anthologia Latina*, Pars I [Carmina in Codicibus Scripta], ed. A. Riese (Leipzig, 1894). Schenkl's "Prooemium" to Proba's *Cento* is extremely useful for a study of both Christian and pagan *centones*, for it lists all the Vergilian *loci* of all the *centones*.

[42] Raby, *Christian Latin Poetry*, p. 14. Prudentius in *C. Symm.* I, 551, names the family in very flattering terms as representing the glorious traditions of the senate begun by Evander.

[43] "Proba's *Cento* is constructed to reflect the symmetry between the Old and New Testaments and the octave ratio between Christ and Adam. 694 lines long, it consists of an introduction, Part One (333 lines, 28 of them introductory), and Part Two (361=333 + 28 lines long). The birth of Christ falls in the exact center; but the events in his life are in many cases described in half the number of

ginning of Genesis, covering Creation, the Fall, and concluding quickly with the Flood. The second paraphrases the
entire life of Christ as presented in the Gospels, concluding
after the Ascension with a brief prayer. A transitional section briefly narrates the Red Sea Crossing. Here the sacramental significance recalls that of the same scene in the
Psychomachia; baptismal cleansing of sins precedes the
Incarnation of Christ, permits the Old Man, the seed of
Adam, to put on Christ.

Why should the Christian poet Proba wish to compose
this sacred story by means of Vergilian borrowings? Some
would attribute the Christian *cento* to tastelessness and
blasphemy,[44] but the poet herself offers a better explana-

---

lines that the corresponding events from the OT require. Lines fall
into groups of 28, 33, 50, 56 (2 × 28) and 100. The most common
mode, 28, permeates the poem, and reflects Pythagorean numerology,
perhaps via the Gnostics, in which it is the second perfect number.
There is a great deal of number symbolism (e.g., the seasons are
described in 12 lines), but the most important numerological aspect
of the poem is the symmetry established between the Old and New
Testaments, pairing the creation of Adam with the birth of Christ,
the temptation of Adam and Eve with that of Christ, the story of
Cain and Abel with the Crucifixion, the Flood (law of justice) with
the Resurrection (law of mercy), and the expulsion of Adam and
Eve from Eden with the descent into Hell."—personal communica-
tion of Gilbert Bagnell. I do not wholly endorse this analysis, but
find it a useful indication of the generally unrecognized sophistication of Proba's *Cento*. The pairing of events is of course typological,
its symmetry resembling Prudentius'. The numerology of Proba is
perhaps a still dubious matter.

[44] Hagendahl, *Latin Fathers and the Classics* (cited above n. 17),
pp. 384-387. On *Psychomachia*, I *et al*.: "I pass on to a more startling
device: prayers to God are couched in the words of a prayer to a
pagan divinity. . . . It is a matter of course that this device above all
is to be found in the *Vergiliocentones*, as in this kind of poetry everything had to be said in the form of Virgilian lines or half lines. . . .
The application is a perfect failure: 'Father of men and gods' does
not agree with the Christian conception of God. . . . What a burlesque
fancy! Christ is substituted for Daedalus, and the Holy Ghost for the
mythical ball of yarn . . . the travesty arouses attention: *altus Apollo*
replaced by *magnus Iesus* and *pater ille deum*, a hint at Jupiter,

tion. In her opening prayer, Proba calls attention to the hiatus between Vergilian and Christian subject matter and between their poetic goals:

Iam dudum temerasse duces pia foedera pacis,
regnandi miseros tenuit quos dira cupido,
diversasque neces, regum crudelia bella
cognatasque acies, pollutos caede parentum
insignis clipeos nulloque ex hoste tropaea,
sanguine conspersos tulerat quos fama triumphos,
innumeris totiens viduatas civibus urbes,
confiteor, scripsi: satis est meminisse malorum:
nunc, deus omnipotens, sacrum, precor, accipe carmen
aeternique tui septemplicis ora resolve
spiritus atque mei resera penetralia cordis,
arcana ut possim vatis Proba cuncta referre.
non nunc ambrosium cura est mihi quaerere nectar,
nec libet Aonio de vertice ducere Musas,
non mihi saxa loqui vanus persuadeat error
laurigerosque sequi tripodas et inania vota
iurgantesque deos procerum victosque penates:
nullus enim labor est verbis extendere famam
atque hominum studiis parvam disquirere laudem:
Castalio sed fonte madans imitata beatos
quae sitiens hausi sanctae libamina lucis
hinc canere incipiam. praesens, deus, erige mentem;
Vergilium cecinisse loquar pia munera Christi:
rem nulli obscuram repetens ab origine pergam,
si qua fides animo, si vera infusa per artus
mens agitat molem et toto se corpore miscet
spiritus et quantum non noxia corpora tardant
terrenique hebetant artus moribundaque membra. (1-28)

---

applied to the Christian God! It is a question of taste whether or not we should take it as a blasphemy." For a recent analysis of Proba's *Cento* as scandalous, blasphemous, and unorthodox, see Ilona Opelt, "Der zürnende Christus im Cento der Proba," *Jahrbuch für Antike und Christentum*, 7 (1964), 106-116.

[A long time ago chiefs who profaned the holy compacts of peace, whom dread desire to rule kept wretched, conflicting murders, kings' cruel wars and battle-lines between kinsmen, shields marked with pollution from parents' gore, and victory-trophies shamefully won, the blood-bespatted triumphs that fame led forth, innumerable cities so often widowed of citizens—I confess it—of this I wrote. It is enough to have remembered these evils. Now, God Omnipotent, I pray you hear a sacred song, open the mouth of your eternal sevenfold Spirit, and unlock the inner rooms of my soul so that I, Proba, as a prophetess may return whole mysteries. I do not care now to seek ambrosial nectar; nor am I pleased to receive the muses from Aonia's peak. Let no vain error persuade me to speak of idols, to pursue laureled tripods and empty offerings and quarreling gods and the conquered penates of noblemen. My task is not to extend men's glory in words and to seek the insignificant praise of men as favors. Imitating the blessed ones, thirsting, I was moistened by the Castalian fountain and drank in libations of holy light; and I would begin to sing from this place. O imminent God, raise up my soul; I will utter a Vergil who has sung the holy gifts of Christ. Returning to a matter obscure to no one, I will go forth from Creation—if faith is in this soul, if true mind infused through the limbs excites the (corporeal) mass and mixes itself with the whole body, if the guilty flesh does not too much retard, and earthly joints and dying members dull, the spirit.][45]

Proba indicates a poetic miracle: she will utter a Vergil who has sung the holy gifts of Christ (23). This can hardly represent her historical assessment of Vergil; it can hardly imply that she believes Vergil to have been inspired by God and to have proclaimed Christ. Such a position would clash with the entire logic of this prayer, with its accumula-

[45] My translation; I am unaware of any other.

tion of contrasting *then/now* and *this/not that* relations which establish irony against Vergil. Proba begins by listing the substance of her earlier poetry. Assuming that she actually wrote this poetry, its disappearance may be explained by its subject matter, which would belong to a preconversion period of Proba's life or of her literary activity. Another interpretation is that Proba here assumes the persona of "the poet" and, in this guise, attributes to herself the grand tradition of Roman poetry. Either way, the subjects treated are those of Vergil, Statius, Lucan. From a Christian point of view, these subjects are all worldly and mirror the state of society in disorder and misery as a result of sin. The impropriety of the epic tradition thus outlined is suggested by the verb *confiteor* (8), "I confess," which may signal admission of guilt before God in addition to acknowledgment of one's works. A similar religious ambiguity may be detected in the phrase *satis est . . . malorum* (8). The worldliness of past poetry is contrasted to the mysterious, inspired, otherworldliness of the poetry to come. This new poetry arises from the miraculous conversion of the poetic tradition, including Vergil, by God's inspirational grace, and its subject matter provides the salvational solution to the condition represented by the earlier themes. All of Vergil's muses are rejected, including (14) that muse of *Georgics* III, 11, who aided in the construction of Caesar's temple. Rejected along with the causes of pagan poetry are its subjects: the quarreling gods, the useless sacrifices, the conquered *penates* of the Roman nobility. Proba's message is clear enough: repudiation of Vergil for Christ. By divine inspiration, the Christian poet will make the pagan Vergil sing the holy gifts of Christ in spite of himself. Having already exposed Vergil's poetic milieu to attack, Proba is able to accomplish two goals at once: as her *cento* unfolds, she not only praises God in a paraphrase of Scripture, but confounds Vergil.

Another early Christian writer, not Proba, has attached to this *cento* an epistolary preface, probably addressed to the bishop of Rome (*Romulidum ductor*).[46] It petitions, "Deign to recognize, through your divine perception, a Vergil changed for the better" (*dignare Maronem / mutatum in melius divino agnoscere sensu*). By the standards of Roman civil religion, such a statement is a blasphemy of sorts, for how could Vergil, the epitome of poets and the voice of *Romanitas*, be changed for the better? Proba's own poetic claim is even more extreme than that of the anonymous writer; she advocates rejection of Vergil as the pre-condition for his forced conversion. What Ausonius says of his own *cento* is true of Proba's (and would seem a basic feature of the genre itself): Vergil is ridiculed in the process of creating something surprisingly new. Where Ausonius is playful, however, Proba is deadly serious. Whatever the poet's purpose, it is the simultaneous perception of the two actions of the puzzle, the picking apart and the piecing together, which makes the *cento* effective. In Proba's *Cento* this simultaneous perception is of error and truth, sin and salvation—in other words, the process of religious conversion in poetry.

The *Psychomachia* is of course not a *cento*, but it is recurrently *cento*-like. Would its several dense clusters of Vergilian quotations have been recognized c. 405 as belonging to the same literary class? We possess no substantive evidence of audience response to Christian *centones*; but we may posit an audience fully sensitive to their basic techniques. Comparetti has rightly pointed to the cultured elite's extensive knowledge of Vergil. Memorization of long passages of the *Aeneid* is widely attested in the fourth century, and one Mavortius is said to have improvised *centones* on the spot.[47] In such a milieu, a Vergilian quotation would be recognized not only as Vergilian, but as having been taken from a particular locus. The obstrusiveness of the contexts

[46] This introductory piece is not in all the MSS, and is not printed in the *Patrologia Latina* edition of Proba. It seems to be nearly contemporary with the composition of the *Cento*, however.

[47] Comparetti, p. 55.

of these quotations often provides their wit or irony, whether the quotations be isolated or condensed in a *cento*. I am sure that a culture producing *centones* would have been alert to related manipulations of Vergil.

The *Saturnalia* supports this line of reasoning by its general characteristic as a repository of Vergil and by specific aspects of its treatment of Vergil. Macrobius' aim, he tells us in his Preface, is to collect in encyclopaedic form a wealth of civilized tidbits worthy to be remembered by his son Eustachius. These are presented in an imaginary dialogue, the occasion of which is a pagan festival, the Saturnalia, actually outlawed years before the work's composition. This festival is observed privately in a pagan household and in a somber, restrained, dignified manner: not with rites but with a discussion of Vergil and evenings reserved for quiet games and pleasantries. The main speakers of the dialogue are Praetextatus, Symmachus, Flavianus, the famous grammarian Servius, and the several other less distinguished pagans.

For all its quiet, nostalgic idealism and its no-longer-militant paganism, the *Saturnalia* is a last-ditch attempt to hold Roman civilization fast against the onslaught of Christianity. Its heroes are highly cultivated, elegant, pedantic, the last survivors of a tired civilization. Macrobius, writing perhaps twenty years after Prudentius, knows well enough that the restoration of the old rites is hopeless, but he is intent on preventing the greatest product of pagan culture from being dragged in the dust. He is not without bitterness, which expresses itself in recurring anti-Christian satire. The pagan heroes of the last generation are apparently defenseless against the rude intrusion of one "Evangelus" into their convivial gathering, for their good manners will not permit them to refuse a place to this Christian boor.[48]

[48] The modern hesitancy to identify "Evangelus" as the butt of anti-Christian satire is difficult to explain except as part of the tendency to see the work as pedantic silliness. Herbert Bloch (cited Critical Introd., n. 6) is exceptionally perceptive of "Evangelus" as a Christian

"Evangelus" displays his perversity whenever he opens his mouth; he interrupts, he misses the gist of the conversation, he petulantly insists upon changing the subject. But of course his major crime is his critique of Vergil as superstitious and as a bad poet. The rest of the speakers agree among themselves that Vergil is not only the greatest of poets, but the repository of all wisdom, the best teacher of grammar, oratory, and the various sciences. On this evidence in the *Saturnalia*, Vergil is the rallying point of aristocratic paganism in the last days of the Empire, and the main object of a cult of *Romanitas*. The characterization of "Evangelus," patently a satiric counterattack, proves that the *Saturnalia* is not the first book engaged in the struggle over Vergil's status.

The *Saturnalia* gives useful secondary information about what Romans c. 430 could discover in Vergil's text, and there is no reason to suppose that this text was interpreted differently in the stormier days when Prudentius worked. First, Vergil was a storehouse of antiquarian lore and, of particular interest to us, of religious lore. The paganism of the late Empire had become infused with the various oriental religions, one effect of which was to put the piety of the *Aeneid* in the category of the old-fashioned. The antiquarian appeal of the Olympian gods and of the rites celebrated by Aeneas had not become entirely a secular matter, however. If nothing else, the religious observances in the *Aeneid* had come almost to symbolize old pagan tradition— one senses this by the meticulous affection attached to these matters in the *Saturnalia*.[49]

Second, the position of Servius in the household of Prae-

---

type. Alan Cameron, in his *Journal of Roman Studies* article (cited Chapter I, n. 44) argues that "Evangelus" is no Christian caricature, but instead a minor and incidental figure recorded in Symmachus' letters, an essentially historical figure.

[49] See especially *Saturnalia* I. 8-24 and III. 1-12. The text used for this work is *Macrobius: The Saturnalia*, trans. Percival V. Davies (New York, 1969).

textatus is made utterly authoritative in matters of interpreting Vergil, which suggests concern over the inviolabil-
ity of the *text* of Vergil. Servius and other speakers often
raise questions about the proper meaning of this word or
that word, and they show an interest in not only the
textual authority of Vergil but its justification. This may
reflect defensiveness against the manipulation of Vergil by
Christians.[50]

Third, among the matters of literary interest is the whole
question of poetic borrowings, influences, quotations, and
imitations. This concern is the key to an appreciation of Prudentius' *cento*-like use of Vergil. Many, many pages of the
Saturnalia are devoted to a complete listing of what lines
and themes Vergil took from Homer, and this includes
evaluation of the success of individual borrowings.[51] It is
most interesting that study of these literary borrowings includes the matter of the context of the quotations in the
original, and that one measure of the worth of such borrowing is whether it fits well into its new context. Given this
extravagant study of Vergil in the late pagan *Saturnalia*, one
including textual matters and the most detailed and intensive
literary concerns, and one supportive of paganism and
Romanitas, it would be hard to err by over-analysis of
Vergilian quotation in embattled Christian poetry of a
slightly earlier period.

VERGIL IN THE *Psychomachia*

The first hexameter of the *Psychomachia* simultaneously
rejects the pagan piety of the *Aeneid* and invokes Christ.
The presence of a nearly intact Vergilian line, and a famous
one, in this prominent position should surely be taken as a
signal of the author's total purpose. What Prudentius accomplishes here in an isolated borrowing is not unlike what

---

[50] For Servius' discussion of linguistic forms, see *Saturnalia* I. 4
and VI. 7-9.
[51] *Saturnalia* V.

he will achieve in his *cento*-like clusters of borrowings. We are reminded of Proba's *Maronem mutatum in melius*—or possibly of "Evangelus" and his misconstruing of Vergil.

The invocation of Christ's inspiration power is also an evocation of the pagan hero Aeneas when, at mid-point of his career and newly arrived in the promised land of Italy, he beseeches the god Apollo for access to the prophetic mysteries of the underworld. There is a certain rhetorical appropriateness in the evocation of the Vergilian context: like Aeneas in Book VI, the poet of the *Psychomachia* is searching for the overarching meaning of human struggle in this world. Comparing the religious prayers of pagan hero and Christian poet, we notice that the rhetorical appropriateness of the borrowing is neither static nor morally neutral, but itself occasions a radical conversion of spirit. Here is Vergil:

> Phoebe, gravis Troiae semper miserate labores,
> Dardana qui Paridis direxti tela manusque
> corpus in Aeacidae, magnas obeuntia terras
> tot maria intravi duce te penitusque repostas
> Massylum gentis praetentaque Syrtibus arva;
> iam tandem Italiae fugientis prendimus oras;
> hac Troiana tenus fuerit fortuna secuta.
> vos quoque Pergameae iam fas est parcere genti,
> dique deaeque omnes, quibus obstitit Ilium et ingens
> gloria Dardaniae.   (VI, 56-65)[52]

> [O Phoebus, who hast ever pitied the heavy woes of Troy, who didst guide the Dardan shaft and hand of Paris against the body of Aeacus' son, under thy guidance did I enter so many seas, skirting mighty lands, the far remote

---

[52] All quotations of Vergil are from *Virgil* (Loeb Classical Library), 2 vols., trans. H. R. Fairclough (London, 1956). I have used this text instead of the authoritative Oxford text because the differences in the Latin are not deemed significant enough to outweigh the advantage of the Loeb text for non-Latinists. (We do not, after all, know what text of Vergil was before Prudentius.)

Massylian tribes, and the fields the Syrtes fringe; now at last we grasp the shores of fleeing Italy; thus far only may Troy's fortune have followed us! Ye, too, may now fitly spare the race of Pergamus, ye gods and goddesses all, to whom Troy and Dardania's great glory were an offence.]

And Prudentius:

Christe, graves hominum semper miserate labores,
qui patria virtute cluis propriaque, sed una,
(unum namque Deum colimus de nomine utroque,
non tamen et solum, quia tu Deus ex Patre, Christe,)
dissere, rex noster, quo milite pellere culpas
mens armata queat nostri de pectoris antro,
exoritur quotiens turbatis sensibus intus
seditio atqua animam morborum rixa fatigat,
quod tunc praesidium pro libertate tuenda
quaeve acies furiis inter praecordia mixtis
obsistat meliore manu.   (1-11)

[Christ, who hast ever had compassion on the heavy distresses of men, who art glorious in renown for thy Father's power and thine own—but one power, for it is one God that we worship under the two names; yet not *merely* one, since Thou, O Christ, art God born of the Father—say, our King, with what fighting force the soul is furnished and enabled to expel the sins from within our breast; when there is disorder among our thoughts and rebellion arises within us, when the strife of our evil passions vexes the spirit, say what help there is then to guard her liberty, what array with superior force withstands the fiendish raging in our heart.]

Simply and directly, Apollo's initial place in the line has been occupied by Christ. The idol has been cast down, the true God is worshipped. As Prudentius has written elsewhere,

273

> torquetur Apollo
> nomine percussus Christi, nec fulmina Verbi
> ferre potest; agitant miserum tot verbera linguae,
> quot laudata Dei resonant miracula Christi.
>
> (*Apo.* 402-405)

[Apollo writhes when the name of Christ smites him, he cannot bear the lightnings of the Word, the lashing tongue torments him sorely whenever the praises of the God Christ's wonderful works are sounded.]

No other text is as good commentary on the first word of the *Psychomachia*.

The special insult tendered to Apollo here at the outset of this poem (and elsewhere) is probably not arbitrary. If Macrobius' presentation of the speech of "Praetextatus" in the *Saturnalia* represents current Roman intellectual trends, Prudentius may be responding directly to pagan theological syncretism: Apollo is the sun according to "Praetextatus," and all the other gods of the Roman pantheon—including the various oriental divinities—are also manifestations of the sun, a single divine power.[53] Another doctrine offered by "Praetextatus" is that Aeneas was the first Roman *pontifex maximus*,[54] an office Prudentius hardly favors. Add to these religious factors the traditional status of Apollo as god of poetry, and Prudentius' substitution makes sense on several levels.

But why is this particular naming of Apollo chosen? We have already marked the hero's general situation at the beginning of Vergil's Book VI. More specifically, Aeneas, by now well established as expert in religious rites and imbued with *pietas*, has made his way to the temple of the Cumaean sibyl. Unlike his earlier religious observances, which were

[53] *Saturnalia* I. 17-23.
[54] *Saturnalia* III. 2. "That Vergil invested Aeneas with the dignity of a pontiff is shown by the very word used for the recital of his hero's woes."

often pragmatic, formal petitions, hurried and crude, what Aeneas is about to experience is the intense, central religious experience of his career. Just before Aeneas' prayer, the sibyl has felt the god's presence. Crying *Deus, ecce, deus* (VI, 46), she enters a state of religious frenzy, and it is in this condition that she urges the hero not to be slow in praying to Apollo "for till then the mighty mouths of the awestruck house will not gape open" (*neque enim ante dehiscent / attonitae magna ora domus*, VI, 52-53). After his prayer, Apollo utters through the sibyl a prophecy of Aeneas' future career. So the prayer was efficacious, and the hero is enlightened by the god and subsequently able to visit the underworld himself, there to witness the significance of his worldly struggles.

Prudentius' situation is analogous to that of Aeneas and the sibyl together. He prays for Christ to reveal the *Psychomachia* through him just as Apollo in former times spoke through the sibyl. His prayer, like that of Aeneas, contains the prominent themes of war, human struggle, the pursuit of some just and good career towards a bright future. The two prayers have a basic similarity of movement. Just as Aeneas addresses first Apollo and then all the divinities collectively, so Prudentius' invocation of Christ becomes an invocation of the Trinity. And the pagan and Christian divinities have parallel relationships with mankind, for they are both proximate enough to be addressed in prayer and powerful enough to alleviate *graves labores*.

Such similarities are not merely rhetorically pleasing; they underscore the radical difference between paganism and Christianity. Christ replaces and obviates Apollo—this is of chief importance; but the substitution of *hominum* for *Troiae* is also significant. The terms of Prudentius' invocatory prayer proclaim the universality of the plot of the *Psychomachia*. Prudentius' outlook is not tribal or national as is Vergil's or as is that of Vergil's contemporary Roman admirers; Prudentius' Romanness shows a certain respect for empire, for political order, but this is dwarfed by the greater

275

aspiration toward the City of God. The founding of New
Troy seems a paltry and misdirected endeavor once the
Gospel is proclaimed; in the hexameters of *Psychomachia*,
Aeneas' great endeavor is superseded by the founding of the
New Jerusalem. The Apollo whom Aeneas invokes as an
active participant in secular warfare is only referable to
human temporal and spatial standards, but Prudentius' God
is at once eternal and historically immanent. Christ's participation in the new moral warfare follows no tribal favoritism but reveals his universal role as man's savior.[55]

Admittedly not all of the borrowings from Vergil are as
suggestive as this first one. There are many phrases in the
Psychomachia, most of them shorter than a hemistich,
which serve no other purpose than to provide incidental
epic conventions of style. As single units of speech, such
borrowings are purely rhetorical and may be seen to contribute unobtrusively to the larger imitation of heroic style.
This minor quotation and imitation of Vergil achieves the
simultaneous heroic (through analogy with Scripture) and
mock-heroic (through emulation of the old Roman tradition) effects already discussed.

My argument by no means denies the rhetorical tradition
of Vergilian quotation in Prudentius; rather, it asserts that
the presence of Vergilian or heroic coloring is not purely
decorative, but works cumulatively to create anti-Vergilian
irony. Throughout Prudentius' works are borrowings of
the order of those in Juvencus and Ambrose, where Vergil's
context backs up the Christian context. But whereas a writer
such as Ambrose will welcome Vergil into his writing just

[55] A second Vergilian quotation in the invocation supports the first.
Combined with the ideas expressed in *exoritur . . . turbatis sensibus*
(7), the word *seditio* recalls the *seditio* of *Aeneid* I, 148. This is the
famous simile of the storm likened to a mob, Neptune calming the
storm to the *virum* of noble character who can quiet a mob. Prudentius implies that Vergil's *virum* is the false pagan version of the necessary Christ, who is the only man who can calm our inner civil
disobedience.

at that point where the subject wants an influx of beauty—
for example, in a description of pre-lapsarian creation, of
Paradise, where Vergil's lines on the Golden Age seem relevant—Prudentius is apt to do just the reverse. Prudentius
marshalls Vergilian phrases for the ugly, the evil, the sinful.
Thus in the *Contra Orationem Symmachi* I, where many of
the satirical hexameters treat the pagan divinities, Vergil
(and Ovid) is ransacked for data on this monstrous subject.
For example, the italicized portion of the following comes
right from *Georgics* II, 380-381:

> his nunc pro meritis *Baccho caper omnibus aris*
> *caeditur.* . . .   (129-130)
>
> [In recognition of these merits a goat is now sacrificed
> to Bacchus on every altar. . . .]

Although the rhetorical technique here is exactly Ambrose's, the persistent choice of falsehood and immorality
as subject matter for Vergilian quotation soon lends the
technique an ironic dimension.[56] A similar usage occurs in
Contra Orationem Symmachi II, but here the subject is less
the actual worship of the pagan gods and goddesses and
more their active role, as claimed by the pagans, in Roman
history. Thus a speech by Juno on the protection of
Carthage is quoted only to show the goddess in error (497-
499); that Vergil himself suggests the same message about
Juno is unacknowledged by Prudentius, with the result that
the error is imputed to Vergil. A similar quotation concerns
Pallas's so-called protection of Ulysses (544), another intervention in human affairs that makes Vergil as well as the
goddess appear foolish. Or again, in the *Hamartigenia*, by
far the heaviest use of Vergil occurs in the description of
the Christian Hell, where we can imagine ourselves with
Aeneas visiting the pagan underworld.

[56] So with the application of *Georgics* to *fallen* Nature. See above
n. 32.

praescius inde Pater liventia *Tartara plumbo*
incendit *liquido* piceasque bitumine fossas
infernalis aquae furvo subfodit Averno,
et *Phlegethonteo* sub *gurgite sanxit* edaces
perpetuis *scelerum poenis inolescere* vermes.
norat enim flatu ex proprio vegetamen inesse
corporibus nostris *animamque* ex ore perenni
formatam non posse mori, non posse vicissim
pollutam vitiis *rursum* ad *convexa reverti*
mersandam *penitus* puteo ferventis abyssi.

(Ham. 824-833)

[Therefore the Father, having foreknowledge, lit the fires
of Tartarus dark-hued with molten lead, and in gloomy
Avernus dug channels for the pitchy bituminous streams
of hell, and down in Phlegethon's gulf ordained that
gnawing worms indwell for the everlasting punishment of
sin. For He knew that the life in our bodies came from
his breath, and that the soul that had its being from everlasting lips could not die, nor again could it return once
more to heaven when it was polluted with sin, but must
be plunged in the depths of the burning pit.]

The italicized words are Vergil's, and most of them occur
in a single passage, *Aeneid* VI, 735-751, where Anchises tells
the hero his son about the mysteries of the underworld.[57]
Prudentius negates Anchises' doctrine while employing his
imagery. Where Anchises says that the soul can return again
to the upper world, Prudentius uses the same language
(*rursum . . . convexa reverti*) preceded by a *non posse*, "it
cannot be." But the major effect here is rhetorical: a sweep
of contextually apt, recognizably Vergilian, allusions. Do
similar allusions occur when the subject is grace and heavenly bliss? Yes, in truth, they do, for Vergil can be abused—
his context inverted, or negated—at will; but they do not
occur so frequently. Vergilian quotations are comparatively

[57] Mahoney, p. 31.

rare, pointed, and carefully selected, when Prudentius writes of divine perfection. The *Hamartigenia*, a poem about the origin of sin, is choked with Vergil, as are other satires against heretical error and paganism, whereas the lyrics are not.[58]

There is an overall tendency in Prudentius' works, then, for Vergil to be rhetorically associated with sin and imperfection. This is borne out in the *Psychomachia*, although here as elsewhere there are important exceptions. Most of the allusions to the *Aeneid* occur during the single combats while the soul is in a state of sin and is struggling to overcome it. This does not mean that Vergilian borrowings must accompany evil. The recollection of events in the *Aeneid* in the temple of Sapientia should alert us against such an oversimplification; so should the fact that during the single combats the virtues as well as the vices are associated with Vergilian borrowings. However, all these borrowings invariably communicate some perspective about the relation of sin, present or distanced, to the action at hand: Vergil reminds us of the city of man.

The comic progress of the soul in the *Psychomachia* is accompanied by progressive shifts in technique vis-à-vis the Roman heroic tradition. Heroic conduct is depicted during the single combats, where its ambiguity is based on the contrast between the moral warfare of scriptural authority and that other futile, immoral, cupidinous warfare of the Roman heroic tradition. Within this large Vergilian imitation are embedded a series of discrete, *cento*-like clusters of quotations, usually one per battle scene. These are formally obtrusive and, in effect, ask to be analyzed in terms of their

[58] There is little obtrusive Vergil in the *Liber Cathemerinon*. Some striking Vergilian borrowing occurs in the martyr poems. The Vergilian "victims" Cassandra and Dido are both recollected in the martyrdom of St. Vincent—high rhetoric? A more ironic usage is in *Peristephanon* X, where the Roman Prefect, as he tortures Romanus, imitates the prophetic speech of Anchises in *Aeneid* VI. See Mahoney, pp. 181-182, for an excellent discussion.

279

composition and function.[59] (They are thematically obtrusive in that no Vergil whatsoever has been quoted in the scriptural "Praefatio.") Near the end of the warfare section occurs a shift in technique that is rather more difficult to assess. This happens as the virtuous army is triumphantly returning to their camp—a false triumph, as is later discovered, yet also a spiritual *transitus*. Here the Vergilian imitation is of a formal sort only, having no quotations or allusions, in the (unique) simile of the Red Sea Crossing. Prudentius' intention here may be simply rhetorical, and it is difficult to judge whether the imitation of a Vergilian simile as a vehicle for this typologically profound scriptural *locus* is meant to convey any irony. Within the city walls occurs another shift of technique. Here there is only very limited Vergilian imitation in the heroic discourse of Fides and Concordia; for the most part, a kind of mystical, scripturally based narrative takes over. As Vergilian imitation dwindles, so does the direct quotation. But at the very end occurs a cluster of forceful allusions again built upon quotations, and these are placed—incongruously, it may seem at first—in the most scriptural scene of the *Psychomachia*. In the course of the whole personification allegory, the transformation of the soul has been immeasurable, from one *status* to another *status*. At the completion of conversion, poignant reminders of Vergil's world confirm the distance between sin and salvation, the pagan heroic world and Christ. Here our perspective on Vergil is distant but clear, unambiguous, and bearing no aesthetic confusion upon the final vision.

In the warfare section of the personification allegory, the

[59] Eighty percent of the borrowings are in clusters: this statistic argues against accidental or unconscious quotation. I assume poetic consciousness when there is (1) a cluster of quotations, (2) a whole line only slightly altered, and (3) a phrase or even a single word which by its special characteristics is markedly Vergilian. Needless to say, this last category is the most liable to my subjective error. How to explain that "Vergilian ring"?

typological scriptural emblems have been counterbalanced by the clusters of quotations. One such cluster occurs during each of the single combats, making seven in all. This one to one correspondence has the important function of systematically connecting the action of the personification allegory with opposing Christian and pagan historical referents. Enough has been said already about the moral hiatus between Scripture and Vergil to suggest that this pairing of opposites is ironic: Vergil is arranged according to a pseudo-order that parodies the scriptural architectonics. The *cento*-like form of the Vergilian clusters is literally a confusion of tongues, a Babylonian language composed of fragments; such an arrangement, simultaneously advertising its coherence and its randomness, sharply contrasts with the aesthetic presentation of the scriptural emblems. Where the Vergil is obscure, the Old Testament type is clear, assuredly conventional, and self-revealing. Again, the virtues explicate their typology; if the vices also explicate their typology, they do so in a visibly backwards logic and with visible perversity of spirit. But the Vergilian quotations have no controlling voice to explain them: they are, so to speak, without authority. To thus offer a Vergil *mutatum in melius* or *cecinisse . . . pia munera Christi* is to deny the literary historical reality of Vergil, to deny his authority. But this does not happen to Scripture which, as itself, explains itself and refers to itself.[60] The opposing moral forces, then, are expressed very differently, and their modes convey their meanings.

This significance of the Vergilian clusters is not a matter of mechanical arrangement. Just as scriptural typology is set among virtues and vices alike—appropriately, for the moral struggle, not its absence, is the substance of Scrip-

---

[60] It is no accident that Prudentius never names Vergil; he would hardly wish to address his own epic as does Statius at the conclusion of the *Thebaid*—

vive, precor; nec tu divinam Aeneida tempta,
sed longe sequere et vestigia semper adora.   (XII, 816-817)

281

ture—so the pagan quotations are set among virtues and vices. It is true that most of the scriptural emblems arise from the virtues; it is equally true that the majority of the Vergil is found near the vices, especially as the vices step into the fray or as they are being killed. But Prudentius has not wished to guarantee the absolute consistency of this pattern, for he is less interested in the simple association of Vergil with sin than in the complex interchanges between Vergil and the Christian moral struggle.

THE BATTLES

I shall examine in detail the Vergilian quotations in the first two battle scenes and shall thereafter restrict myself to more general remarks about certain contextually relevant quotations. This treatment, though incomplete, should suffice to indicate Prudentius' method.

Fides versus Cultura Deorum Veterum.—This single combat has already been discussed in relation to the idea of the heroic, and it has been observed that while the entry of Faith upon the Prudentian battlefield is in many respects un-Vergilian, her execution of the vice is pointedly Vergilian. This sudden transformation of Faith's conduct is emphasized by the infusion of quotations:

> ecce lacessentem conlatis viribus audet
> prima ferire Fidem *Veterum* Cultura *Deorum.*
> illa hostile caput phalerataque *tempora vittis*
> *altior insurgens* labefactat, et ora cruore
> de pecudum satiata *solo adplicat* et pede calcat
> *elisos* in morte *oculos*, animamque malignam
> fracta intercepti commercia *gutturis* artant,
> *difficilemque obitum* suspiria longa fatigant.   (28-35)

[Lo, first Worship-of-the-Old-Gods ventures to match her strength against Faith's challenge and strike at her. But she, rising higher, smites her foe's head down, with its fillet-decked brows, lays in the dust that mouth that was

sated with the blood of beasts, and tramples the eyes
under foot, squeezing them out in death. The throat is
choked and the scant breath confined by the stopping of
its passage, and long gasps make a hard and agonizing
death.]

A number of these tags are thematically relevant to the death
of the vice, for their sources in the *Aeneid* pertain to pagan
piety and religious sacrifice. The very name of the vice
derives from the speech of Evander in Book VIII.[61] Evander
is Vergil's hoary representative *par excellence* of pious
pagan devotion. Here is the opening of his discourse to
Aeneas:

> rex Euandrus ait: non haec sollemnia nobis,
> has ex more dapes, hanc tanti numinis aram
> *vana superstitio veterumque ignara deorum*
> imposuit: saevis, hospes Troiane, periclis
> servati facimus meritosque novamus honores.

(VIII, 185-189)

[King Evander spoke: These solemn rites, this wonted
feast, this altar of a mighty Presence,—'tis no idle superstition, knowing not the gods of old, that has laid them
on us. As saved from cruel perils, O Trojan guest, do we
pay the rites, and repeat the worship due.]

The full force of Prudentius' irony in thus choosing the
vice's name depends upon recollection of its verbal context
within the line, that is, *vana superstitio . . . ignara*. Readers
or listeners who missed this verbal irony—perhaps Evander's speech was one passage they had *not* memorized in
school—would remember its themes anyhow. They would
surely remember that the religious rites celebrated are re-

---

[61] Mahoney does not identify this allusion. Unless indicated, all
following borrowings have been identified by Mahoney. Others not
treated by me are treated by Mahoney; therefore I urge readers to
supplement my treatment by reference to his.

lated to Hercules, the genius of the place, whose execution of the monster Cacus is related by Evander later on in Book VIII. Prudentius in fact reminds us of Cacus' death at the hands of Hercules by quoting the words *elisos oculos* from Evander's speech (VIII, 261). Another allusion to pagan religion is in the words *tempora vittis*, an apt image of Roman ritual. The words could suggest any number of sacrifices in the *Aeneid*. Among these is that spoken of by Sinon, the Greek secret agent against the Trojans. Sinon uses this phrase (II, 133) referring to the fillets meant for his own temples when, according to his fabricated story, he was to have been sacrificed to Apollo by his countrymen. This context may not have been perceived by Prudentius' audience, but another more serious allusion to what is indeed a pagan human sacrifice is present in the quotation of *difficilemque obitum* from *Aeneid* IV, 694. No one would miss this allusion to Dido's death or fail to observe Vergil's manner of representing Dido's suicide upon her pyre as a ceremony of religious sacrifice. In the source, Juno pities Dido's difficult death and sends Iris down from heaven to release the soul; in the *Psychomachia* there is an abrupt change in tone as the difficult death of paganism is cheered by a thousand martyrs. These martyrs have experienced just as difficult dying, but to good ends.[62]

The Vergilian quotations so far examined are thematically apt. A series of ironies are put into motion by them, ironies of varying magnitude of effectiveness, and, it must be admitted, of varying chances of being recognized. But there can be no doubting the relevance of this cluster of quotations to the idea of an anti-pagan struggle. But further complexities arise in consideration of the applicability of the allusions to the personifications themselves. It certainly makes sense (if the sense is intended) for Cultura Deorum

[62] See above, n. 53 and Mahoney's discussion; there remains a question as to whether this usage in the *Psychomachia* sheds light on the other. Perhaps Dido is, in *Peristephanon* V, exposed as the martyr to futility.

Veterum to be like Sinon. A likeness to Dido is also appropriate, for from a Christian point of view there is nothing sentimental about illicit sexual passion or suicide for any reason; nor would Vergil's ritual overtones during Dido's death elicit sympathy in a Christian. And the likeness to Cacus is especially apt: the name means "bad" in Greek (κακός), and paganism was strongly felt to be a monstrous devourer of innocent blood (the martyrs). But here the analogy becomes clouded: is Fides therefore like Hercules? Prudentius elsewhere describes Hercules also as a fiend, a cruel pagan divinity,[63] so perhaps his intent here is to convey that Vergil's world is turned upside down. Along the same lines, Fides' gesture of rising up higher than her antagonist (*altior insurgens*) is like that of Turnus in Book XII, 902. In the phrase *solo adplicet* she is like Coryneus killing the Trojan Ebysus, Book XII, 303. In the face of three such inversions of the *Aeneid*, it would seem overly cautious to argue that Fides simply puts on Turnus' anger and Turnus' bravery, or that her gesture is simply an arbitrarily heroic gesture with no fixed associations with Turnus. There seems to be an equal likelihood that Aeneas' enemies will accompany a virtue as that they will accompany a vice. A Christian virtue may reflect an Italian as well as a Trojan: neither (pagan) side is favored. In respect to this cultivated illusion of arbitrariness, the Vergilian clusters have more than a formal likeness to *cento* composition.

Pudicitia versus Libido.—The second cluster confirms what the first has suggested: that a limited rhetorical appropriateness of theme is contaminated by the purposeful confusion of mingled fragments. Here the cluster is at the beginning of the episode:

exim *gramineo in campo* concurrere prompta
virgo Pudicitia speciosis *fulget in armis,*

[63] Hercules is attacked by the martyr Romanus in *Peristephanon* X; and in *Contra Orationem Symmachi* I, 116-121, where his homosexual love is stressed. Compare Lactantius' *Divinae Institutiones* I, 17-18.

quam patrias *succincta faces*, Sodomita Libido
adgreditur *piceamque* ardenti sulpure *pinum*
ingerit in faciem pudibundaque *lumina* flammis
adpetit, et taetro temptat subfundere *fumo.*
sed *dextram* furiae *flagrantis* et ignea dirae
tela lupae *saxo ferit inperterrita* virgo,
excussasque *sacro taedas depellit* ab *ore.*   (40-48)

[Next to step forth ready to engage on the grassy field is
the maiden Chastity, shining in beauteous armour. On her
falls Lust the Sodomite, girt with the fire-brands of her
country, and thrusts into her face a torch of pinewood
blazing murkily with pitch and burning sulphur, attack-
ing her modest eyes with the flames and seeking to cover
them with the foul smoke. But the maiden undismayed
smites with a stone the inflamed fiend's hand and the
cursed whore's burning weapon, striking the brand away
from her holy face.]

The iconography of Libido is basically scriptural, of course,
the firebrands suggesting both passion itself and the destruction by fire of the city of Sodom. But the various torches
of the *Aeneid* also would seem to contribute their thematic
meanings. Many of these quoted words and phrases come
from Book IX, where the Rutulians attempt to fire the
Trojan fleet with torches. Additionally, the word *pinum*
may recall the episode in Book VII, 398, where the frenzied
Amata carries a flaming pine torch to the Bacchic rites. In
Book VII, 456, Allecto hurls a torch (*faces*) at Turnus in
order to incite him to wrath over his thwarted marriage.
Torches in the *Aeneid* are associated either with destruc-
tive burning or with the passions of love. Both Amata and
Turnus are consumed with passion related to their opposition to the marriage of Aeneas and Lavinia—so in a round-
about way the association of these characters with torches
may bear on the character of Libido. But again, whatever
thematic unity such quotations may cement is broken apart

by the majority of the allusions. These seem purposefully irrelevant or based on inversion. Thus Pudicitia is unafraid (*inperterrita*) like Mazentius in Book X, 770—whom she hardly resembles! Whereas in the previous battle Fides killed Cultura Deorum Veterum much in the manner Corynaeus is said to kill Ebysus (*Aeneid* XII, 287-310), now these roles are reversed. Libido the vice now acts like Corynaeus, who in his first attack against Ebysus assaults him with a charred brand.[64] More confusions and contradictions are visible. Pudicitia on the grassy field (*gramineo in campo*) recalls Aeneas during the games in Book V, 287. Is there any appropriateness here? From Vergil's point of view, Mazentius and Aeneas are polar opposites; either will serve Prudentius' purpose. That Prudentius consciously aims at this mishmash effect is indicated in line 41: *virgo Pudicitia speciosis fulget in armis*. Admittedly a few different warriors "gleam in their armor" in the course of the *Aeneid*, but by far the most noteworthy are Caesar and Pompey. Like the difficult death of Dido, Anchises' prophetic account of Roman history revealed to Aeneas in Hades must have been deeply ingrained in the memories of Prudentius' audience. The phrase *fulget in armis* would recall these lines:

illae autem, paribus quas fulgere cernis in armis,
concordes animae nunc et dum nocte premuntur,
heu! quantum inter se bellum, si lumina vitae
attigerint, quantas acies stragemque ciebunt!

(VI, 826-829)

[But they whom thou seest gleaming in equal arms, souls harmonious now, while wrapped in night, alas! if they but reach the light of life, what mutual war, what battles and carnage shall they arouse!]

---

[64] The virtue Fides has acted like Corynaeus in the previous battle, certainly within the reader's memory.

That both antagonists in the civil war shine equally suggests, once this context is brought into the *Psychomachia*, a truly absurd ambiguity. Just this sort of purposeful irrelevance undercuts the *Aeneid* rather than the *Psychomachia*, and the technique (*de seriis ludicram*), it cannot be overemphasized, comes straight from the *cento*. The insult is repeated every time Prudentius uses Vergil thus irrelevantly or irreverently: it is as if Prudentius were flaunting his lack of respect for Vergil's content, as if he were saying, "I can use you for any purpose whatever."[65]

Patientia versus Ira.—Here there is a much more extended but still dense concentration of Vergilian quotations from line 109, the beginning of the episode, to line 150. Little point would be served by my quoting the passage—neither here nor in later battle scenes does Prudentius' method change significantly. From here on I shall point to certain thematic associations and, where they seem especially striking, the *cento*-like fragmentations. The vice Ira is linked to wrathful warriors of the *Aeneid*. From *Aeneid* X, 644, is the phrase *teloque et voce lacessit* (115), which is said of the phantom "Aeneas" constructed by Juno in order to taunt Turnus into anger. The martial iconography of Ira is certainly consistent with her ethical nature; she is of all the vices the best armed (with conventional edged weaponry,

---

[65] Perhaps the extreme case of this is—

XXXV. PER MARE AMBULAT CHRISTUS

It mare per medium Dominus flųctusque liquentes
calce terens iubet instabili descendere cumba
discipulum, sed mortalis trepidatio plantas
mergit; at *ille manum regit et vestigia firmat.* (*Ditt.* 137-140)

Christ walks on the sea actually—in Vergil the phrase occurs in two similes: the first about the hero Aeneas moving into battle as when a storm cloud moves through mid-ocean; the second about Camilla, who might have crossed the sea's waves without wetting her feet. Here we have obvious contextual reminders which are, additionally, not without anti-Vergilian irony. Now Christ guides Peter, making his steps firm just like the pine trunk that guided the hand of the blinded Polyphemus.

that is), and thus she contrasts fittingly with the unarmed Patientia who is only protected by a corselet. Two of Ira's weapons certainly come from the *Aeneid*. The whistling spear thrown at Patientia (121-124) is identical with that thrown at Aeneas by the savage Mazentius (X, 776); and Ira's shattered sword (146-149) is an apt recollection of Turnus' shattered sword near the end of the epic. But Ira's helmet-plumes (*vertice cristas*, 117) are exactly those of Aeneas (XII, 493), the point being, once again, that all the warriors of the *Aeneid* are children of wrath. Other quotations reflect designed disorder. Patientia (112) is like Aeneas leaving the sibyl's cave (VI, 156) with downcast (*defixus*) eyes; the detail fits Patientia's character, but there is probably no contextual significance. Again, the three-ply corselet (124-125) of Patientia may symbolize the Trinitarian armor of the Christian, but its source, the *loricam trilicem* worn by an unnamed Latin warrior (VII, 639), given by Helenus to Aeneas (III, 467) and given by Aeneas as second prize for the ship race (V, 259), is a paltry prize indeed.

Mens Humilis and Spes versus Superbia.—Here a dense cluster of Vergilian language for clothing and equestrian behavior (186-193) has been attached to the entry of Superbia, prior to the appearances of Mens Humilis and Spes. Additional quotations are scattered throughout the episode. The lion's skin (*pelle leonis*, 179) would be familiar to Prudentius' audience; mentioned six times in the *Aeneid*, where it functions as a saddle-blanket, it is always a hero's gift, either to or from Aeneas. In the *Psychomachia* it is Superbia's saddle-blanket. In her fine cambric mantle, Superbia cuts a handsome figure. Like Dido's horse before the hunt in Carthage (IV, 135), Superbia's horse chomps the bit. This vice is probably the most "heroic" of all the vices. Her speech, the longest in the *Psychomachia*, is modeled on that of Juturna to the Rutulians in *Aeneid* XII, 228ff.[66] Superbia appeals to all the heroic virtues of the vices, to their courage, their aristocratic pride of lineage, even their manhood

[66] Or possibly that of Remulus, Book IX, 598ff.

(252)! She is extremely silly, this Vergilian heroine. In order to present a superior figure, *tumido despectans agmina fastu* (182), she seats herself well upon her horse's neck! Superbia's demise is no cause for boasting; she and her horse fall into a ditch dug by her own follower, Fraus (259). It seems generally less the case here than in previous battles that Prudentius employs strikingly irrelevant quotations. In costume, gesture, and rhetoric of discourse, Superbia has been made to subsume the norms of heroic style in her character. The Vergilian material employed for this purpose consists mostly of single words and short phrases that would not usually recall a specific heroic context. The *cento* structure of the cluster is obvious enough, but its function is largely rhetorical.

Sobrietas versus Luxuria.—There are really two small clusters of quotations during this episode, the first (329-337) as Luxuria is defeating the armies of the virtues with her "strange warfare," the second (407-416) as she is being killed at the hands of Sobrietas. The two most seductive females of the *Aeneid*, Venus and Dido, contribute to the character of Luxuria. As Luxuria is winning on the field of battle, we are reminded of an especially apt comparison from Vergil. An entire line, *inspirat tenerum labefacta per ossa venenum* (329) is Vergilian but is composed of two elements: *labefacta per ossa* (VIII, 390) is an obvious allusion to Venus's seduction of Vulcan, her softening of her husband's will in order to gain Aeneas' armor; *inspirit . . . venenum* comes from *Georgics* IV, 236, and gives the sober and not irrelevant advice that if you are stung by a bee, rest will absorb the poison. The words *obstupefacti* (333) and *mirantur* (335) are both in *Aeneid* I, 494, where the hero is dumbfounded by Dido's pictures of the Trojan War. Now wonderment is common enough in the *Aeneid* that I should not wish to place the context in this *locus* were it not that one of the pictures viewed by Aeneas is the model for Luxuria's death later on. Meanwhile another typically snide quotation: the words *bratteolis crepitantia* (335) unmistakenly suggest the golden bough in *Aeneid* VI, 209. This marvelous talisman has been beaten into gold foil as adornment for Luxuria's chariot; no longer sacred, its deceptive beauty may still speed one's entry into the Christian Hades. Now the death of Luxuria is related. When Sobrietas holds up the cross of Christ in the faces of Luxuria's horses, the horses panic and bolt. Luxuria is thrown out of her chariot, befouled by dust, and crushed under the wheels. This scene is a conflation of a number of violent passages in Vergil: the storm-tossed ship in *Aeneid* I, 115-117, Turnus's dream of a dusty, defiling death for his enemy Aeneas in *Aeneid* XII, 99-100, the simile of Mars rampaging over Europe like a chariot race out of control at the end of *Georgics* I. Amidst this *cento* of Vergilian destruction occurs the death of Troilus pictured on the walls in Carthage:

> parte alia fugiens amissis Troilus armis,
> infelix puer atque impar congressus Achilli,
> fertur equis curruque haeret resupinus inani,
> lora tenens tamen; huic cervixque comaeque trahuntur
> per terram et versa pulvis inscribitur hasta.   (I, 474-478)

[Elsewhere Troilus, his arms flung away in flight—unhappy boy, and ill-matched in conflict with Achilles—is carried along by his horses and, fallen backward, clings to the empty car, yet clasping the reins; his neck and hair are dragged over the ground, and the dust is scored by his reversed spear.]

This is Luxuria's death also. By copying this scene, Prudentius is able to transform pathos into ridicule and to do so openly in good Christian faith.

Ratio versus Avaritia.—This episode of combat is formally the least *cento*-like, for it contains no grouping of quotations dense enough to remind us convincingly of this genre,[67] and the content of these quotations is nearly always

[67] Discounting density, there are discernible groupings at 464-466 and 475-482.

thematically related to the vice. And there is a striking Vergilian imitation where about fifty lines of the *Psychomachia* (549-595) follow the action of *Aeneid* II, 389-430: the disguising of Avaritia follows that of the Trojans at Coroebus' urging.[68] Avaritia's followers include three personifications, Cura, Famis, and Metus (464), to be found in Vergil's underworld (*Aeneid* VI, 274). Other rhetorically apt allusions emphasize the essential greed of Avaritia, thus revealing Prudentius atypically drawing upon the moral philosophy of the pagan poet in a straightforward manner. Thus King Evander's criticism of *Amor Habendi* (VIII, 327) as having terminated the Saturnian Golden Age is recalled by the presence of this term in the *Psychomachia* (464). Especially striking is the belt buckle, *fulgentia bullis / cingula* (475-476), which according to Prudentius a son would steal even from his father's corpse on account of the sin of Avaritia. In *Aeneid* IX, 359, Vergil presents the adolescent Euryalus foolishly stealing armor and other trophies, including *aurea bullis cingula*, from the dead Latins. Euryalus' greed will shortly bring about his death, and this same booty is to figure most prominently in the tragedy of Turnus. It goes without saying that Prudentius deflates the spirit of Vergilian tragedy, but up to a point of morality Prudentius is not un-Vergilian here.

Fides and Concordia versus Discordia.—There is extensive Vergilian quotation in this last and dramatic battle— dramatic on account of the plot reversal, its occurrence after the triumphal procession. Here Prudentius has reinstated his *cento*-like technique. If we remember that this fragmentation of Vergil follows closely on the heels of a grand Vergilian simile containing no distracting quotations and having an exclusively scriptural content, we may appreciate what is also a stylistic reversal. Prudentius, that is to say, is careful to remind us that the recrudescence of sin is aesthetically as well as morally jarring. And of course the

[68] Discussed by Thomson, "The *Psychomachia* of Prudentius," quoted above, p. 239; see also Mahoney, p. 52.

existence of a *cento*-like cluster here is especially appropriate in a larger rhetorical sense, given the name and character of the vice. Vergil also personifies Discordia in association with the idea of religious conflict (which is not to say heresy); Discordia as pictured on Aeneas' shield appears to embody the sense of religious perversion, for she is set among the Egyptian goddesses hostile to Apollo (not yet assimilated into the Roman pantheon):

> omnigenumque deum monstra et latrator Anubis
> contra Neptunum et Venerem contraque Minervam
> tela tenent. saevit medio in certamine Mavors
> caelatus ferro, tristesque ex aethere Dirae,
> et scissa gaudens vadit Discordia palla,
> quam cum sanguineo sequitur Bellona flagello.
>
> (VIII, 698-703)

[Monstrous gods of every form and barking Anubis wield weapons against Neptune and Venus and against Minerva. In the midst of the fray storms Mavors, embossed in steel, with the fell Furies from on high; and in rent robe Discord strides exultant, while Bellona follows her with bloody scourge.]

Prudentius advertises his indebtedness to Vergil for the personification by also clothing her in a rent robe, presenting her with Bellona's whip to boot:

> *scissa* procul *palla* structum et serpente *flagellum*
> multiplici media camporum in strage iacebant. (685-686)

[Her torn mantle and her whip of many snakes were left lying far behind amid the heaps of dead on the field of battle.]

Unlike the Augustan enemies of Rome, it is in the nature of Prudentius' Discordia to appear otherwise than she really is. She leaves her iconography behind in order to attempt an entry into the holy city. In Book VIII of the *Aeneid* the

enemy of Discordia (on the hero's shield of Roman history)
is Actian Apollo; by reminding us of his Vergilian *locus*,
Prudentius may be commenting ironically upon the place of
Apollo in the fourth-century pagan pantheon where he has
joined Anubis and the other *deum monstra* in a discordant
throng. Prudentius uses thematic parallelism when (699-
715) he imitates *Aeneid* II, 67 and following.[69] Sinon (who
may also be present in Fides' first contest versus Cultura
Deorum Veterum) is a good model for Discordia. He is a
dissembler, attempting to gain entry for the Greeks into the
city of Troy—an entry which will result in great discord
as well as religious crimes against the temple of Athena. In
Prudentius' source the Trojans surround this secret agent,
listen to him, and are convinced. But the followers of Fides
and Concordia soon discover Discordia and tear her to
pieces; the citadel is built, not razed; Wisdom's temple is
adored, not violated.[70] This imitation, thus ironically altered,
shows the Christians to be far wiser than Aeneas' countrymen. Another thematically related quotation is *conscius
audacis facti* (703), Discordia being "conscious of a reck-
less deed" after she has wounded Concordia. She is just like
the wolf in Vergil's simile (XI, 812), the wolf who attacks
and kills a shepherd. The Christian significance of such
imagery needs no explanation, being well attested in the
Gospels. The likening of heresy to a wolf is also a fourth-
century commonplace. The same quotation also seems to
draw us away, as in earlier battles, from the thematically
relevant to the absurd. The simile of the wolf is applied by
Vergil to Arruns, who has just murdered Camilla. Arruns,
like Discordia, is sneaky; but is Camilla like Concordia, and
if so in what respect? Within the Sinon imitation also there
seems to be an allusion to Camilla: the phrase *convertere
oculos* (700) recalls the same action just before Camilla's

[69] Discussed by Mahoney, pp. 53-54.
[70] The death of Rufinus in Claudian's *In Rufinum* II, 405ff., is so
close to the death of Discordia that it would be difficult not to assume
some influence.

death. In Books XI and XII of the *Aeneid*, turning the eyes to gaze upon something is generally a signal that the object of vision will be a dying hero or a hero about to die. Is this relevant to the last battle of the *Psychomachia*? Perhaps so, if it is intended to create suspense or if it is intended to heighten the contrast between Concordia's surface wounds and the fatal wounds suffered by Vergil's heroine. Yet the comparison is at best far-fetched and other quotations tend to further confuse thematic clarity with crosscurrents of associations. Prudentius has once again refused to allow Vergil's epic to illuminate his own by any direct means; rather, he offers certain thematically appropriate allusions alongside of thematically inappropriate ones. Vergil's heroic world again is permitted to confound itself.

Perhaps the most paradoxical feature of these clusters—a feature embodied in the *cento* genre—is that even as they are constructed out of the language of the most classical of poets they disregard classical decorum. We have examined certain quotations where the original context is brought into the *Psychomachia*: thus Turnus' rage is felt in Ira, and Avaritia acts like Euryalus despoiling corpses. Such rhetorically fit quotations are isolated. It is not just the enemies, fools, and monsters of the *Aeneid* that crowd around the Christian vices. Evander in a pious speech names the vice of false religion. Aeneas' lion skin serves as Superbia's saddle-blanket. Aeneas' mother, Love herself, is incarnated in that old alcoholic whore Luxuria. And the virtues share attributes and actions with some of the worst characters in the *Aeneid*, Mazentius among them. Thus features decorously separated and morally distinct in Vergil are mixed and contaminated.[71]

The result of such an unclassical mixture is that the total

[71] Mahoney consistently employs the term *contaminationes* to denote Prudentius' Vergilian clusters. According to Roman rhetorical thinking, however, a *contaminatio* is a construction of one plot out of two or more plots from another author—the term is not applied to words, but to actions.

mythos of the *Aeneid*, the interpretation of historical progress in terms of the struggle to found and build Rome, the
City of Man, loses that clarity which is the prerequisite of
belief. It is this clarity which Macrobius in the *Saturnalia*
attempts to preserve against Christianity—Christianity epit-
omized by the rude and obfuscating "Evangelus," the
deprecator and contaminator of Vergil. *Contra paganos*,
Prudentius asserts in the *Psychomachia* that there is room
for only one *mythos*, one belief, and that this has been
revealed for the salvation of man in Scripture. He puts forth
Vergil in *cento*-like fragmentation in order to summon up
an image of the City of Man disordered by sinful strife: if
Vergil is the architect of this city, so much the worse for
him.

In Sapientia's Temple

The final Vergilian presence in the *Psychomachia* confirms the destruction of the old city and the construction of
the new; or, to be more exact, it intones the conversion of
Rome to Christ by reminding us of the distance traversed
by this conversion. There are none except very sparsely
scattered and unimportant Vergilian quotations between
the death of Discordia and the final vision of Sapientia enthroned. Here occurs another cluster of quotations, still
structurally very like a *cento* but alluding with far greater
clarity than heretofore to major moments of pathos in the
Aeneid.

> stridebat gravidis funalis *machina vinclis*
> inmensas rapiens alta ad fastigia gemmas.
> *ad domus interior* septem *subnixa columnis*
> crystalli algentis vitrea de *rupe recisis*
> *construitur*, quarum tegit edita calculus albens
> in conum caesus capita et sinuamine subter
> subductus conchae in speciem, quod mille talentis
> margaritum ingens, opibusque et censibus hastae
> addictis, animosa Fides mercata pararat.

hoc *residet solio* pollens Sapientia et omne
consilium regni celsa disponit ab aula,
tutandique hominis *leges* sub corde retractat.
in manibus dominae *sceptrum* non arte politum
sed ligno vivum viridi est, quod *stirpe recisum*,
quamvis nullus alat terreni caespitis umor,
fronde tamen viret incolumi, tum *sanguine* tinctis
intertexta *rosis* candentia *lilia miscet*
nescia marcenti florem submittere collo.
huius forma fuit sceptri *gestamen* Aaron
floriferum, sicco quod *germina cortice trudens*
explicuit tenerum spe pubescente decorem
inque novos subito tumuit virga arida fetus.   (866-887)

[The crane was creaking with the weight on its chains as
it whirled the vast gems up to the heights. An inner
chamber, too, is constructed, which rests on seven pillars
cut from a glassy rock of ice-like crystal and topped with
a white stone cut cone-wise and curved on the lower part
into the likeness of a shell, a great pearl to buy which
Faith had boldly sold at auction all her substance and her
property, and paid for it a thousand talents. Here mighty
Wisdom sits enthroned and from her high court sets in
order all the government of her realm, meditating in her
heart laws to safeguard mankind. In the sovereign's hands
is a sceptre, not finished with craftsman's skill but a living
rod of green wood; severed from its stock, it draws no
nurture from moist earthly soil, yet puts forth perfect
foliage and with blooms of blood-red roses intermingles
white lilies that never droop on withering stem. This is
the sceptre that was prefigured by the flowering rod that
Aaron carried, which, pushing buds out of its dry bark,
unfolded a tender grace with burgeoning hope, and the
parched twig suddenly swelled into new fruits.]

I have already discussed this passage in relation to its rich
scriptural imagery and typology. Just as the typological
emblems of the seven battle scenes are paired off with

clusters of Vergilian quotations, so are these scriptural features here. The gems of the heavenly Jerusalem are hoisted with chains, and by means of a *machina*, so as to remind us of the dragging of the Trojan horse into the city (II, 235-238).[72] Here the horse itself is called a *machina*, and has been described as drawn with some effort by means of chains: *scandit fatalis machina muros, / feta armis* ("The fateful engine climbs our walls, big with arms"). To be thus reminded of such a line from within the temple of Wisdom, where arms and warfare are excluded, heightens our consciousness of the distance from Vergil and the distance from the previous action of the poem. And notice the continuation. The words *at domus interior* ring forth with unmistakable echoes of Priam's palace burning during the destruction of Troy (*Aeneid* II, 486) and of Aeneas' shocked recognition of the defilement taking place in the inner chambers. Yet this *domus*, we know simultaneously, is the House of the Lord, is Christ, is the Christian soul at peace with God. Now a succession of other words, *subnixa* (868), *resident solio* (875) and *leges* (877), from *Aeneid* I, 506ff., allude to Dido as the magnificent queen of Carthage. Sapientia dispenses the New Law within the soul—we cannot avoid comparing this with Dido's presence upon her briefly occupied throne, from which she dispenses laws for her faithful citizens. Again, the roses and lilies from the Song of Songs, allegorized Christologically by the Church Fathers, further related to the blood of Christ and the sacrament of the Eucharist—these positive religious associations have as their Vergilian counterparts the manifestations of grief over the fate of Turnus as shown in Lavinia's face:

> accepit vocem lacrimis Lavinia matris
> flagrantis perfusa genas, cui plurimus ignem
> subiecit rubor et calefacta per ora cucurrit.
> Indum sanguineo veluti violaverit ostro

[72] I am indebted to John Arthur Hanson for pointing out this allusion.

si quis ebur, aut mixta rubent ubi lilia multa
alba rosa: talis virgo dabat ore colores.   (XII, 64-69)

[Lavinia heard her mother's words, her burning cheeks
steeped in tears, while a deep blush kindled its fire, and
mantled o'er her glowing face. As when one stains Indian
ivory with crimson dye, or as when white lilies blush
with many a blended rose—such hues her maiden features
showed.][73]

All Vergilian allusions at the end of the *Psychomachia* are
to moments of considerable pathos, moments when the
pagan reader (or the sympathetic modern reader) of Vergil is overwhelmed by the cost of empire in terms of its
birthpangs of human suffering. As a Christian, and especially
as a Christian c. 400, when Vergil's status is a central issue
in the anti-pagan struggle of the Church, Prudentius must
respond differently. He converts the tragic vision of Vergil
into his own and the Church's positive Christian vision. The
final allusion is telling. Here Prudentius has us recollect
King Latinus during his last moment as a ruler in his native
land. The king swears an oath by his scepter, stating in the
figure of an *adunaton* that it would be impossible for this
scepter to grow foliage—

ut sceptrum hoc (dextra sceptrum nam forte gerebat)
numquam fronde levi fundet virgulta nec umbras,
cum semel in silvis imo de stirpe recisum
matre caret posuitque comas et bracchia ferro;
olim arbos, nunc artificis manus aere decoro
inclusit patribusque dedit gestare Latinis.   (XII, 206-211)

[even as this sceptre (for haply in his hand he bore his
sceptre) shall never burgeon with light leafage into
branch or shade, now that once hewn in the forest from
the nether stem, it is reft of its mother, and beneath the

[73] Not in Mahoney. This allusion is identified by Gnilka, *Studien
zur Psychomachie des Prudentius* (cited Critical Introd., n. 36), p. 121,
in the context of standard classical erotic imagery (e.g., Ovid).

steel has shed its leaves and twigs; once a tree, now the craftsman's hand has cased it in seemly bronze and given it to sires of Latium to bear.]

A greater craftsman, Prudentius tells us, has nullified the King Latinus' oath and has thereby nullified the supremacy of Roman civilization conferred by Vergil through this oath. What concord has King Latinus with Christ the King? In this early Christian context, Latinus' scepter seems all the more brazen, all the more barren, against the fruition of Aaron's rod in the hand of Sapientia.

INDEX

Aaron, 205, 216, 217, 300
Abel, 169
Abraham, 80, 107, 110, 114, 126,
    168, 197 n.25, 241; typology of,
    in *De Abraham* (St. Ambrose),
    222-32; typology of, in *Psycho-
    machia*, 26, 112, 173, 184, 194,
    206-22
Adam, 180, 189, 194, 224
*Adversus Ioannem Hierosolymi-
    tanum* (St. Jerome), 85n
Adversus Marcionem (Tertul-
    lian), 123n
Aeneid (Vergil), Avitus' use of,
    257-58, 259; Juvencus' imitation
    of, 248-50; Pope Damasus' use
    of, 252-54; St. Augustine's
    treatment of, 245-48, 257-59;
    as symbol of pagan tradition,
    270-71. Quotations: I, *278-
    279, 257*; I, *474-478, 291*; VI,
    52-53, 275; VI, *56-65, 272*; VI,
    724-729, 255; VI, *826-829, 287*;
    VIII, *698-703, 293*; VIII, *702, 153*;
    XII, *64-69, 298-99*; XII, *206-211,
    299-300*. *See also* Typology, in
    Psychomachia, negative; Vergil
Against the Christians (Por-
    phyry), 71
Agar, 218
Alain de Lille, 25 n.32
Alaric, 8, 20
Alföldi, A., 95 and n
Allegory, 105-106, 109, 141;
    medieval, 10-11, 150; personifi-
    cation, 3-4, 6-7, 23-24, 25, 26,
    109-110, 111, 188, 209-210;

scriptural, 13, 24-26, 27; theories
    of, 23-24. *See also* Personifica-
    tion; *Psychomachia*, and sacred
    history; Typology
Ambrose, Saint, 50, 61, 83, 122
    n.10, 172n, 175; as hymnist, 9,
    16, 57, 62, 103; influence of, on
    Prudentius, 83, 222-33; and
    Symmachus, 46, 91; Vergil used
    by, 251-52; 276-77. Works: *De
    Abraham*, 195, 222-32; *De Bono
    Mortis*, 136-37; *De Interpella-
    tione Job et David*, 183; *De
    Isaac et Anima*, 136; *Hexae-
    meron*, 251-52
Anastasius II (pope), 86
Apollinarianism, 80-83, 86-87,
    88, 136
Apollinarius (bishop of Laodi-
    cea), 80
Apotheosis, 37 n.13, 53, 71, 88n,
    114 n.5, 195 n.22, 197 n.25; and
    Nicene orthodoxy, 30, 31, 50,
    72, 74, 80, 82, 84-86; and
    paganism, 106-107, 274; and
    patristic tradition, 175-77;
    structure of, 120, 122-25; typol-
    ogy in, 176-77. Quotations:
    Hymn, 123; *Hymn 2, 194*;
    Hymn 7-9, 82; *22-27, 80*;
    330-337, 176-77; *376-405, 106-
    107, 402-405, 274*; *446-448, 241*;
    512-513, 133 n.22; *786-793*,
    85-86; *915-917, 86*; *924-933*,
    87-88
Arator, 18
Arcadius (emperor), 8, 43
Arevalo, 3 n.1, 12n

301

Library of Congress Cataloging in Publication Data

Smith, Macklin, 1944-
Prudentius' Psychomachia: A Reexamination

Includes index.
1. Prudentius Clemens, Aurelius. Psychomachia.
I. Title.
BR65.P783S6   233'.7   75-29436
ISBN 0-691-06299-4

DATE DUE

DEMCO 38-297